Reform of Eyewitness Identification Procedures

Reform of Eyewitness Identification Procedures

Edited by **Brian L. Cutler**

American Psychological Association · Washington, DC

Published by
American Psychological Association
750 First Street, NE
Washington, DC 20002
www.apa.org

To order
APA Order Department
P.O. Box 92984
Washington, DC 20090-2984
Tel: (800) 374-2721; Direct: (202) 336-5510
Fax: (202) 336-5502; TDD/TTY: (202) 336-6123
Online: www.apa.org/pubs/books
E-mail: order@apa.org

In the U.K., Europe, Africa, and the Middle East, copies may be ordered from
American Psychological Association
3 Henrietta Street
Covent Garden, London
WC2E 8LU England

Typeset in Goudy by Circle Graphics, Inc., Columbia, MD

Printer: United Book Press, Baltimore, MD
Cover Designer: Mercury Publishing Services, Rockville, MD

The opinions and statements published are the responsibility of the authors, and such opinions and statements do not necessarily represent the policies of the American Psychological Association.

Library of Congress Cataloging-in-Publication Data

Reform of eyewitness identification procedures / edited by Brian L. Cutler.
    p. cm.
  Includes bibliographical references and index.
  ISBN 978-1-4338-1283-5 — ISBN 1-4338-1283-5 1. Eyewitness identification.
I. Cutler, Brian L.

  HV8073.R483 2013
  363.25'8—dc23
                                    2012035436

British Library Cataloguing-in-Publication Data
A CIP record is available from the British Library.

Printed in the United States of America
First Edition

DOI: 10.1037/14094-000

CONTENTS

CONTRIBUTORS

Shannon M. Andersen, MA, Department of Psychology, University of Oklahoma, Norman

Jacqueline L. Austin, BA, John Jay College of Criminal Justice, City University of New York, New York

Steven E. Clark, PhD, Department of Psychology, University of California, Riverside

Brian L. Cutler, PhD, Faculty of Social Science and Humanities, University of Ontario Institute of Technology, Oshawa, Ontario, Canada

Gary Dalton, BS, Psychology Department, University of London, Egham, Surrey, England

Charles A. Goodsell, PhD, Department of Psychology, Canisius College, Buffalo, NY

Scott D. Gronlund, PhD, Department of Psychology, University of Oklahoma, Norman

Ruth Horry, DPh, Psychology Department, Flinders University, Adelaide, South Australia

Margaret Bull Kovera, PhD, John Jay College of Criminal Justice, City University of New York, New York

Amina Memon, PhD, Psychology Department, University of London, Egham, Surrey, England

Rebecca Milne, PhD, Centre of Forensic Interviewing, Institute of Criminal Justice Studies, Portsmouth, Hampshire, England

Molly B. Moreland, MA, Department of Psychology, University of California, Riverside

Jeffrey S. Neuschatz, PhD, Department of Psychology, University of Alabama in Huntsville

Colton Perry, BS, Department of Psychology, University of Oklahoma, Norman

Lindsey Rhead, MA, John Jay College of Criminal Justice, City University of New York, New York

Ryan A. Rush, MA, Department of Psychology, University of California, Riverside

Laura Smalarz, MS, Department of Psychology, Iowa State University, Ames

Andrew M. Smith, MA, Department of Psychology, Queen's University, Kingston, Ontario, Canada

Nancy K. Steblay, PhD, Department of Psychology, Augsburg College, Minneapolis, MN

Gary L. Wells, PhD, Department of Psychology, Iowa State University, Ames

Stacy A. Wetmore, MA, Department of Psychology, University of Oklahoma, Norman

Miko M. Wilford, MS, Department of Psychology, Iowa State University, Ames

Daniel B. Wright, PhD, Department of Psychology, Florida International University, Miami

David M. Zimmerman, MA, John Jay College of Criminal Justice, City University of New York, New York

ACKNOWLEDGMENTS

I wish to thank Nawal Ammar for her continued professional and social support throughout this project. I also wish to thank Claire Sookman for being there for me in all respects.

Reform of Eyewitness Identification Procedures

INTRODUCTION: IDENTIFICATION PROCEDURES AND CONVICTION OF THE INNOCENT

ANDREW M. SMITH AND BRIAN L. CUTLER

Innocence advocacy organizations such as the Innocence Project (http://www.innocenceproject.org) in the United States and the Association in Defense of the Wrongly Convicted (http://www.aidwyc.org) in Canada have uncovered hundreds of cases of wrongful conviction. Researchers at these organizations have concluded that mistaken eyewitness identification is a leading precursor to wrongful conviction. Meanwhile, experimental psychologists have been conducting research on eyewitness identification for several decades. This research is regularly published in refereed journals and is summarized in meta-analyses, books, and book chapters. Psychologists now have a solid understanding of such issues as the effects of suggestive questioning on eyewitness reports, the suggestibility of children, methods of improving eyewitness interviews, the effects of crime factors on identification accuracy, the relation between confidence and identification accuracy, methods of improving identification accuracy, and the effectiveness

DOI: 10.1037/14094-001
Reform of Eyewitness Identification Procedures, B. L. Cutler (Editor)

of safeguards designed to protect defendants from wrongful conviction in eyewitness cases.

In this volume, authors focus narrowly on methods of improving identification accuracy. Several factors point to the need for a thorough treatment on this topic. First, research on the effects of trial-related safeguards designed to protect defendants from wrongful conviction following mistaken eyewitness identification is lacking. This finding points to the need to reduce the risk of mistaken identification at the investigation stage. Second, a growing number of judicial and law enforcement organizations have embraced the psychological research findings on eyewitness identification and have made significant reforms to the identification procedures in their jurisdictions, including the U.S. Department of Justice and the states of New Jersey, New York, North Carolina, and Wisconsin. Reforms have also taken place in smaller jurisdictions and are under review in other states. Third, some of the procedural reforms, such as the use of sequential presentation and double-blind administration, remain controversial and unsettled. Fourth, research on identification procedure continues, and there is a need for new and updated literature reviews. Fifth, although much has been written on the various reforms in research articles and review articles, the time is right for a new volume in which authors collectively review the research underlying the reforms. This edited volume, which should fulfill this need, should be of significant use to students, eyewitness researchers, and law enforcement and legal practitioners who desire to know more about the reform movement and underlying research.

Human memory has been the subject of scientific study for over a century. *Eyewitness memory* is a subset of human memory pertaining to the memory for people and events experienced by an observer. The scientific study of eyewitness memory began in earnest in the 1970s with classic works by psychologists Elizabeth Loftus (1974, 1976; Loftus & Palmer, 1974), Ray Bull (Clifford & Bull, 1978), and Robert Buckhout (1974), though one can find much earlier scholarship in the historical archives (e.g., Whipple, 1909). A seminal article by Gary Wells (1978) shaped the direction of much eyewitness research from the time of its publication to the present. Wells drew the distinction between estimator and system variables. *Estimator* variables are factors that are *not* under the direct control of actors within the criminal justice system, for example, the conditions under which an eyewitness views a crime. *System* variables, by contrast, are factors that *are* under the control of the criminal justice system, such as the manner in which eyewitnesses are interviewed and the procedures used to obtain eyewitness identifications. Wells recommended that future research focus on system variables with the objective of developing procedures for improving the accuracy of eyewitness testimony and minimizing errors. Wilford and Wells (see Chapter 1, this volume) revisit this historically important distinction.

Since the publication of Wells's (1978) article, research on system variables has burgeoned. Psychologists now have a large body of research devoted to procedures used to obtain eyewitness identifications, including show-ups, photo arrays, and lineups. Psychologists now also have a large body of research on system variables associated with other aspects of eyewitness testimony, such as methods of interviewing child and adult eyewitnesses, but this volume is devoted to eyewitness identification procedures. The research on eyewitness identification addresses such issues as whether showups are more or less effective than photo arrays and lineups. The research also addresses such issues as how various instructions to an eyewitness prior to an identification test and the composition and presentation procedures for photo arrays and lineups influence the accuracy of eyewitness identification. The goal of this volume is to present a contemporary review of the extant research on the most commonly examined system variables to date.

Why is it important to review the contemporary research on system variables at this time? It is important for several reasons. It has a very real impact on the criminal justice system. Eyewitness identification affects the course of criminal investigations and prosecutions, and mistaken eyewitness identification leads to miscarriages of justice, as noted previously. Furthermore, research on eyewitness identification system variables has grown and matured profoundly in the past 30 years. This research has had an impact on public policy and criminal justice procedures in many U.S. districts and internationally. Scientists must help synthesize the research to guide their own future research and to provide input to justice personnel who strive to improve their procedures. And last, research conclusions are not static. As scientists drill down further into the nuances of their techniques, examine qualifying factors, refine their methods, incorporate new psychological theories and findings outside of eyewitness research, and recruit new scientists to this exciting field, they sometimes find that commonly held views need to be reexamined and modified. In such an environment, it is beneficial to step back; review and integrate literature; and communicate summaries, conclusions, challenges, limitations, and directions for future research that go beyond the typical content of peer-reviewed journal articles.

In the next two sections of this introduction, we expand on these reasons for studying system variables. Next, we review some basic explanations of eyewitness research that are common to the chapters. Last, we provide an overview of the book chapters.

ESTABLISHING THE NEED FOR A SYNTHESIS OF SYSTEM-VARIABLE RESEARCH

We begin this section by summarizing a compelling case of mistaken identification in the conviction of two innocent men. We follow with our own analysis of known wrongful convictions. Next, we acknowledge the growth of system-variable research, identify some areas in need of review, and discuss the impact of system-variable research on policy and practice. Finally, we conclude this section of the chapter by discussing areas of eyewitness identification in which our understanding continues to evolve.

The Role of Mistaken Identification in Conviction of the Innocent

On January 11, 1993, two men broke into a house in La Centre, Washington, while the housekeeper was cleaning. They blindfolded her with tape, bound her to the kitchen table, threatened her with a knife and cut off all of her clothes. One man penetrated her with a foreign object before raping her while the other man held her down. The men did not steal anything from the house and left immediately after the attack. Because she was blindfolded she was able to give only a very vague description of her assailants—one had dark hair, and the other was blonde (http://www.innocenceproject.org).

Law enforcement personnel released the description to the public—two men, one with dark and the other with blonde hair. Someone called in and said that Larry W. Davis and Alan G. Northrop were friends who fit that general description. Law enforcement personnel developed photo arrays containing the two men and presented them to the victim. Although the victim could only describe the hair colors of the two men, she made a tentative identification of Davis but did not identify the other suspect. She was later presented with a live lineup identification procedure containing both men and identified them as her attackers. They were the only two men included in the previous photo arrays that were presented to her. Furthermore, immediately before the identification procedure a friend of the eyewitness provided her with a description of the two men who were questioned by the police. Although no physical evidence connected either man to the crime, they were convicted solely on the eyewitness's testimony in 1993. They spent 16.5 years in prison before being exonerated in 2010 (http://www.innocence project.org).

The case of Davis and Northrop is a compelling example of how mistaken identification can lead to conviction of the innocent. There are many more such cases. Over the past century, several researchers have examined the role of mistaken eyewitness identification in wrongful convictions (e.g., Borchard, 1932; Gross, Jacoby, Matheson, Montgomery, & Patil, 2005).

These and other such studies share a general framework: They present a set of compelling cases of wrongful conviction (typically following the familiar theme described previously), review the antecedents of each given wrongful conviction, and ultimately recommend legal reforms (Leo, 2005). Mistaken eyewitness identification figures prominently in all of these works (e.g., Gross et al., 2005; Rattner, 1988).

How often does mistaken identification lead to conviction of the innocent? To address this question, we analyzed known cases of conviction of the innocent (see Table on pp. 8–9). We identified six independent published and unpublished databases. The existing literature included books, journal articles, and unpublished reports. We included only literature that presented unique cases of wrongful conviction to avoid double counting of cases. One of these databases (Rattner, 1988) was itself a compilation of previous databases (e.g., Borchard, 1932; Frank & Frank, 1957). In this instance, we included the Rattner results but not the databases already compiled by Rattner. Also, for the case to be included in our analyses, we had to have a clear analysis of the antecedents of the case so that we could know for sure whether mistaken identification was a factor. Huff, Rattner, and Sagarin (1996), building on the work of Rattner (1988), identified in excess of 500 wrongful convictions. The first 205 cases identified by Rattner are included in our study, but the approximately 300 additional wrongful convictions identified by Huff et al. (1996) could not be included in our study because the authors did not present a systematic analysis of the antecedents of these cases (though they did offer approximations of the antecedents).

We mined each database for several variables. We recorded the authors' definitions of wrongful convictions, their sources of data, the range of dates covered, the total number of wrongful convictions, and the percentage of cases that included mistaken eyewitness identification. In total, we found five sources that presented original catalogues of wrongful conviction, which ranged in date from 1900 to 2011.

In five of six of the sources, *wrongful conviction* was defined as verified actual innocence—instances in which individuals were convicted of crimes that they did not commit and for which they were later exonerated (e.g., http://www.innocenceproject.com; W. Wahrer, personal communication, May 6, 2011). The definition used by Radelet, Bedau, and Putnam (1994), however, differed from those in the other sources in two distinct ways. First, the authors only examined cases in which the defendant was convicted of murder or received a death sentence for rape—capital cases. Second, in the instance in which an individual had not received a formal exoneration but the authors believed, in consensus, that the individual was likely wrongly convicted, the case was included by Radelet et al. (1994).

In total, we identified 1,213 unique cases of wrongful conviction across all databases. Of those cases, 1,198 were valid, meaning that there was

Mistaken Identification and Wrongful Conviction

Study	Definition of wrongful conviction	Source of data	Years covered	Role of mistaken eyewitness identification
Rattner (1988)	"A person was convicted of a felony but later was exonerated" (p. 284).	Radin (1964) 29.3% ($N = 60$) Borchard (1932) 26.3% ($N = 54$) Frank & Frank (1957) 14.1% ($N = 29$) Gardner (1952) 6.3% ($N = 13$) Block 0.5% ($N = 1$) Loftus (1979) 1% ($N = 2$) Ehrman 2.4% ($N = 5$) Newspaper and law reports 20% ($N = 41$) Total: $N = 205$; $N = 191$ valid	1900–1988	Most prominent type of error 48.8% or 52.4% of valid cases (cases in which such information was available) ($n = 100$)
Radelet, Bedau, & Putnam (1994)	Miscarriage of justice—"(a) the defendant was convicted of homicide or sentenced to death for rape; *and* (b) when either (i) no such crime actually occurred, *or* (ii) the defendant was legally and physically uninvolved in the crime." Inclusion of any and all cases based on author consensus.	*New York Times* index (1900–1987) Announcements in newspapers for (a) criminologists, (b) litigating defense attorneys in capital cases, and (c) opponents of the death penalty Capital punishment holdings in several libraries Letters to 47 governors and the mayor of the District of Columbia Total: $N = 424$	1900–1987	19.34% ($n = 82$)

Gross et al. (2005)	Exonerated defendants (144 cleared by DNA, 196 by other means)	From media database (N = 340–144 = 196[a])	Not listed–2003	Most prominent type of error 55.1% of cases (n = 108)
Canadian Wrongful Convictions (Received from Win Wahrer, Director of Client Services, AIDWYC; personal communication, May 6, 2011)	Factual innocence	Win Wahrer at AIDWYC (N = 45; valid N = 44)	1959–present	36.36% of valid cases (cases in which such information was available) (n = 16)
Innocence Project	DNA-based exoneration (5 exonerated by other means)	Innocence Project (N = 289)	1974–present	Most prominent type of error 73.36% of cases (n = 212)
Conroy & Warden (2011)	A person has been convicted of a crime for which he or she would later be found legally innocent (excludes legal innocence). Confined to murder, sexual assault, attempted murder, and armed robbery	Court documents, state and county public records, and news articles in Illinois (N = 85–31 = 54[b])	1978–present	18.15% of cases (n = 46–20 = 26)
Totals		N = 1,213; valid N = 1,198	1900–present	45.41% of cases (n = 544)

Note. AIDWYC = Association in Defense of the Wrongly Convicted.
[a]The total number of cases included in this article is 340; however, 144 of those cases are already included in the Innocence Project database and, therefore, were not included under Gross et al. (2005).
[b]The total number of cases included in the report is 85; however, 31 of the cases are already included in the Innocence Project database and, therefore, were not included under Conroy and Warden (2011).

sufficient information about the case to determine what antecedents were associated with the wrongful conviction. Because we could not determine the antecedents associated with the 15 invalid cases (one in W. Wahrer, personal communication, May 6, 2011; 14 in Rattner, 1988), we could not include them because we do not know how many of them included mistaken eyewitness identification. In total, 544 cases (45.41% of valid cases) involved mistaken eyewitness identification. If we had included Huff et al.'s (1996) full database and relied on their estimations, we would have had a total of 1,513 cases of wrongful conviction with approximately 724 (47.85%) cases involving mistaken identification, so the results do not change much by including or excluding those cases.

How does this estimate compare with other known estimates of the role of mistaken identification in conviction on the innocent? The percentage of wrongful convictions that involve mistaken eyewitness identification in the present database might appear low at first glance, especially in comparison with Innocence Project data, which suggest that mistaken eyewitness identification occurs in approximately 75% of all wrongful convictions (see Table on pp. 8–9). Our analysis of case characteristics provides some clues as to the variability of estimates. For example, Radelet et al. (1994) included only capital cases ($N = 424$)—cases in which individuals were convicted for murder or rape and received capital sentences. It is quite possible that in many of these murder cases the only eyewitnesses were the murder victims. If so, it is not surprising that only 82 (19.34%) of these cases involved mistaken eyewitness identification. The Innocence Project cases are sexual assault cases in which DNA was available for analysis and exoneration. Given this restricted sample of types of cases, it would be risky to generalize the results from this sample to other types of crimes without further empirical validation.

Also, with respect to case selection, it is important to consider the role of post appellate review in selection bias. Post appellate review is almost always reserved for the most serious offences, murders and rapes. Robberies and assaults are both crimes for which eyewitnesses are likely to proffer evidence; however, because these cases are less serious than murder and rape cases and given that the number of wrongful conviction claims far exceeds the human resources available to review them, it is unlikely that these cases will ever receive post appellate review. It is possible that mistaken identification is more common in robbery and assault cases—both case types that are less likely to receive post appellate review than sexual assault or murder cases.

Gross and Shaffer's (2012) recent analysis of 873 exonerations between 1989 and 2003 sheds some light on the issue of selection bias. Gross and Shaffer found that mistaken eyewitness identification was an antecedent to 43% of all exonerations, 27% ($n = 416$) of homicide exonerations, 80% ($n = 203$) of sexual assaults, 26% ($n = 102$) of child sexual abuse cases, 81% ($n = 47$)

of robbery cases, 51% ($n = 47$) of other violent crimes, and 19% ($n = 58$) of nonviolent crimes.

We find some comfort in knowing that Gross and Shaffer (2012) reached a similar estimate of the role of mistaken eyewitness identification in wrongful convictions. However, some of this comfort might be illusory considering the degree of overlap between the cases included in our analysis and the cases included in theirs (see http://www.exonerationregistry.org). Gross and Shaffer's estimate of 43% of wrongful convictions entailing mistaken eyewitness identification is substantially smaller than the 55.1% figure reported at the outset of this project (Gross et al., 2005). In attempting to explain this discrepancy, Gross and Shaffer began to distinguish between eyewitnesses who mistakenly identified an innocent suspect and those who perjured (deceitfully implicated an innocent suspect). Past research has not uniformly made this distinction (e.g., Gross et al., 2005). We excluded mistaken eyewitness identifications from our analysis only when it was possible to determine that the eyewitness was not mistaken but had perjured. For instance, case profiles provided by the Innocence Project often list the antecedents associated with a wrongful conviction but provide no case description or the description is not thorough enough to distinguish between deceitful and mistaken eyewitnesses. Thus, we too may have misclassified some deceitful eyewitnesses as mistaken.

We estimate that about 50% of known cases of conviction of the innocent involved mistaken eyewitness identification. The problem of mistaken identification is compounded by the ineffectiveness of safeguards that are designed to prevent mistaken identification from becoming a wrongful conviction. Mistaken identifications need not lead to conviction of the innocent. After all, eyewitnesses do not convict people; judges and juries issue convictions. The judicial system has in place various safeguards designed to prevent mistaken identifications from becoming wrongful conviction. These safeguards, however, are not fully effective. Most suspects do not have legal representation during the identification procedures through which they are identified (Devenport, Kimbrough, & Cutler, 2009). Motions to suppress suggestive identifications rarely succeed, in part because of inherent problems with the legal standards by which they are evaluated and the psychological processes that influence eyewitnesses (Wells & Quinlivan, 2009). Cross-examination, which is believed to be an effective safeguard against wrongful conviction, requires a level of knowledge and sensitivity to the factors that influence eyewitness identification on the part of attorneys, judges, and jurors. This knowledge and sensitivity, however, is lacking (Devenport et al., 2009).

In conclusion, the powerful contribution of mistaken eyewitness identification to conviction supports the importance of continued attention to reform of eyewitness identification procedures and is one of the key reasons for the current volume.

The Growth of System-Variable Research and Its Impact on Policy and Practice

Some of the earliest system-variable research, published in the early 1980s, focused on instructions given to eyewitnesses prior to a lineup or photo array (see Chapter 3, this volume). Since that time, however, considerable system-variable research has been published. One sign of the volume of research is the availability of meta-analyses. *Meta-analyses* are quantitative reviews of a set of studies aimed at answering a general question such as the overall effects of lineup instructions on eyewitness identification performance. Meta-analyses are often conducted when there is a group of studies to be reviewed. Eyewitness researchers have published meta-analyses on the comparison of eyewitness performance from showups and lineups (Steblay, Dysart, Fulero, & Lindsay, 2003), the effects of lineup instructions (Steblay, 1997) and lineup presentation methods (Steblay, Dysart, Fulero, & Lindsay, 2001; Steblay, Dysart, & Wells, 2011) on identification performance, and the effect of postevent feedback on eyewitness confidence (Douglass & Steblay, 2006). There are several factors, such as the effect of lineup composition and blind presentation, for which there is a growing body of research but as of this writing no published meta-analyses. In short, there are scores of published studies of system variables. These studies are published in peer-reviewed journals and call out for fresh reviews of their findings.

The psychological research on system variables is having an effect on practice and policy. One of the earliest instances of this effect is the publication of the U.S. Department of Justice's *Eyewitness Evidence: A Guide for Law Enforcement* (DOJ guide; U.S. Department of Justice, Office of Justice Programs, National Institute of Justice, 1999). The DOJ guide was inspired by U.S. Attorney General Janet Reno, who formed a technical working group of attorneys, law enforcement personnel, and eyewitness researchers to develop a practical set of guidelines based on the scientific research on eyewitness identification. The psychologists involved in the effort included Ron Fisher, Solomon Fulero, Rod Lindsay, Roy Malpass, John Turtle, and Gary Wells. The efforts of the working group are described in Wells et al. (2000).

The DOJ guide launched a wave of reform of eyewitness identification procedures that continues to this day. Shortly after the publication of the DOJ guide, the attorney general of New Jersey issued a statewide set of guidelines for eyewitness identification procedures. Some other states and police departments within various states issued guidelines as well. Many of these guidelines are summarized in the Conclusion of this volume.

The wave of reform of eyewitness identification procedures puts a special demand on eyewitness scientists to continue their research efforts, to better understand the cognitive processes underlying eyewitness identification, to more fully flesh out the impact and qualifying factors of system variables, and to continually integrate and synthesize this research to ensure that they are providing policymakers and practitioners with valid conclusions and advice. This volume is the latest such synthesis. Because system-variable research is alive and well, it will not be the last such synthesis!

Psychologists' Evolving Understanding of Eyewitness Identification

The third reason given in the preceding section for the need for the latest synthesis is that the understanding of the effects of system variables and their qualifying factors continues to evolve. For example, although psychologists have a good understanding of the deleterious influence of instructions to eyewitnesses that do not explicitly acknowledge that the perpetrator might not be present in a lineup (see Chapter 3, this volume), the effects of other types of instructions, such as warning the eyewitness that the perpetrator's appearance might have changed between the crime and the identification test, are less clear (yet the appearance change instruction is a common feature in reform procedures). Psychologists' understanding of the relative benefits and drawbacks of showup identifications and the factors that influence performance in field identification tests continues to evolve. The use of sequential presentation is common in newly established reforms (see Conclusion, this volume), yet it continues to be hotly debated (Clark, 2012; Newman & Loftus, 2012; Wells, Steblay, & Dysart, 2012).

In sum, the demonstrated role of mistaken identification in conviction of the innocent, the growth of system-variable research, and the evolving understanding of eyewitness identification processes and system variables establish the need for this volume. It is our hope that this new synthesis conveys to researchers and practitioners the most current understanding of the psychological research, the implications of this research for psychologists' practices, and directions for future research.

BASIC ELEMENTS OF EYEWITNESS RESEARCH

Some basic elements common to eyewitness research are necessary for understanding the content of these chapters. The content of this section will be common knowledge to eyewitness researchers, but to new researchers and practitioners, the concepts explained here are essential. Some of these concepts are explained in the various chapters as well. The editor of this volume

(Brian L. Cutler) encouraged some redundancy in this respect because he recognized that many readers would review individual chapters rather than the full volume from start to finish.

Identification Tests

Throughout this volume, the reader will find references to showups, photo arrays, and lineups. *Showups* are one-on-one identification tests normally conducted in the field. In practice, showups are usually live, meaning that the eyewitness is shown the suspect and is asked whether he or she is the perpetrator, though sometimes an eyewitness might be shown a photograph of a single suspect.

Photo arrays and (live) *lineups* differ from showups in that they contain, in addition to a suspect, fillers. *Fillers* are people (or photos of people) who are not suspects in the crime. They are included in the identification test to make it difficult for the witness to identify the suspect by guessing or deduction. In practice, photo arrays are used more commonly than live lineups, in part because photo arrays are more practical. There is little research differentiating photo arrays from live lineups. The psychological processes underlying identifications from photo arrays and live lineups and the factors that influence identification performance using the two procedures are assumed to be the same or similar, and for this reason the terms *photo array* and *lineup* are often used interchangeably. In some instances, photo arrays or lineups have contained more than one suspect (e.g., the Duke Lacrosse case; see Wells, Cutler, & Hasel, 2009). The inclusion of multiple suspects—or worse, only suspects—in a photo array or lineup is problematic, and guidelines generally recommend the inclusion of only one suspect in an identification procedure (see Conclusion, this volume).

Eyewitness Identification Decisions

Eyewitnesses attempt identifications from identification tests (showups, photo arrays, lineups). In these tests, the suspect is either guilty (i.e., the suspect is the actual perpetrator) or innocent (the suspect is not the actual perpetrator). When participating in a showup identification wherein the eyewitness is shown one suspect, several outcomes are possible. First, if the suspect is the perpetrator, the eyewitness might say "that's him." One would refer to this decision as a *correct identification*. In contrast, the eyewitness may mistakenly say "that's not him." One would refer to this decision as a *miss* or an *incorrect rejection*. If the suspect is *not* the perpetrator, the eyewitness may nevertheless say "that's him." One would refer to this decision as a *false identification*. If the suspect is not the perpetrator and the eyewitness says "that's not him," one would refer to this decision as a *correct rejection*. In any eyewitness identification test an eyewitness might also say "I don't know." *Don't know* responses have sometimes been permitted and sometimes not permitted in eyewitness research, and when permitted, they are either omitted from analyses or analyzed separately.

Research Methodology

Most of what researchers know about eyewitness identification comes from laboratory research. In laboratory research, eyewitnesses (often university students) view live or videotaped enactments of crimes and attempt identifications from showups, photo arrays, or lineups. Laboratory experiments have several benefits. They enable researchers to hold factors constant while manipulating a single factor of interest. For example, researchers can expose hundreds of eyewitnesses to the same viewing conditions but manipulate the procedures used to obtain eyewitness identifications. They can collect repeated observations and subject their observations to statistical analyses. The degree of experimental control and statistical precision enables them to draw causal conclusions about the effects of system variables on eyewitness identification performance.

It is common, indeed expected, in laboratory research to include both target-present and target-absent identification tests. *Target-present identification tests* are those in which the perpetrator from the simulated crime is included among the fillers. These identification tests resemble situations in which the suspect is the perpetrator. A *target-absent identification test* is one in which the perpetrator has been replaced by an innocent suspect. Target-absent identification tests resemble situations in which the suspect is not the perpetrator. The inclusion of both target-present and target-absent identification tests is necessary to examine the impact of system variables on the full range of eyewitness identification decisions, as defined previously.

Laboratory experiments have drawbacks too. They have been criticized as unrealistic, and questions have been raised about the extent to which laboratory results generalize to what occurs in actual crimes (Yuille, Ternes, & Cooper, 2010). In recognition of this concern, some researchers now conduct studies of actual crimes to empirically examine the extent to which laboratory findings replicate in the field. Chapter 8 of this volume is devoted to field research.

OVERVIEW OF CHAPTERS IN THIS VOLUME

Wilford and Wells (Chapter 1) provide a historic overview of eyewitness research and explain the importance of key distinctions that have guided and continue to guide eyewitness research. These distinctions include the estimator–system variable distinction and the distinction between general impairment and suspect bias factors. They remind one of the importance of base rate of guilty suspects in lineups and make a compelling case for defining eyewitness confidence as accuracy. Wilford and Wells give considerable attention to the processes by which eyewitness science translates from the lab to practice and policy, noting the importance of knowing the system in which psychologists are trying to apply their research and the power of contemporary media for effecting change. There are valuable lessons here for applied psychologists who wish to see the results of their research affect practice and policy. Wilford and Wells identify the need for a new class of variables—system-diagnostic variables—and call for more research on this new class of variables in the hopes that future eyewitness scientists can help identify indices that assist psychologists in correctly classifying accurate and inaccurate eyewitnesses.

Goodsell, Wetmore, Neuschatz, and Gronlund (Chapter 2) explain how and why showups, or field identification tests, are used. They review the relevant law behind showups. They also review the empirical work to date, most of which focused on the comparison of identification performance from showups and lineups but some of which examined factors affecting showup identifications. They conclude that the results are rather mixed and do not clearly favor one procedure over the other. They note that these findings conflict with the opinions of many eyewitness experts and provide direction for more research with a particular aim toward theory, factors affecting showup identifications, and use of showups and live lineups on scene.

Steblay (Chapter 3) provides a detailed review of the previous research on lineup instructions and an updated meta-analysis of the effects of lineup instructions on identification performance. Her review compares the use of a may-or-may-not-be-present instruction with an instruction that implies that the culprit is present. In data from over 3,000 witnesses to simulated crimes, her new analyses confirmed that the presence of the may-or-may-not instruction significantly and substantially reduced the risk of misidentifications from perpetrator-absent lineups. The may-or-may-not instruction also significantly reduced the risk of filler picks from perpetrator-present lineups but did not significantly influence the likelihood of a correct identification of the perpetrator. Combining these results, Steblay demonstrates that lineups that use the may-or-may-not instruction produce identifications that are more diagnostic of the suspect's guilt than do culprit-present instructions. The may-or-may-not instruction reduces witnesses' tendencies to make positive identifications and increases their willingness to conclude that the perpetrator is not present in the lineup. This reduction in choosing leads to both a reduced chance of false identification of innocent suspects and a reduced rate of filler identifications.

Clark, Rush, and Moreland (Chapter 4) review the existing research on lineup construction with specific emphasis on filler selection. Guided by the WITNESS model, they compare decision outcomes from lineups that vary with respect to the degree to which the fillers match the description of the perpetrator and compared fillers selected on the basis of their match to the description of the perpetrator versus their match to the suspect's characteristics. Clark et al. conclude that when fillers better match the description (as opposed to match less or mismatch), the risk of false identification decreases, the likelihood of correct identification increases, and the probative value of the identification increases. When comparing outcomes from description- and suspect-matched lineups, Clark et al. conclude that description-matched lineups reduce both the correct and false identification rate compared with suspect-matched lineups. This conclusion contradicts earlier thinking that description-matched lineups reduce the risk of false identification without impacting the rate of correct identification. Clark et al. suggest that the optimal filler selection procedure might be one that uses a combination of description- and suspect-matched lineups. Importantly, they identify numerous lineup compositions that require a more solid understanding to further inform police practices.

Gronlund, Andersen, and Perry (Chapter 5) review the most recent research on lineup presentation methods with particular emphasis on simultaneous versus sequential presentation. They conclude that the extant evidence suggests that sequential presentation reduces the risk of false identification and the likelihood of correct identification, thus creating a criterion shift, or more conservative decision making on the part of the eyewitness. Gronlund et al. suggest that this sequential shift explanation better fits the data than does the sequential advantage explanation. They further articulate some of the issues that policymakers should consider when deciding which presentation method to adopt. They also identify key research questions associated with sequential and simultaneous presentation as well as other lineup presentation issues that should be addressed going forward.

Addressing the issue of double-blind lineups, Austin, Zimmerman, Rhead, and Kovera (Chapter 6) review basic psychological research on experimenter expectancy effects as a foundation for understanding the benefits of double-blind lineups. They then review the small but on-point research examining double-blind lineups and conclude that the risk of false identification increases when the lineup administrator knows the identity of the suspect. The adverse effects of double-blind administration are more serious with simultaneous presentation and biased instructions. Their further research will continue to articulate factors that qualify the influence of double-blind lineups. Meanwhile, they continue to support the use of double-blind lineups in criminal investigations.

Smalarz and Wells (Chapter 7) review research on one of the most commonly studied factors in eyewitness identification: eyewitness confidence. They examine the importance of eyewitness confidence, the relation between confidence and accuracy, and the conditions under which confidence predicts accuracy. Smalarz and Wells conclude that contrary to early beliefs that confidence was unrelated to accuracy, the extant research shows a moderately strong correlation and a stronger correlation among eyewitnesses who make positive identifications from lineups (choosers). They review the literature concerning the confidence malleability problem—the well-established finding that confidence levels can be inflated through certain investigator procedures—and suggest the need for unbiased identification procedures and the recording of confidence statements to address this problem.

The nearly exclusive reliance on laboratory research to study the factors affecting eyewitness identification has long been acknowledged and has met with calls for more field research. Wright, Memon, Dalton, Milne, and Horry (Chapter 8) address the laboratory–field study distinction and discuss methodological issues associated with both types of studies. They then provide contemporary examples of field archival and experimental studies and show how questions addressed in field studies may differ from those addressed in the lab. In keeping with the call for more field research, Wright et al. close the chapter with some concrete recommendations for field research methods.

Finally, in the Conclusion to this volume we (Smith & Cutler) review the successful application of eyewitness research from the lab to the police station. In our analysis of the eyewitness reform movement, we review adopted and recommended best practice procedures at national, state, and municipal levels of government in Canada, Great Britain, and the United States. Among the most commonly adopted and recommended best practices are the use of neutral lineup instructions (100%), the documentation of lineup procedures (92%), and the assessment of eyewitness confidence without postidentification feedback (84.6%). We conclude that the adoption of best-practice identification procedures is spreading, but cooperation and information sharing among eyewitness scientists, policymakers, and investigators will be essential to maintaining the positive momentum.

In sum, eyewitness scientists have brought an impressive amount of research to bear on practice- and policy-relevant questions concerning how best to conduct eyewitness identification tests to increase the likelihood of correct identification of perpetrators and decrease the risk of false identification. Although some sets of findings (e.g., that for lineup instructions) are generally well accepted and unlikely to change, other research conclusions (e.g., the confidence–accuracy relation, presentation methods) have continued to be refined over time and will likely be revisited again in the lab and in review articles. Still other sets of findings (e.g., showups, lineup composition, double-blind presentation) are based on relatively small amounts of research and will likely garner further research attention. In all cases, the authors provided insightful directions for research and addressed the policy implications of their findings. The common call for field research is addressed and clarified by Wright et al. (Chapter 8), who provide useful guidance for conducting field research.

REFERENCES

Borchard, E. M. (1932). *Convicting the innocent: Sixty-five actual errors of criminal justice*. Garden City, NY: Garden City.

Buckhout, R. (1974, December). Eyewitness testimony. *Scientific American, 231*(6), 23–31.

Clark, S. E. (2012). Costs and benefits of eyewitness identification reform: Psychological science and public policy. *Perspectives on Psychological Science, 7*, 238–259. doi:10.1177/1745691612439584

Clifford, B. R., & Bull, R. (1978). *The psychology of person identification*. London, England: Routledge & Kegan Paul.

Conroy, J., & Warden, R. (2011). *The high costs of wrongful conviction*. Retrieved from http://www.bettergov.org/investigations/wrongful_convictions_1.aspx

Devenport, J. L., Kimbrough, C. D., & Cutler, B. L. (2009). Effectiveness of traditional safeguards against erroneous conviction arising from mistaken eyewitness identification. In J. L. Devenport, C. D. Kimbrough, & B. L. Cutler (Eds.), *Expert testimony on the psychology of eyewitness identification* (pp. 51–68). New York, NY: Oxford University Press. doi:10.1093/acprof:oso/9780195331974.003.003

Douglass, A. B., & Steblay, N. K. (2006). Memory distortion in eyewitnesses: A meta-analysis of the post-identification feedback effect. *Applied Cognitive Psychology, 20*, 859–869. doi:10.1002/acp.1237

Frank, J., & Frank, B. (1957). *Not guilty*. London, England: Gallancz.

Gardner, E. S. (1952). *The court of last resort*. New York, NY: Sloane.

Gross, S. R., Jacoby, J., Matheson, D. J., Montgomery, N., & Patil, S. (2005). Exonerations in the United States, 1989 through 2003. *Journal of Criminal Law and Criminology, 95*, 523–560. Retrieved from http://papers.ssrn.com/sol3/papers.cfm?abstract_id=753084

Gross, S. R., & Shaffer, M. (2012). *Exonerations in the United States, 1989–2012: Report by the National Registry of Exonerations*. Retrieved from http://globalwrong.files.wordpress.com/2012/05/exonerations_us_1989_2012_full_report.pdf

Huff, C. R., Rattner, A., & Sagarin, E. (1996). *Convicted but innocent: Wrongful conviction and public policy*. Thousand Oaks, CA: Sage.

Leo, R. A. (2005). Rethinking the study of miscarriages of justice: Developing a criminology of wrongful conviction. *Journal of Contemporary Criminal Justice, 21*, 201–223. doi:10.1177/1043986205277477

Loftus, E. F. (1974). Reconstructing memory: The incredible eyewitness. *Psychology Today, 8*(7), 116–119.

Loftus, E. F. (1976). Unconscious transference in eyewitness identification. *Law & Psychology Review, 2*, 93–98.

Loftus, E. F. (1979). *Eyewitness testimony*. Cambridge, MA: Harvard University Press.

Loftus, E. F., & Palmer, J. C. (1974). Reconstruction of automobile destruction: An example of the interaction between language and memory. *Journal of Verbal Learning & Verbal Behavior, 13*, 585–589. doi:10.1016/S0022-5371(74)80011-3

Newman, E. J. & Loftus, E. F. (2012). Clarkian logic on trial. *Perspectives on Psychological Science, 7*, 260–264.

Radelet, M. L., Bedau, H. A., & Putnam, C. E. (1994). *In spite of innocence: Erroneous convictions in capital cases*. Boston, MA: Northeastern University Press.

Radin, E. D. (1964). *The innocents*. New York, NY: Morrow.

Rattner, A. (1988). Convicted but innocent: Wrongful conviction and the criminal justice system. *Law and Human Behavior, 12*, 283–293. doi:10.1007/BF01044385

Steblay, N. (1997). Social influence in eyewitness recall: A meta-analytic review of lineup instruction effects. *Law and Human Behavior, 21*, 283–297. doi:10.1023/A:1024890732059

Steblay, N., Dysart, J. E., Fulero, S., & Lindsay, R. C. L. (2001). Eyewitness accuracy rates in sequential and simultaneous lineup presentations: A meta-analytic comparison. *Law and Human Behavior, 25*, 459–473. doi:10.1023/A:1012888715007

Steblay, N., Dysart, J. E., Fulero, S., & Lindsay, R. C. L. (2003). Eyewitness accuracy rates in police showup and lineup presentations: A meta-analytic comparison. *Law and Human Behavior, 27*, 523–540. doi:10.1023/A:1025438223608

Steblay, N. K., Dysart, J. E., & Wells, G. L. (2011). Seventy-two tests of the sequential lineup superiority effect: A meta-analysis and policy discussion. *Psychology, Public Policy, and Law, 17*, 99–139. doi:10.1037/a0021650

U.S. Department of Justice, Office of Justice Programs, National Institute for Justice. (1999). *Eyewitness evidence: A guide for law enforcement*. Retrieved from http://www.nij.gov/pubs-sum/178240.htm

Wells, G. L. (1978). Applied eyewitness-testimony research: System variables and estimator variables. *Journal of Personality and Social Psychology, 36*, 1546–1557. doi:10.1037/0022-3514.36.12.1546

Wells, G. L., Cutler, B. L., & Hasel, L. E. (2009). The Duke-lacrosse rape investigation: How not to do eyewitness identification procedures. In M. L. Siegel (Ed.), *Race to injustice: Lessons from the Duke University lacrosse players' rape case* (pp. 307–322). Durham, NC: Carolina Academic Press.

Wells, G. L., Malpass, R. S., Lindsay, R. C. L., Fisher, R. P., Turtle, J. W., & Fulero, S. M. (2000). From the lab to the police station: A successful application of eyewitness research. *American Psychologist, 55*, 581–598. doi:10.1037/0003-066X.55.6.581

Wells, G. L., & Quinlivan, D. S. (2009). Suggestive eyewitness identification procedures and the Supreme Court's reliability test in light of eyewitness science: 30 years later. *Law and Human Behavior, 33*, 1–24. doi:10.1007/s10979-008-9130-3

Wells, G. L., Steblay, N. K., & Dysart, J. E. (2012). Eyewitness identification reforms: Are suggestive induced hits and guesses true hits? *Perspectives on Psychological Science, 7*, 264–271. doi:10.1177/1745691612443368

Whipple, G. M. (1909). The observer as reporter: A survey of the psychology of testimony. *Psychological Bulletin, 6*, 153–170. doi:10.1037/h0071084

Yuille, J. C., Ternes, M., & Cooper, B. S. (2010). Expert testimony on laboratory eyewitnesses. *Journal of Forensic Psychology Practice, 10*, 238–251. doi:10.1080/15228930903550590

1

EYEWITNESS SYSTEM VARIABLES

MIKO M. WILFORD AND GARY L. WELLS

Over 30 years ago the term *system variable* was first introduced in application to the realm of eyewitness evidence (Wells, 1978); this term has since evolved to a level of universality often requiring no reference or definition. System variables are those that affect the accuracy of eyewitness accounts for which the criminal justice system has (or can exert) control. A prototypical example, and one that has received significant attention, is instructions provided to eyewitnesses prior to their viewing of a lineup (see Chapter 3, this volume). System variables were originally contrasted with *estimator variables*, which, although also affecting the accuracy of eyewitness evidence, cannot be controlled by the criminal justice system. A prototypical example of an estimator variable is whether the race of the eyewitness and the perpetrator match or do not match (i.e., own race bias).

Many events have transpired since the original introduction of the system–estimator variable distinction, so it seems timely to review and

This chapter is based on work supported by the National Science Foundation Graduate Research Fellowship Grant No. 202-18-94-00.

DOI: 10.1037/14094-002
Reform of Eyewitness Identification Procedures, B. L. Cutler (Editor)

revisit this concept. In 1992, a nonprofit legal clinic now known famously as the Innocence Project was born and dedicated its resources to the exoneration of the innocent and the prevention of future injustice. To date, nearly 300 people have been exonerated through postconviction DNA tests. The Innocence Project has proven (far better than any study could) that the flaws of the criminal justice system extend beyond the lab to the real world. One of the important characteristics of the cases overturned with forensic DNA testing is that approximately 75% are cases involving mistaken eyewitness identification (see Introduction, this volume, for additional analyses of the relation between mistaken identification and wrongful conviction). The individuals freed through the efforts of the Innocence Project provide a unique gift to what were previously thought to be abstract scientific causes: They provide a face to research and reform efforts. Thus, the forward progress of research in the domain of eyewitness evidence has led to actual policy change in several precincts across the United States (see Conclusion, this volume).

We begin this chapter with a discussion of some nuances of the system–estimator variable distinction, and position the system–estimator variable distinction among other important variable classifications. We then note some ways in which the domain of system variables has grown to include variables not anticipated in 1978 and discuss why system variables continue to resonate. In the second half of the chapter, we move from the identification and definition of system–estimator variables to their application and discuss several avenues (and their limitations) by which system-variable knowledge is transferred to the legal system. The importance of this transfer cannot be exaggerated; without transfer from the research to actual practices and policies, the promise of the system-variable idea would remain unfilled. System variables by their very nature identify better policies and practices by which the legal system can improve current procedures.

THE SYSTEM–ESTIMATOR VARIABLE DISTINCTION: A DEEPER LOOK

System variables are variables under the control of the justice system that affect eyewitness accuracy. In contrast, estimator variables are variables that affect eyewitness accuracy over which the justice system has no control. The *functional relation* between estimator and system variables is one of asymmetric subsets. In the original conceptualization, the term *estimator variable* was coined as a reference to the fact that these variables can only be used to estimate accuracy of eyewitnesses in actual cases; they cannot control accuracy. It is also the case, however, that all system variables are also estimator variables in the sense that they too can be used to estimate the likely accuracy of eyewitnesses. In other words, system variables can serve the same function as estimator variables (the estimation function), but estimator variables cannot serve the same function as system variables (controlling accuracy in actual cases).

It is also worth noting that the original system–estimator variable article (Wells, 1978) approached estimator variables rather pessimistically, being somewhat dismissive of estimator variables. For example, it was originally argued that the estimator approach might be futile given the number of possible estimator variables and their interactions. In support of this argument, a hypothetical was offered to illustrate the difficulty of using a mere subset of 10 estimator variables to postdict accuracy (e.g., lighting, distance, attention, presence or absence of weapons, witness–culprit race, exposure duration, delay between witnessing and testing, lineup instructions, filler similarity, and appearance change). To test just this set of 10 variables (with only two levels of each variable) and their interactions empirically, the experiment would require 2^{10} (i.e., 1,024) cells. More realistically, at least 20 estimator variables have been clearly noted in the eyewitness literature, which would require an experiment with 1,048,576 cells to test all main effects and interactions. Clearly, these are impossible studies to conduct.

Fortunately, this originally dismissive attitude toward estimator variables did not fully deter researchers from doing estimator-variable research. Consequently, the unheeded progression of this research has been valuable for a number of originally unanticipated reasons. The first reason is that the aforementioned hypothetical ignores the role of theory and the understanding of psychological processes in understanding how these estimator variables will behave without the need to test over a million conditions. For instance, psychologists' theoretical understanding of how the weapon-focus effect occurs permits educated opinions regarding how the effect could be moderated by exposure duration, even in the absence of studies specifically examining that interaction. Second, some variables have boundaries that if exceeded, would supersede the possible effects of other variables. For example, if the distance between the witness and the perpetrator reaches a certain length, no amount of lighting, attention, exposure duration, or other factor could possibly be sufficient to produce a reliable identification (G. R. Loftus & Harley, 2005). Finally, eyewitness experts do not use estimator variables to estimate the probability of eyewitness accuracy in court anyway. In fact, U.S. courts will not permit an eyewitness expert to articulate the probability that any given witness is accurate or mistaken. Instead, estimator-variable information (e.g., regarding *direction* of influence) is provided to triers of fact (e.g., judges, juries) for them to use in their considerations of reliability. E. F. Loftus (1979) made this latter point in her defense of the utility of estimator variables in expert testimony.

Although estimator variables cannot be controlled by the justice system in actual cases, they can be controlled in experiments. In other words, estimator variables can be manipulated, and participant-witnesses can be randomly assigned to predetermined estimator-variable conditions. For that reason, the internal validity of estimator variable experiments can be theoretically comparable to the internal validity of system-variable experiments. External validity for estimator variables, on the other hand, might not be as great as external validity for system variables. The difference is that estimator variables in the real world are fraught with multicollinearities that are not represented in lab experiments (see Chapter 7, this volume). For instance, researchers might find that stress impairs witness performance in the lab when all other factors are held constant (or randomized out of the treatment effect). In actual cases, however, stress might be correlated with distance—the closer the witness is to the witnessed event, the more stressed the witness might become. Hence, the effects of distance and stress might cancel out such that neither is predictive of eyewitness accuracy in actual cases. In other words, in a well-controlled experiment stress is uncorrelated with distance (because the experimental design holds distance constant), but in actual cases stress and distance might be routinely correlated.

Unlike estimator variables, system variables are operationalized in the lab (random assignment to levels) in the same way they are operationalized in the real world (an agent assigns the level without regard to levels of other variables). For example, a strong prelineup admonition (instruction) remains the same regardless of whether it is presented in the real world versus in an experiment. Therefore, its presence or absence should be orthogonal to other accuracy-driving variables. Although the argument might seem subtle, it is actually quite important. Consider the recent experiment by Wells, Steblay, and Dysart (2011) using real-life witnesses to serious crimes. The manipulated system variable in that experiment (simultaneous vs. sequential procedure) was unrelated to the host of estimator variables present in each case (e.g., victim vs. bystander, view, attention, lighting, stress). Hence, the effects of the system variable were not confounded with other witness-relevant variables. The same cannot be said of the estimator variables. Stress, for instance, was likely correlated with the status of the witness (i.e., victim vs. bystander) which, in turn, was correlated with whether there was a weapon visible and so on. Thus, research examining system rather than estimator variables is more conducive to the generalization of lab studies to the real world. This difference in generalizability stems from the fact that system variables can be controlled in both the lab and the real world, whereas estimator variables can be controlled in the lab but not in the real world (see Seelau & Wells, 1995 for a more extended treatment of this argument).

General Impairment Versus Suspect-Bias Variables

Although the system–estimator distinction has been useful, it has perhaps overshadowed other important distinctions in eyewitness research. One such distinction is that made between general-impairment variables and suspect-bias variables in eyewitness identification (Wells & Loftus, 2003). *General-impairment variables* are those that interfere with eyewitness identification performance but do not have any inherent tendency to direct an identification error in the direction of the suspect. *Suspect-bias variables*, in contrast, influence witness identifications in the direction of the suspect. An example of a general-impairment variable would be lighting conditions at the time of the witnessed event. Although poor lighting conditions would impair the witness's ability to make an accurate identification, this is not a variable that would bias the witness toward the suspect in a lineup. On the other hand, a suspect-bias variable, like using lineup fillers who fail to match the witness's description of the culprit, directs errors toward the suspect. This distinction is quite important because general-impairment variables fail to address why the witness identified the suspect from the lineup rather than one of the fillers. Consider the previous example of a general-impairment variable, lighting conditions: If the lighting conditions were so poor, why did the witness even make an identification? Further, why was the identification directed at the suspect? Cross-race identifications provide another example of a general impairment variable. Cross-race identifications are less reliable than same-race identifications, but that fact does not address the critical question: Namely, how did the Caucasian witness manage to identify the African American suspect from the lineup and avoid picking a filler? After all, every member of the lineup was African American. These issues are critical from an applied standpoint; even if juries comprehend the effects of general-impairment variables, general-impairment variables do not explain why a witness picked the suspected person (rather than one of the fillers).

Importantly, the suspect-bias versus general-impairment distinction is largely orthogonal to the system–estimator distinction. A general-impairment variable could be either an estimator variable (e.g., amount of time between the witnessed event and the identification) or a system variable (e.g., presence or absence of a prelineup admonition). Moreover, a suspect-bias variable could be either an estimator variable (e.g., source confusion resulting in the identification of a bystander) or a system variable (e.g., suggestions from a lineup administrator). General-impairment variables and suspect-bias variables are both important, just as estimator variables and system variables are both important. System variables are unique in their ability to articulate specific reforms that can reduce chances of mistaken identifications. Suspect-bias variables are unique in their ability to explain why the witness made the mistake of identifying the suspect specifically, rather than the mistake of identifying a filler.

Certainty as a System Variable

The domain of system variables has expanded in several ways since its introduction. Consider witness certainty (confidence), for example. In the original system–estimator variable article, witness certainty was only mentioned near the end and was categorized as a special kind of estimator variable. Rather than something that affects accuracy over which the justice system has no control (which is the general definition of an estimator variable), certainty could be construed as a postdiction variable. Like other estimator variables, certainty can (at least theoretically) be used to estimate the likely accuracy of the witness. For the most part, witness certainty primarily held this postdiction/estimator-variable status for many years. However, two considerations began to change how eyewitness researchers thought about certainty. The first consideration involved the recognition that eyewitness identification testimony is not automatically persuasive to triers of fact in and of itself. Instead, eyewitness identification testimony in which the witness is certain or highly confident is what people find persuasive; people are quite willing to be dismissive of an eyewitness who is uncertain about his or her identification. Accordingly, it is not mistaken identifications themselves that result in convictions of the innocent; instead, convictions of the innocent occur when an eyewitness is both highly certain and mistaken.

We propose that the definition of eyewitness accuracy should be construed more broadly to include certainty. This broader definition would consider mistaken eyewitnesses who are highly certain to be more inaccurate than witnesses who make the same mistake but are not at all certain. Given this definition of eyewitness accuracy, other effects related to eyewitness certainty can be construed as system variables. A dominant example of this would be the postidentification feedback effect (Wells & Bradfield, 1998; see also Conclusion, this volume). Feedback from a lineup administrator (e.g., "Good, you identified the suspect") drives up the certainty of eyewitnesses who have made mistaken identifications (see the meta-analysis by Douglass & Steblay, 2006). The postidentification feedback effect provides one of the important foundations for lineup reform recommendations. These include the recommendation for double-blind procedures as well as the related recommendation that the double-blind administrator secure a statement of the witness's certainty at the time of the identification (before certainty can be inflated by feedback). In this way of construing eyewitness certainty (as influenced by the procedures used to collect eyewitness identification evidence), the concept of system variables has grown to include variables affecting not just the accuracy of the identification but also the certainty with which that identification is expressed (for more discussion of eyewitness certainty, see Chapter 7, this volume).

Culprit Present or Absent Base Rate as a System Variable

A second important example of the system-variable concept expanding to other variables is the base rate for perpetrator-present versus perpetrator-absent lineups. The importance of the present–absent base-rate variable in lineup identification has long been known in the eyewitness research area (e.g., Wells & Lindsay, 1980). In their treatment of lineup models, Wells and Turtle (1986) noted that the single-suspect model (one suspect embedded among known-innocent fillers) creates a situation in which mistaken identifications of innocent suspects cannot occur if the actual perpetrator is in the lineup (the only mistaken identifications are of known-innocent fillers). Further, of course, accurate identifications of the perpetrator cannot occur when the actual perpetrator is not in the lineup. Bayesian analyses show that the base rate for the presence or absence of the perpetrator drives mistaken identification and accurate identification rates more than perhaps any other variable (Wells & Turtle, 1986). Early treatments of the base-rate issue tended to treat the base rate as a fixed and unknown value in the real world and, accordingly, graphed the results on Bayesian curves across all possible values. By 1993, however, the base rate was treated as a variable that had no single value in the real world but instead was likely to vary across jurisdictions or even across detectives within a given jurisdiction on the basis of their practices (Wells, 1993).

Consider, for example, two hypothetical law enforcement jurisdictions. In one jurisdiction, which we will call the Lax Police Department, the detectives require little to no justification for placing a suspect in a lineup (hence, lax criterion for deciding to place a possible suspect in a lineup). Detectives in Lax will present these lineups to witnesses on the basis of a mere hunch that the crime might have been committed by a particular person. In the other jurisdiction, which we will call the Strict Police Department, the detectives will not put a suspect in a lineup unless they have some reasonable cause, which, although difficult to define, would require some kind of evidence against the person beyond a mere hunch. Over a given series of lineups (e.g., 100 lineups), the practices of the Lax jurisdiction are likely to result in a much lower base rate (e.g., 50 of the 100) for how often the actual perpetrator is in the lineup compared with the more conservative Strict jurisdiction (e.g., 85 of the 100 lineups). The consequences of these two different base rates are huge. When witnesses view perpetrator-absent lineups, bad things tend to happen. There is not only an obvious increased risk of a mistaken suspect identification but also an increased chance of witnesses picking fillers. When witnesses pick fillers, it spoils the witnesses for any later identification tests should the actual perpetrator be located later.

On the basis of this analysis, the base rate of perpetrator-present versus perpetrator-absent lineups is a system variable. This base rate is under the (probabilistic) control of the justice system and affects the accuracy of eyewitness identification evidence. This provides yet another example of the system-variable domain expanding in ways that were not anticipated in 1978.

This discussion of the culprit present or absent base rate as a system variable is a convenient place to make another point. There is a tendency for some people to think about the study of eyewitness identification as studies of memory variables. Although memory is a big aspect of the study of eyewitness identification, the reliability of eyewitness identification is influenced by much more than just the mental operations of human memory. The base-rate variable, for example, is not itself a memory variable in the traditional sense of the term. Many other eyewitness identification variables are also not memory variables in the traditional sense of the concept of memory. Some are social influence variables that might affect responding but not affect memory per se. Others, such as the single-suspect versus all-suspect lineup model, are structural variables that protect innocent suspects by distributing mistakes to less harmful errors (identification of known-innocent fillers). Hence, neither system variables nor estimator variables are restricted to memory variables per se.

The Resonance of System Variables

The system–estimator distinction has resonated among eyewitness researchers. Of course, system-variable research would have been conducted even without the label and in fact was conducted before the label was created. Much of the groundbreaking work of Elizabeth Loftus involving misleading questions, for instance, clearly preceded the 1978 system-variable article (e.g., E. F. Loftus & Palmer, 1974). Further, more than 35 years before the system-variable article, Snee and Lush (1941) described the results of their experiments showing the advantages of narrative over interrogatory methods of obtaining testimony. Even Munsterberg's (1908) discussions of suggestion qualify as system-variable concerns.

Although we will never know the extent to which this distinction biased the post-1978 literature toward system variables rather than estimator variables, we do know that system-variable research grew at a rapid pace after 1978. The generic interpretation for this rapid growth of system-variable research is the straightforward observation that such research can inform the justice system of ways to improve the reliability of eyewitness evidence.

But there is another characteristic that differs between system and estimator variables as well, one that relates back to the earlier observation that system variables can also serve as estimator variables. Although eyewitness researchers use both estimator and system variables to educate jurors about the reliability of eyewitness evidence, it can be argued that estimator variables and system variables maintain some qualitative differences at the level of expert testimony. Specifically, unlike estimator variables, the discussion of system variables in court can carry a *responsibility* or even a *blame* component. When an expert discusses a weapon-focus effect on the stand, for example, there is no sense of someone being responsible or blameworthy for the effect. In contrast, when discussing the failure to give the witness a prelineup admonition, there is a responsibility component—the investigators *should* have provided an admonition.

As a result of the responsibility or blame component of expert testimony focused on system variables, which is absent in estimator-variable expert testimony, some experts have expressed a preference for being retained only in cases for which there is a system-variable problem. The preference is not likely to be based on an interest in assigning blame per se but rather on trying to push two positive effects. One effect is to assist the defendant by convincing the jury not to overweigh the eyewitness evidence and to consider factors that could have led the witness to make a mistaken identification. The other effect, unique to expert testimony on system variables, is to put pressure on the system by encouraging reforms that can reduce the chances of mistaken identification in future cases.

Another reason that system variables resonate is that they commonly (though not always) involve some component of suggestion. Failure to give a prelineup admonition, failure to use lineup fillers who fit the description of the perpetrator, postidentification feedback, and so on are all construed as suggestion. Judicial law in the United States tends to regard suggestive identification procedures with more concern than it does other (nonsuggestive variables) procedures, especially when the suggestion is the result of state action. The primary judicial law governing U.S. courts' admissibility assessments of eyewitness identification evidence appears to treat suggestive identification procedures as a special category (*Manson v. Brathwaite*, 1977). In accordance with this treatment as a special category, eyewitness identification evidence is judged differently with a different set of criteria.

A final reason why system variables resonate loudly is that they represent a constructive, cooperative approach between science and the legal system. Actors in the legal system (as in many other domains) often take the attitude, "do not come to me with problems; come to me with solutions." This does not mean that suggested solutions to the eyewitness problem will always be accepted (or even greeted as welcome) by everyone in the legal system. But at the very least, there is a difference between merely documenting eyewitness reliability problems (estimator variables) and offering ways to improve eyewitness reliability (system variables). Whereas estimator variables provide useful insights regarding the limitations of eyewitness testimony, system variables are necessary to provide clearer guidance and actual remedies. By definition, estimator variables cannot be controlled through policy or in practice. System variables, on the other hand, offer avenues toward improvement, making the translation of research into the real world possible.

SYSTEM VARIABLES AND THE TRANSFER OF RESEARCH TO PRACTICE

Transferring system-variable research findings to actors in the legal system is important. After all, if the system-variable findings remain limited to writings in scholarly psychology journals, the primary idea behind system-variable research is rendered moot. In this part of the chapter, we describe four main channels by which psychological science has been disseminated to the legal system and some of the difficulties with each.

Most American universities have long concerned themselves with what is commonly called *technology transfer*. The concern has been that research conducted in universities was being buried in scientific journals and not being translated and transferred into products. In fact, the creation of so-called research parks, which are connected to universities (and use the scientific expertise of the universities), was partially inspired by the mission to bridge this gap. Research park entities could connect to businesses configuring research into practical products that can enter the public market. This movement has been highly successful in certain disciplines, such as genetics, computer science, and materials science. The transfer of social science findings to the real world typically has not been construed as one of the missions of university research parks. Perhaps the time has come to explore the idea of social science research parks that would facilitate the transfer of social science to practical applications.

It is rather obvious that publication of empirical studies in the scientific literature through the journal process per se has little to no chance to directly impact the legal system. Eyewitness system variables, for example, are primarily relevant for law enforcement, trial attorneys, and judges. Yet, these empirical articles are nearly invisible to police and attorneys, the journals are relatively inaccessible to them, and the articles themselves are usually not written in a way that can be understood by nonscientists. One solution would be for eyewitness scientists to write more articles in police publications and law review journals. This approach has been increasingly used in recent years, but its effect is still limited. Law review journals tend to be read by law professors rather than practitioners, and police publications rarely reach the practitioner audience of detectives.

Expert Testimony as a Research Transfer Avenue

In theory, expert testimony at the trial level should be an effective way to transfer system-variable information to policymakers. Consider, for example, a case in which the detectives failed to give a prelineup admonition to the witness and/or used fillers who failed to fit the description the eyewitness had given of the perpetrator. Suppose further that an expert carefully described the problems with the failure to give the admonition and the suggestiveness of the lineup composition. This might be done at a pretrial hearing or at trial. This would seem to create an ideal situation for the purposes of disseminating information and applying pressure in that jurisdiction for law enforcement to reform their policies, aligning them more closely with science-based recommended practices. The mechanism for this transfer would likely occur through the prosecutor who could inform the law enforcement agency that it needs to reform procedures to reduce the potential criticism or suppression of these eyewitness testimonies.

Undoubtedly, this type of expert-testimony driven feedback has had effects in some jurisdictions. But there are factors that undermine the efficacy of this path. Perhaps the biggest factor is the fact that judges in the United States routinely rule that any suggestive identification procedure, almost regardless of how extreme it might be, is not grounds for considering the identification unreliable. In part, the blame for American courts' trivialization of suggestive identification procedures stems from the flawed architecture for evaluating identifications obtained through suggestive procedures. This architecture was set forth by the U.S. Supreme Court (*Manson v. Brathwaite*, 1977) and continues to guide U.S. courts to this day. The *Manson v. Brathwaite* criteria have been largely discredited in eyewitness research literature, and these problems are not discussed in detail here (but see Wells & Quinlivan, 2009).

In 2012, the U.S. Supreme Court further clarified its position on suggestiveness in eyewitness identification procedures (*Perry v. New Hampshire*, 2012). Going into that case, eyewitness researchers hoped that the Court would revise its previous stance regarding the criteria with which to judge eyewitness accuracy; instead, the outcome of the decision was decidedly narrow in scope. In this case, Perry was identified late at night in a parking lot by a witness who claimed to have seen him breaking into cars. The identification situation was clearly suggestive because Perry was the only person in the parking lot not in police uniform; there were police surrounding him; and the witness knew that the police were investigating the break-ins. However, even the defense admitted that the suggestive circumstances were not arranged or orchestrated by the police. Instead, they were the result of happenstance. Further, the police did not ask the witness to make an identification, but instead she volunteered the identification. The defense requested the right to have a pretrial hearing assessing the reliability of the witness on the basis of the suggestive circumstances. From a reliability perspective, a suggestive circumstance arranged by police versus one that occurs by happenstance matters little, if at all. But the Court was dealing with a constitutional question regarding due process and ruled that due process does not require a reliability hearing when law enforcement did not itself procure the suggestive circumstances. This decision essentially narrowed the applicability of *Manson v. Brathwaite* (1977) to cases in which the state is somehow responsible for the suggestive circumstances leading to the eyewitness identification. Unfortunately, this case did nothing to update the criteria by which eyewitness testimony is judged to be reliable (as outlined in *Manson v. Brathwaite*, 1977), which researchers have long awaited.

Perry v. New Hampshire (2012) provides a good illustration of the limits on the U.S. Supreme Court's role in eyewitness reform. This decision represents the first instance in over 30 years in which the Court even discussed eyewitness evidence. In the intervening 30 years, researchers have been extremely productive in revising their understanding of eyewitness evidence, yet this progress went unrecognized by the Court. Reform is unlikely to come about through a sweeping decision made by the U.S. Supreme Court, which could be a good thing. After all, research has a fluidity that courts cannot recognize or afford. Whereas research seeks to discover new knowledge, the courts seek to interpret old knowledge in new situations. Given the inherent conflict in the goals of these two institutions, it should not be surprising that few changes have occurred in eyewitness procedure as a result of court verdicts. Courts represent an ill-equipped instrument for the consistent renovation needed if policy is to reflect research. Talk of total reform with a single U.S. Supreme Court decision would be both odd and dangerous; the consistent success of such a decision would be contingent on the stagnation of scientific discovery or the constant updating of judicial precedent.

The main point, however, is that the net result of using the *Manson v. Brathwaite* (1977) criteria is that suggestive eyewitness identification procedures (even the most extreme violations of system-variable ideas) rarely result in the suppression of eyewitness identification. Judges rarely even provide warnings to jurors regarding the suggestiveness of these procedures. The routine admission of highly suggestive procedures, therefore, emboldens law enforcement and prosecutors to believe that their procedures are fine because they are constitutionally acceptable. Because identifications obtained using suggestive and suboptimal procedures are almost never suppressed, strong messages back to the police (e.g., through the prosecutor) about the unacceptability of the procedures are extremely rare. In fact, law enforcement will really only receive this message in cases in which the defendant is acquitted and the acquittal is attributed to problems with the identification procedure. Even if the defendant is acquitted (an uncommon event if the witness was certain), prosecutors can often point to other things (e.g., an inconsistency in the witness's testimony, a defendant-biased jury) as the reason for the outcome. Additionally, a common reaction for a prosecutor is to prepare for future cases by finding new arguments to exclude expert testimony or to find better ways to cross-examine and neutralize the expert. In fact, prosecutors routinely go so far as to attack the expert and attempt to trivialize his or her research during cross-examination of the expert. This then tends to make it even more unlikely that the prosecutor would suggest that police use the expert's recommended procedures posttrial—this would seem a dissonant act. Furthermore, few prosecutors want to risk creating an atmosphere of conflict between their office and the police department by criticizing the police and suggesting that a deficiency in their procedures resulted in an acquittal.

Popular Media as a Research Transfer Avenue

Surprisingly, much of the dissemination of system-variable findings to practitioners and policymakers has come through mass media. The Innocence Project often garners this interest from mass media after its orchestration of high-profile exoneration cases. Although anecdotal, a couple of examples help to illustrate this point. A number of years ago, an author of this chapter (Gary L. Wells) was on *The Oprah Winfrey Show*, which had roughly 25 million viewers at the time. In the weeks that followed, dozens of law enforcement agencies called Wells with an interest in improving their eyewitness identification procedures on the basis of system-variable ideas that were discussed on the program. (Some admitted that they did not see the program but had been told about it by their spouse or an acquaintance.) The response from law enforcement as a result of that show was significantly greater than the response resulting from any article that Gary L. Wells had published, including an article in a law review. Similar effects were observed following a segment on the program *60 Minutes*, articles in *The New York Times*, interviews on National Public Radio, and so on. The point is that much of the social science information that enters the "attention agenda" of policymakers and practitioners in the United States is presented through popular media. Although this probably should not surprise us, we are nonetheless typically surprised.

Because popular media are so effective in reaching millions of people, it is important to ensure that complex ideas are expressed in relatively simple ways to maximize these effects. In fact, it could be argued that the key to the transfer of system-variable findings into actual practice is the communication of those ideas in everyday language. The success of transferring system-variable research findings to affect actual practices relies on the ability of researchers to bridge the communication gap. We suggest that this bridge can be broken down into three key components. First, it is generally best to use the language of the audience (e.g., police, prosecutors) rather than the language of the researchers. For instance, eyewitness identification researchers historically used the word *distractor* to refer to the nonsuspects in a lineup. But law enforcement and others in the legal system never use that term. In fact, the term *distractor* (spelled with the *-or* ending) was largely invented by cognitive psychology researchers from the past and is not even a recognized word in the English language. For the most part, eyewitness researchers have now shifted to the common language of police and others in the legal system in calling these nonsuspects in the lineup *fillers*.

Second, to communicate effectively through popular media, ideas must be expressed in ways that relate to matters with which people are already familiar. The use of metaphor and analogy is particularly powerful. For example, eyewitness research has made great use of the idea that human memory is not like a camera (e.g., memory is a reconstruction rather than a playback), the analogy between physical trace evidence and memory trace evidence (e.g., concern about contamination, the need for a clear protocol, preservation), and the lineup as a multiple-choice test (in which the correct answer might be "none of the above"). Without analogy or metaphor readily available to the eyewitness expert, the communication of complex ideas is sometimes too awkward or too wordy for journalists and for practitioners.

Third, communication from researchers to popular media always needs to have elements of a proper "story." In the case of system variables, for example, this means that the story should typically begin with convincing evidence that there is a problem. One of the most common approaches has been to cite the Innocence Project reports, which show that 75% of the people exonerated with DNA testing were mistakenly identified (Scheck, Neufeld, & Dwyer, 2000). The next element of the story should convince listeners that using better procedures can prevent some of these mistakes. (Notice that the term *system variables* is not actually needed to tell this story. Why introduce a term that requires one to offer up a definition when the term is not needed?) In keeping with the idea that popular media have relatively low limits for length and complexity, communication should be restricted to two or three easily described examples. In the case of system variables, this might mean mentioning the prelineup admonition instruction or double-blind lineups and forgoing discussion of complex rules for selecting fillers. The idea is not that popular media will itself be the source for new policies or procedures but that the media coverage will increase interest and motivation. This increase will then lead policymakers and practitioners to take the next step and seek more detailed information. In fact, going from a media story on eyewitness identification to a Google search of key terms produces results that could easily put policymakers and practitioners in direct contact with eyewitness experts.

Working With Policymakers

Generally, the successful transfer of system-variable research to policies and practices by law enforcement agencies has materialized through policymakers initiating contact with eyewitness researchers, not vice versa. Consider the examples of numerous U.S. jurisdictions that have made reforms by adopting the best eyewitness instructions (see Chapter 3, this volume), research-based methods of selecting lineup fillers (see Chapter 4), double-blind procedures (see Chapter 6), and so on. States such as New Jersey, North Carolina, Wisconsin, Texas, and Connecticut, for example, had already decided to explore the idea of eyewitness identification reforms (e.g., through commissions) before turning to eyewitness identification researchers for advice regarding the scientific foundations for various reform options. The same is true for various cities and counties such as Dallas, Denver, Boston, Santa Clara County (California), Hennepin County (Minnesota), and others. The primary driving force in these jurisdictions was a combination of recent DNA exonerations (clearly the precipitating factor in the states of New Jersey, North Carolina, Wisconsin, Texas, and Connecticut as well as the city of Boston) plus media coverage of eyewitness system variables as a possible way to prevent these wrongful convictions. See the Conclusion for more discussion of eyewitness identification reforms in practice.

Policymakers necessarily have to think at a much broader level than do researchers. This is because their constituencies and their policy domains tend to be very broad. Consider a police chief, for example. The police chief has to weigh the effects of a policy change not only on the rates of mistaken identifications but also on potential financial and time costs. Will switching to double-blind lineups, for example, become a resource problem? Will this mean that two detectives would have to be available for trial, not just the case detective but also the blind lineup administrator? How will the detectives perceive imposing a new procedure on them, such as the double-blind procedure? Might they construe this requirement as an indication that the detectives are not to be trusted? How can detectives be "bought in" to the procedure so that they do not simply interpret it as a new bureaucratic order?

In most jurisdictions across the United States, no police department would significantly change their eyewitness identification procedures without getting buy-in from the district attorney's office. Further, district attorneys will want their assistant prosecutors to be on board as well. In fact, prosecutors are always represented on task forces or commissions assembled to address eyewitness identification reform issues. Furthermore, to the extent that there is stiff resistance to reform, it tends to come from prosecutors more than from police (see Wells et al., 2000).

Why more resistance from prosecutors than from police? Some of this greater resistance from prosecutors than from police stems from the fact that police commonly observe witnesses identifying known-innocent fillers from lineups (which tend to account for 30%–40% of all identifications made by eyewitnesses), whereas prosecutors almost never see these erroneous identifications. Hence, police see eyewitness mistakes frequently, whereas prosecutors only tend to see the "successful" identifications that make it to trial. Another reason for prosecutors' resistance is that they have traditionally "battled" eyewitness experts in court (eyewitness experts being typically called by the defense) and have honed arguments discrediting the research. Such arguments often question the application of the research to actual eyewitnesses in the real world. Thus, there is something almost dissonant about prosecutors endorsing reform recommendations from the very eyewitness experts that they often attempt to discredit.

Understanding the likely thoughts, reservations, and motives of policymakers is critical for a successful dialogue. Policymakers are just like everyone else in the sense that they want to know how or why something is in their best interest. Of course, people in the justice system should be motivated purely by a desire for justice, and they are for the most part. But pointing out additional benefits of reform can still help move the ball forward. Prosecutors, for instance, find the idea that reforms to eyewitness identification procedures could help to keep eyewitness experts out of the courtroom (or undermine the "bite" of their testimony) appealing. Oddly, most seem not to consider this benefit until it is pointed out to them. Another benefit that appeals to prosecutors is that pristine eyewitness identification procedures can result in more guilty pleas from defendants and their attorneys,)who consequently see less opportunity to pick holes in identification evidence at trial. Further, one could argue that the jurors will find the identification evidence more compelling if the procedures are not being called into question because of suggestive procedures.

For police, the perceived benefits are somewhat different. One benefit of systemic reforms is that they can prevent criticism of the detective on the witness stand. For example, defense attorneys are becoming quite proficient in cross-examining detectives and suggesting that detectives' behaviors somehow cued or led the witness or inflated the witness's certainty. If double-blind procedures were used, however, that entire line of criticism or suggestion is jettisoned from the trial.

An additional benefit recognized by police relates to the idea that factors such as including prelineup cautionary instructions and using the sequential procedure reduce the chances of witnesses identifying fillers. This is something that experienced detectives immediately see as a huge benefit because most experienced detectives have had a situation in which a witness identified a filler and later a new suspect was discovered. Unfortunately, because the witness identified a filler earlier, that witness is no longer credible to identify the new suspect. Had the witness identified no one from the earlier lineup, however, the witness would still be credible for viewing the new lineup with someone who is likely the actual culprit.

Many police and prosecutors tend to be naturally (and understandably) dismissive of academics, researchers, and others who have not themselves investigated and prosecuted criminal cases. This potentially dismissive attitude is all the more reason researchers should immerse themselves in knowledge of the investigation and prosecution of crime to avoid coming across as naïve or making unrealistic recommendations. Consider some key examples. Some eyewitness researchers have suggested that police should cease conducting showups (a one-on-one identification procedure) because witness errors always "load up" on the suspect (see Chapter 2, this volume, for a review of research on showups). Lineups, on the other hand, allow errors to be distributed across known-innocent fillers. Despite the greater safety to an innocent suspect afforded by lineups compared with showups, it is naïve to suggest that showups should be eradicated. There are several legitimate reasons why it could be bad policy to advocate the abolition of showups despite what the research might show. For example, in most cases it is impossible to actually conduct a lineup when a person who fits the description has been detained near the scene of a crime. This is because similarity to a description is not justification for an arrest, and the relatively short time that one can legally detain someone (without arrest) is insufficient for composing a lineup. If showups were not permitted, the detained person would have to go free, which could mean setting free a dangerous person. Furthermore, calling for the abolition of showups ignores the fact that showups often result in rejections (witnesses see the detained person and say that is not the person), which quickly frees the innocent from suspicion.

Consider another example in which a myopic view of the research findings could lead to a naïve recommendation or otherwise problematic interaction with police or prosecutors. Most lab studies conduct sequential lineups such that the procedure is stopped as soon as the witness makes an identification (see Chapter 5, this volume, for a review of research on sequential presentation). If an eyewitness expert suggested that this *stopping rule* be used in actual cases, however, both police and prosecutors would dismiss the expert as someone out of touch with the realities of the real world. Consider the prosecutor's perspective, for example. Suppose the witness picks someone in Position 2 who turns out to be the suspect and the procedure is stopped in concordance with the stopping rule. When the prosecutor takes the case to trial, the defense will hammer the procedure, "You only showed the witness photos of two people?!" Even worse, suppose the suspect is in Position 1, the witness chooses him, and the procedure is stopped. The stopping rule for sequential lineups, although prevalent in research experiments, is a totally unrealistic procedure in actual cases. Notice again the importance of understanding the environment in which police and prosecutors operate. It is critical to understand the broader context in which policies and procedures must work for the actors in the legal system to constructively and credibly work with policymakers.

SUMMARY AND FINAL REMARKS

The system-variable concept continues to resonate among researchers and those in the legal system for a variety of reasons, primarily because it communicates a positive, constructive message of how to improve the reliability of eyewitness identification evidence. The system-variables domain has expanded from its original construal to include factors such as certainty inflation and base rates for perpetrator-present versus perpetrator-absent lineups. Some might criticize the substantial emphasis researchers have placed on system variables to the extent that it has come at the cost of furthering knowledge of important estimator variables. Regardless, there is little denial that the system-variable emphasis in the eyewitness research literature has fostered a working relationship between eyewitness researchers and actors in the legal system that could not have been achieved otherwise.

The relatively large numbers of highly motivated and well-trained young eyewitness identification researchers who are now in the field (compared with the small number of researchers who started this literature) ensure that the future of system-variable research will be a bright one. However, one could also look pessimistically at the ability of the traditional system-variable approach to yield the fuller solutions needed for improving eyewitness identification evidence. Consider the recent field experiment reporting the results of 497 lineups given to actual eyewitnesses in which all the very best system procedures were used (e.g., the best prelineup instructions, double-blind procedures, sequential presentation; Wells et al., 2011). The results show that 42% of those who made an identification from a simultaneous lineup identified a known-innocent filler. The sequential procedure fared better than the simultaneous, yielding 31% filler identifications among those making an identification. Despite better results from the sequential procedure, it is shocking that using all the best system-variable practices still resulted in nearly one of every three actual eyewitnesses making a mistaken identification. What does this say about the prospects for system variables to prevent wrongful convictions in eyewitness cases? Is it possible that traditional system-variable solutions are running up against the inherent limitations of human memory?

One direction that might prove fruitful is to begin thinking more about a third type of variable, which, for the moment, we call *system-diagnostic variables*. These are variables that the justice system can create (hence the term *system*) that help diagnose the likelihood that an identification was accurate versus mistaken. Perhaps the greatest potential for a system-diagnostic variable is the video recording of eyewitness identifications while they occur. This is certainly not a new idea (e.g., see Kassin, 1998). But much of the research that might confirm the efficacy of this idea has not actually been done. The question concerns whether certain witness behaviors could help sort (diagnose) the likely accuracy or inaccuracy of that witness. Obvious examples include the speed of the identification, eye movements, pupil dilation, and spontaneous verbal comments. We call these system-diagnostic variables because the justice system does not currently use methods to preserve this information, but there is potential to do so in the future. What can we learn from the utterings, the hems and haws, the facial expressions, and the gesturing of eyewitnesses while they perform an identification task? We already know that speed of an identification is related to eyewitness identification accuracy, and yet we know of no jurisdictions in the United States that are measuring this variable. Accordingly, there are system-level recommendations to be made regarding the collection and preservation of this type of evidence.

System-diagnostic research is not just estimator-variable research in the traditional sense because it involves information that the justice system could (but is currently not) collecting and preserving. In that sense, it is a system variable; it is something over which the justice system has control (they could videotape) but currently chooses not to exert that control. This means that system-diagnostic research shares some qualities that system-variable research has in that it translates into policy recommendations regarding best practices and procedures. At the same time, system diagnostics are not synonymous with traditional system variables because they do not prevent mistaken identifications but rather attempt to diagnose them.

Our idea is that a full treatment of the eyewitness identification problem requires a tripartite approach that involves traditional estimator variables (e.g., lighting, distance, same race, other race), traditional system variables (e.g., double-blind procedures, prelineup admonitions), and system-diagnostic variables (e.g., video recording identifications and using objective assessment tools for analyzing the video). Putting all our faith in any one of these three approaches is not likely to produce the success that we hope to achieve, that is, the prevention of convictions of the innocent on the basis of mistaken identification. Taken together, however, the system-variable, system-diagnostic, estimator-variable approach has great promise for reducing convictions of the innocent.

REFERENCES

Douglass, A. B., & Steblay, N. (2006). Memory distortion in eyewitnesses: A meta-analysis of the post-identification feedback effect. *Applied Cognitive Psychology, 20*, 859–869. doi:10.1002/acp.1237

Kassin, S. M. (1998). Eyewitness identification procedures: The fifth rule. *Law and Human Behavior, 22*, 649–653. doi:10.1023/A:1025702722645

Loftus, E. F. (1979). *Eyewitness testimony*. Cambridge, MA: Harvard University Press.

Loftus, E. F., & Palmer, J. C. (1974). Reconstruction of an automobile destruction: An example of the interaction between language and memory. *Journal of Verbal Learning & Verbal Behavior, 13*, 585–589. doi:10.1016/S0022-5371(74)80011-3

Loftus, G. R., & Harley, E. M. (2005). Why is it easier to identify someone close than far away? *Psychonomic Bulletin & Review, 12*, 43–65. doi:10.3758/BF03196348

Manson v. Brathwaite, 432 U.S. 98 (1977).

Munsterberg, H. (1908). *On the witness stand: Essays on psychology and crime*. New York, NY: Doubleday.

Perry v. New Hampshire, 132 S. Ct. 716 (2012).

Scheck, B., Neufeld, P., & Dwyer, J. (2000). *Actual innocence*. New York, NY: Doubleday.

Seelau, S. M., & Wells, G. L. (1995). Applied eyewitness research: The other mission. *Law and Human Behavior, 19*, 319–324. doi:10.1007/BF01501663

Snee, T., & Lush, D. (1941). Interaction of the narrative and interrogatory methods of obtaining testimony. *The Journal of Psychology: Interdisciplinary and Applied, 11*, 229–236. doi:10.1080/00223980.1941.9917031

Wells, G. L. (1978). Applied eyewitness testimony research: System variables and estimator variables. *Journal of Personality and Social Psychology, 36*, 1546–1557. doi:10.1037/0022-3514.36.12.1546

Wells, G. L. (1993). What do we know about eyewitness identification? *American Psychologist, 48*, 553–571. doi:10.1037/0003-066X.48.5.553

Wells, G. L., & Bradfield, A. L. (1998). "Good, you identified the suspect:" Feedback to eyewitnesses distorts their reports of the witnessing experience. *Journal of Applied Psychology, 83*, 360–376. doi:10.1037/0021-9010.83.3.360

Wells, G. L., & Lindsay, R. C. L. (1980). On estimating the diagnosticity of eyewitness nonidentifications. *Psychological Bulletin, 88,* 776–784. doi:10.1037/0033-2909.88.3.776

Wells, G. L., & Loftus, E. F. (2003). Eyewitness memory for people and events. In A. Goldstein, (Ed.), *Comprehensive handbook of psychology: Vol. 11. Forensic psychology* (pp. 149–160). New York, NY: Wiley.

Wells, G. L., Malpass, R. S., Lindsay, R. C. L., Fisher, R. P., Turtle, J. W., & Fulero, S. (2000). From the lab to the police station: A successful application of eyewitness research. *American Psychologist, 55,* 581–598. doi:10.1037/0003-066X.55.6.581

Wells, G. L., & Quinlivan, D. S. (2009). Suggestive eyewitness identification procedures and the Supreme Court's reliability test in light of eyewitness science: 30 years later. *Law and Human Behavior, 33,* 1–24. doi:10.1007/s10979-008-9130-3

Wells, G. L., Steblay, N. K., & Dysart, J. E. (2011). *A test of the simultaneous vs. sequential lineup methods: An initial report of the AJS national eyewitness identification field studies.* Unpublished manuscript, American Judicature Society. Retrieved from http://www.ajs.org/wc/pdfs/EWID_PrintFriendly.pdf

Wells, G. L., & Turtle, J. W. (1986). Eyewitness identification: The importance of lineup models. *Psychological Bulletin, 99,* 320–329. doi:10.1037/0033-2909.99.3.320

2

SHOWUPS

CHARLES A. GOODSELL, STACY A. WETMORE,
JEFFREY S. NEUSCHATZ, AND SCOTT D. GRONLUND

Ms. Winton received a phone call from her security company that her back door alarm had been triggered. She was concerned and called Mr. Fletcher, who lived close to the residence, to check on her house. He parked near the back of the residence and noticed a man in the backyard stuffing items into a bag. As Mr. Fletcher approached the house, the man heard him and took off running. Mr. Fletcher took chase, but the suspect disappeared into the woods behind a neighbor's home. Mr. Fletcher went back to Ms. Winton's house, where he met with her and police officers to discuss what happened. Later Mr. Fletcher was driving home and thought he saw the suspect again and immediately called the police. The police apprehended a man, Mr. Ellerby, who matched the description they had been given, although he was wearing a

This work was supported by the National Science Foundation Grants SES-1060913 to Charles A. Goodsell, SES-1060921 to Jeffrey S. Neuschatz, and SES-1060902 to Scott D. Gronlund. Any opinions, findings, and conclusions or recommendations expressed in this material are those of the authors and do not reflect the views of the National Science Foundation. The authors thank John Wixted and H. Lloyd Perkins for their helpful comments.

DOI: 10.1037/14094-003
Reform of Eyewitness Identification Procedures, B. L. Cutler (Editor)

hat and sunglasses, which was not part of the original description. Mr. Ellerby was placed in the backseat of a patrol car, and Mr. Fletcher was brought to the scene and positively identified him as the man he chased from the home. Fortunately for Mr. Ellerby, the actual perpetrator was later arrested for an unrelated crime and confessed to the burglary.

This one-person identification performed in the Ellerby case is termed a *showup*. In this chapter, we review how showups are used and discuss the relevant law regarding their use. The most important questions surrounding showups involve whether they are unduly suggestive and how they compare with lineups in that regard. Therefore, we review how showups and lineups should be compared and what factors complicate that comparison. This discussion moves into an analysis of variables likely to have a greater effect on showups than on lineups. These variables include clothing bias, expectation, and presentation mode (live vs. photographic). Finally, we conclude with suggestions for best practice guidelines for showups and policy implications regarding their use.

Apprehending a suspect near the scene of a crime and asking a witness to make an identification about that suspect are common actions. According to several sources (e.g., Dysart & Lindsay, 2007), showups are the most common form of eyewitness identification. In their archival study of the Sacramento Police Department and the surrounding metropolitan area, Behrman and Davey (2001) reported that of the 689 identifications conducted from 1987 to 1998, 271 (40%) were showup identifications. Similarly, Flowe, Ebbesen, Burke, and Chivabunditt (2001) found that showups constituted 55% of the 488 identifications from 1991 to 1995 in metropolitan areas in the western United States. The estimates of showup identifications as a percentage of all identifications range from 30% to 77% (Gonzalez, Ellsworth, & Pembroke, 1993; McQuiston & Malpass, 2001).

Showup identification procedures have advantages over traditional multiperson lineups. First, showups have the potential to be conducted hastily, relative to lineups, and therefore can help law enforcement personnel to quickly detain criminals and free innocent people of suspicion. Second, as has been well documented in the literature, memory performance decreases with time (e.g., Light, 1996). Research on eyewitness identification demonstrates that witnesses tend to perform more poorly at identifying guilty suspects as time progresses (Clark & Godfrey, 2009). Therefore, it is better to test memory (i.e., administer an eyewitness identification procedure) after a short than a long delay. Thus, if a showup can be conducted sooner than a lineup could be, better memory performance could be achieved as a result of the reduced delay between the incident and the administration of the identification procedure.

But there are potential disadvantages to showup identifications. Garrett (2011) reviewed 160 DNA exoneration cases and found that 34% (53/160) involved misidentifications from showups. Furthermore, in a survey of eye-witness identification experts, Kassin, Tubb, Hosch, and Memon (2001) reported that 74% of the respondents endorsed the statement that showups increased the likelihood of a false identification relative to lineups. We turn next to a discussion of the factors that ostensibly enhance the suggestibility of showups.

SHOWUPS IN THE FIELD

Showups are used in the field when the police can apprehend a suspect who matches the victim's description of the perpetrator and who is within a reasonable distance (e.g., a few blocks, miles radius) and a reasonable time frame (i.e., less than 2 hours) of the incident. Cases in which these criteria are not met typically result in a lineup (H. Lloyd Perkins,[1] personal communication, January 23, 2012). Although showups are typically administered within a short time after a crime, there are instances in which showups have been used much later. For example, in October 1985, a woman was attacked in her home in Alexandria, Virginia. She gave the police a description of a man wearing a gray hooded sweatshirt and red shorts. A few weeks later the police showed the witness a photo array that included a neighbor, Walter Snyder, who happened to own red shorts. She did not identify anyone. Two months later Snyder went to the police department to ask for his shorts back. Police officers brought the victim in and asked her if Snyder was her attacker. She indicated that he was, and he subsequently was convicted and sentenced to 45 years in prison. He served 7 years before DNA evidence exonerated him (Mid-Atlantic Innocence Project, 2012).

Several procedural safeguards for conducting eyewitness identification procedures have been recommended by social science researchers (e.g., U.S. Department of Justice, Office of Justice Programs, National Institute of Justice, 1999; Wells et al., 1998). Recommendations for unbiased instructions (see Chapter 3, this volume) and double-blind administration (see Chapter 6) have made their way into police departments around the United States. But because lineups typically are conducted in a controlled environment, it is easier for the officers to follow a regimented protocol in the administration of a lineup. Moreover, the nature of administering an identification procedure in the field means that officers must rely more on their training and experience when conducting a showup (H. Lloyd Perkins, personal communication, January 23, 2012). In other words, whereas a lineup can be conducted in

---

[1]Chief of police, Skaneateles Police Department, Skaneateles, New York.

a similar manner each time it is given, the conduct of a showup may fluctuate as a result of many different factors.

This variability is evident in how showups are administered. Ideally, a witness or victim will be transported to where the suspect has been detained and asked to indicate if the suspect is or is not the perpetrator (H. Lloyd Perkins, personal communication, January 23, 2012). To minimize suggestion, police try to avoid having the suspect in handcuffs, wearing identifying clothing (e.g., the witness describes the perpetrator as wearing a hooded sweatshirt, so the officer has the suspect remove the sweatshirt), standing next to a uniformed officer, or sitting in the back of a police car. However, this is not always possible. Suspects who are uncooperative can become a flight risk or violent, and they must be restrained to ensure the safety of everyone involved (H. Lloyd Perkins, personal communication, January 23, 2012). Furthermore, there are circumstances in which the witness or victim cannot be transported (e.g., when medical attention is needed) and the suspect must be brought to the witness.

What does the law have to say about the impact of these factors on showup identifications? To examine how the U.S. Supreme Court views the admissibility of showup identifications, we use the following major Court decisions: in *Stovall v. Denno* (1967), *Neil v. Biggers* (1972), and *Manson v. Brathwaite* (1977). After reviewing these criteria, we evaluate whether they achieve the purpose they were created to accomplish: preventing the admission of suggestive eyewitness procedures and unreliable eyewitness evidence in court. Wells and Quinlivan (2009) have already started this important work, and we summarize and expand on their findings.

RELEVANT LAW REGARDING SHOWUPS

Stovall v. Denno

The landmark case regarding showups is *Stovall v. Denno* (1967). In *Stovall*, the Supreme Court opined that due process forbids any pretrial identification that is suggestive and conducive to misidentification. The facts of the case were as follows: During an attack, Dr. Paul Behrendt was stabbed to death, and his wife was critically injured. A shirt and keys left at the scene led to the arrest of Theodore Stovall. Two days after the attack, Stovall was brought to Mrs. Bherendt's hospital room for a showup identification. Mrs. Behrendt identified him as her attacker. At the time of the identification, Stovall did not have any legal representation and was handcuffed to a police officer for the entire hospital confrontation. Stovall was convicted and sentenced to death. He appealed the decision, arguing that his due process rights were violated because he was not represented by counsel during identification. In identification proceedings, due process means that the police must not use unduly suggestive procedures (*Foster v. California*, 1969). The appeal reached the U.S. Supreme Court, which affirmed the conviction, ruling that the identification procedure, although suggestive, was necessary because of the injured state of the witness. Doctors had informed the investigators that the witness had a small chance of surviving surgery. The court decision in *Stovall* was to acknowledge that showups are more suggestive than lineups and to restrict showups only to case of emergencies.

As seen in *Stovall*, just because an identification is suggestive does not mean that a defendant's due process rights have been violated or that the identification is unreliable. The Court has held that whether a due process violation has occurred should be determined by the totality of the evidence. Under this standard, the U.S. Supreme Court has ruled that showups do not violate due process in the following situations:

- The showup was held a short time after the crime was committed. The courts have upheld such showups because memory is best immediately after a crime occurs as it affords officers the chance to quickly arrest or release persons of interests.
- The witness is in critical condition and may not survive long enough to view a lineup.
- The suspect is in criminal possession of property stolen from the witness.

Shortly after the *Stovall* decision, the U.S. Supreme Court decided that reliability was the lynchpin for the admissibility of identification evidence. In the 1970s, the Court developed a two-pronged test of reliability for all identification procedures (*Manson v. Brathwaite*, 1977; *Neil v. Biggers*, 1972). In the first prong, the Court evaluated the suggestiveness of the identification procedure. In the second prong, the Court attempted to determine whether the identification was accurate in spite of any biased procedures that were used. For example, a police officer may influence an eyewitness during the showup, but if the witness was the neighbor of the defendant for 20 years, the court might recognize that the identification is still likely to be accurate and allow the testimony. The second prong was activated only if the identification procedures were suggestive or failed the first prong.

First Prong—Suggestiveness or Bias

A *biased identification* is defined as one in which people who did not witness the event can choose the suspect at a rate greater than $1/n$, where

n is the number of individuals in the identification procedure (Neuschatz & Cutler, 2008).

Preidentification instructions are one factor that bias identifications. Biased instructions imply that the perpetrator is in the lineup, whereas unbiased instructions explicitly state that the perpetrator may or may not be in the lineup. The effect of these instructions can be dramatic (see Chapter 3, this volume). Steblay (1997) meta-analyzed the studies examining the effects of lineup instructions on identification accuracy and found a clear, consistent pattern. With perpetrator-absent lineups, unbiased instructions led to fewer false identifications (35%) than did biased lineup instructions (60%). However, unbiased instructions also can lead to a decrease in correct identifications when the perpetrator is present (Clark, 2005). If the identification procedure has been determined to be highly suggestive, the evaluation process proceeds to the second prong.

Second Prong—Five Factors

The U.S. Supreme Court has endorsed five factors for jurors to use in evaluating the reliability of eyewitness identifications. These factors are (a) opportunity to view, (b) attention, (c) description, (d) time to identification, and (e) certainty. The idea is that if a witness had ample opportunity to view the perpetrator, paid attention to the perpetrator as the crime was occurring, gave an accurate description of the perpetrator, and was confident that he or she had identified the correct person as the perpetrator, then the jurors can trust that the eyewitness is accurate in his or her identification. However, as Wells and Quinlivan (2009) suggested, these factors are only weakly related to identification accuracy, can be misleading as indices of identification accuracy, and therefore can be detrimental to juror decision making.

Postidentification feedback, for example, weakens the correlation between confidence, view, and attention with accuracy. *Postidentification feedback* refers to statements made to the witness from the lineup administrator regarding the accuracy of the identification. Wells and Bradfield (1998) had participants watch security footage and make an identification from a perpetrator-absent lineup. Following the identification, some of the participants were given erroneous confirming information from the experimenter ("Good, you identified the culprit"), and others were given no or negative feedback. Participants who were given confirming feedback subsequently reported that they paid more attention to the perpetrator, were more certain in their identification, and had a clearer view of perpetrator compared with participants who were not given feedback. Of course, these are the same factors that jurors are instructed to use as indicators of eyewitness accuracy.

Conclusion

In *Stovall*, the U.S. Supreme Court argued that showups are a suggestive identification procedure and should be avoided to the extent that other means of identification are available. The Court suggested that lineups be used instead of showups whenever possible. The Court, however, acknowledged that in certain situations showups may be the only option. Although the Court's decision in *Stovall* seemed to restrict showups to only emergency situations, *Neil v. Biggers* (1972) made it clear that law enforcement officials could conduct showups even if there was no emergency as long as there was no due process violation. Therefore, because the courts have raised the issue regarding the potential bias of a showup, it seems prudent to compare the empirical evidence evaluating showups and lineups to see if one technique is superior (i.e., more correct identifications of the perpetrator and/or fewer false identifications of the innocent suspect). If identification performance is similar between lineups and showups, then they should continue to be used given their advantages (discussed previously). However, if lineups consistently outperform showups, then the U.S. Supreme Court's decision in *Stovall* (use in emergency situations only) would be preferred. In the next section, we review the psychological literature on showup and lineup identifications.

SHOWUP VERSUS LINEUP

The scientific research regarding showups versus lineups is difficult to interpret. Although some researchers have indeed found a negative impact of showups (i.e., more false identifications than in lineups; Lindsay, Pozzulo, Craig, Lee, & Corber, 1997; Wagenaar & Veefkind, 1992; Yarmey, Yarmey, & Yarmey, 1994; Yarmey, Yarmey, & Yarmey, 1996), others have reported more correct identifications in showups when the perpetrator is present and higher correct rejection rates when the perpetrator is absent (Beal, Schmitt, & Dekle, 1995). Meta-analyses by Steblay, Dysart, Fulero, and Lindsay (2003) and Clark and Godfrey (2009) have examined the existing data to determine which identification procedure is the best. The best identification procedure should lead to more correct identifications when the perpetrator is present and fewer false identifications when the perpetrator is absent.

Analysis of Steblay et al. (2003)

Steblay et al. (2003) analyzed eight published articles that included 12 tests of identification performance in showups and lineups. The results from the meta-analysis revealed that the choosing rate, collapsed over perpetrator-present and perpetrator-absent conditions, was significantly higher in lineups (54%) than in showups (27%). Despite a lower choosing rate, the laboratory data indicated that showup choices were more accurate: Correct decisions (perpetrator identifications from perpetrator-present conditions + correct rejections from perpetrator-absent conditions) were significantly higher in showups (69%) than in lineups (51%). Witnesses in showups did not choose more often, and contrary to expert opinion (Kassin et al., 2001), when witnesses did choose from showups, they made more correct decisions. In addition, the number of incorrect identifications was significantly lower in showups (15%) than in lineups (43%). Showups appear to be superior.

Before we continue, we need to make a distinction between two types of incorrect identifications. A *false identification* refers to the identification of an innocent suspect who mistakenly is thought to have committed the crime; *filler identifications* refer to identifications of people in the lineup who are known to be innocent. The former is considered a dangerous error because of the potential for an innocent person to be prosecuted. But because there are six ways to make a filler identification (in a six-person lineup without a designated innocent suspect) but only one way to make an innocent suspect identification, we estimated an innocent suspect rate by dividing the filler identification rate by the number in the lineup to make these two types of incorrect identifications comparable (Clark, Howell, & Davey, 2008).

Steblay et al. (2003) argued that comparing incorrect decisions was misleading because filler identifications from lineups were not dangerous errors. Instead, they argued that it made more sense to compare errors involving only the identification of an innocent suspect. But only five of the 12 experiments included a designated innocent suspect. When Steblay et al. focused on just those studies (Dekle, Beal, Elliott, & Honeycutt, 1996; Yarmey et al., 1994, 1996), they found that the false identification rate from showups (23%) was higher than that for lineups (10%). One issue with this conclusion is that it only takes into account correct identifications in perpetrator-present and correct rejections in perpetrator-absent lineups. Clark and Godfrey (2009) pointed out that this comparison places lineups at a disadvantage because witnesses can choose a filler in a lineup but cannot do so in a showup. For example, assume that 40% of witnesses are willing to choose the innocent suspect from a showup, which results in a 60% correct rejection rate. But in a fair lineup, some of the 60% of witnesses who would have rejected the showup may choose to select one of the lineup fillers. Every filler choice reduces the correct rejection rate of the lineup. Therefore, they argued for the use of conditional probability to compare two identifications procedures.

Analysis of Clark and Godfrey (2009)

In their review, Clark and Godfrey (2009) included the five comparisons from Steblay et al. (2003) described previously (Dekle et al., 1996; Yarmey et al., 1994, 1996) with the addition of Dekle (1997), Lindsay et al. (1997), and Wagenaar and Veefkind (1992). The result was a total of 15 showup–lineup comparisons. Contrary to Steblay et al., Clark and Godfrey found that correct identification rates in perpetrator-present conditions and innocent suspect identifications from perpetrator-absent conditions were not significantly different between lineups and showups.

Clark and Godfrey (2009) argued that the joint consideration of correct and false identification rates was a better measure of identification performance (see also Gronlund, Carlson, Dailey, & Goodsell, 2009). Clark and Godfrey argued that a measure of probative value like the conditional probability of a suspect identification affords a more appropriate comparison between different identification procedures because it is unaffected by the filler response rate, which showups cannot have. Conditional probability is the probability of choosing the guilty suspect given that a suspect (innocent or guilty) was chosen (= [(guilty suspect identifications from perpetrator-present lineups)/(guilty suspect identifications from perpetrator-present lineups + innocent suspect identifications from perpetrator-absent lineups)]). Clark and Godfrey found that the conditional probability for lineups (.79) was significantly higher than for showups (.69), indicating that showups put an innocent suspect at greater risk of being falsely identified.

But conditional probability is not without its problems. It is influenced by response biases (see Clark, Erickson, & Breneman 2011; see also Chapter 5, this volume). That is, it covaries with the choosing rate: An identification procedure could have a higher conditional probability because it results in better performance or because it exacts a higher level of confidence (i.e., a more conservative rate of choosing). That makes conditional probability, or any measure of probative value, problematic for comparing performance across different testing procedures that differ in choosing rates. There is evidence that showups produce less conservative choosing, which would contribute to finding a lineup advantage (see Meissner, Tredoux, Parker, & MacLin, 2005). Thus, the use of measures like conditional probability may confuse, rather than inform, researchers' ability to determine which identification procedure is superior.

Wixted and Mickes (2012) supported this view. Wixted and Mickes used the simultaneous–sequential lineup debate (see Chapter 5, this volume) as the backdrop for their proposal that receiver-operating characteristic (ROC) curves should replace traditional measures like correct identification rate, false identification rate, and diagnosticity (correct or false) as well as other probative value measures like conditional probability. ROC analyses are standard practice for testing between diagnostic procedures in the medical literature, especially radiologic decision making (e.g., Lusted, 1971; Pisano et al., 2005, compared the performance of film vs. digital mammography using ROC analysis). Their use is long overdue in the eyewitness domain. Unfortunately, ROC curves comparing showups and lineups do not yet exist.

Where does this leave us? Some might conclude that lineups appear to result in more accurate identifications. However, we believe that the evidence on that point is not definitive given the limited number of tests comparing showups and lineups and the issues raised regarding performance measures like conditional probability. This point underscores the need for more research on the topic. And if more research is needed, there are three factors that must play a role: (a) the expectation that the suspect is the perpetrator, (b) the effect of clothing on the identification, and (c) live versus photographic identifications. These factors are important to decisions regarding which identification procedure is superior because these factors likely have a greater impact on showups. In other words, to the extent that these factors confound comparisons of showups versus lineups, they could inflate the purported benefit of lineups over showups.

VARIABLES CONFOUNDING THE SHOWUP VERSUS LINEUP COMPARISON

Expectation

Quinlivan et al. (2012) examined the effect of expectations in lineups. After watching a mock video crime, participants were given biased or unbiased lineup instructions. Half of each of the instruction groups were given the expectation that the perpetrator would be in the lineup by suggesting to the witness that they would be able to pick out the "right person." All lineups were perpetrator absent so the correct choice was not to make an identification. In the no-expectation control condition, participants who received biased lineup instructions chose significantly more often than participants who received unbiased instructions (100% and 39%, respectively). This is the typical effect of unbiased instruction—a reduction in false identifications (Malpass & Devine, 1981; Neuschatz & Cutler, 2008). However, when participants were given the expectation that the perpetrator was in the lineup, the choosing rate in the unbiased condition increased to 83%, which was not significantly different from the 100% choosing in the biased condition. Given that showups typically occur shortly after a crime has been committed, it is reasonable to assume that a witness believes there is a very strong chance that the police found the perpetrator. In fact, a victim might be brought to the location where the suspect was found or where the suspect is presented in handcuffs or sitting in the back of a police car. Thus, expectations likely are higher that a showup includes the perpetrator. That means that expectations exert a greater impact on showups than lineups. However, more research is needed to make this determination.

Clothing Bias

Clothing bias poses a greater problem for showups than lineups. Clothing plays a bigger role in showups in that a suspect might be apprehended because he matches the description of the perpetrator, and clothing is one of the most frequent descriptors given by witnesses (Lindsay, Martin, & Webber, 1994). Thus, innocent people dressed in clothing similar to the perpetrator are at risk of being apprehended and falsely identified. On the other hand, lineups are more likely to feature individuals wearing prison scrubs or clothing different than what was worn at the time of the crime.

Clothing can bias a witness into making a false identification of an innocent suspect. The case of Arthur Carmona demonstrates the danger. The police found Carmona near the scene of a robbery and put him in a showup. Before asking the witness to make an identification decision, police had him put on a Lakers' cap linked to the crime. Largely on the basis of this identification, Carmona was convicted and spent 2 years in prison before being released (Carmona, 2007). Two studies have examined this issue. In Yarmey et al. (1996), the perpetrator approached volunteers in public places and asked for directions. After varying retention intervals the volunteers completed a showup. In one condition the perpetrator and the suspect wore the same clothing; in the other condition the suspect wore a sweater that differed in color and style from the one worn by the perpetrator. The results revealed more false identifications in the perpetrator-absent condition when the clothing matched. However, Dysart, Lindsay, and Dupuis (2006) found a clothing bias effect only when the suspect wore distinctive clothing (e.g., a Harley-Davidson t-shirt); there was no clothing bias when suspects were dressed in typical clothing (e.g., blue button-down dress shirt).

The events in the aforementioned studies took place under optimal conditions (i.e., good lighting, clear view, no weapons, etc.). Optimal viewing conditions likely mitigate the effect of clothing bias. Real crimes, however, often occur in situations that do not offer optimal viewing conditions (e.g., low light, extreme stress, disguises). In fact, according to the *outshining hypothesis* (Smith, 1988, 1994), clothing bias should have a greater effect when typical cues like hairstyle and eyes are less salient because strong retrieval cues outshine weaker cues. Moreover, if retrieval cues that ordinarily are present are degraded, other context cues could be substituted. Facial cues are strong retrieval cues in eyewitness identification. If these cues are encoded well, contextual cues like clothing should have little impact on identification accuracy. But if the facial cues are degraded, cues like clothing may be called on to aid memory. Thus, according to the outshining hypothesis, a clothing bias should be more pronounced when the facial cues of the perpetrator are degraded, as would frequently occur in the real world. In other words, poor encoding of the face would increase reliance on clothing, which is more likely to match in a showup.

Photograph Versus Live

In addition to expectation and clothing bias, the mode of presentation of the identification task (e.g. a live presentation, photo, video) may differentially influence showups and lineups. Because showups are conducted relatively soon after the crime, they are typically live. Lineups, however, are often conducted as photo arrays as a result of the fact that digital photo databases make them easier to create. It is reasonable to assume that a live identification task like a showup would provide more cues to memory compared with a static image. In addition, lineup photos often can be dated and may not necessarily match how a perpetrator looked at the time of the crime. The issue is that different modes of presentation may convey different characteristics, or cues, about the perpetrator. Valentine and Heaton (1999) examined the differences between individuals who were asked to make an identification from a live or videotaped identification task. They found that 25% of the participants were able to select the suspect from the live lineup; however, only 15% of the participants were able to select the suspect from a video lineup. Cutler and Fisher (1990) found no significant differences in correct identifications between a live lineup, a videotaped lineup, or a photo lineup. However, both the live and video format resulted in fewer false identifications (see also, Kerstholt, Koster, & van Amelsvoort, 2004). In contrast, Morgan et al., (2004) found that the live lineup resulted in fewer correct identifications. More research is needed to understand how mode of presentation may affect showup and lineup performance given the confounding in the literature.

Despite important questions remaining concerning the differential contributions of expectations, clothing bias, and mode of presentation, the police still frequently conduct showups and will continue to do so. Therefore, it behooves psychologists to make sure that best practices are being followed until a more definitive recommendation can be made regarding which identification procedure is superior. For that reason we conclude this chapter by outlining some best practice guidelines and policy implications.

BEST PRACTICE GUIDELINES

In 1999, under the leadership of U.S. Attorney General Janet Reno, the U.S. Department of Justice published a best practices guide for conducting identification procedures (U.S. Department of Justice, Office of Justice Programs, National Institute of Justice, 1999), which included a section on showup identifications. The guide acknowledged the potential suggestive nature of showups and recommended the following procedures to avoid biasing the witness. First, the investigator should document the witness's description of the perpetrator prior to the identification procedure. Thus, viewing the suspect during the identification will not influence the witness's description. Second, if multiple witnesses are involved, the person conducting the identification should keep the witnesses separate so that they do not influence one another's identification or description. Furthermore, in the case of multiple witnesses, if one witness makes a positive identification from a showup, then the investigator should consider a different identification procedure for the remaining witnesses (e.g., lineup). Third, inform witnesses that the suspect they are about to view may or may not be the perpetrator. Unbiased instructions reduce the increase in false identifications from lineups, but the same findings have yet to be demonstrated in the showup literature (Clark, 2005; Malpass & Devine, 1981). Fourth, after an identification (or nonidentification) has been made, the investigator should record the witness's confidence assessment before it can be influenced by other events (e.g., other witness statements, the media) to preserve a record for trial. This is very important because jurors often rely on confidence as an indication of accuracy of the identification (Cutler, Penrod, & Dexter, 1990; Fox & Walters, 1986). Confidence can be influenced by a host of factors that are not related to the witness's memory of the event (see Chapter 7, this volume). We suggest one additional best practices guideline: The investigator should provide no feedback to the witness regarding the accuracy of the identification. As was mentioned earlier, feedback, both confirming (e.g., "Good, you identified the suspect") and even seemingly innocuous (e.g., "Take your time"; Clark, Marshall, & Rosenthal, 2009), can affect a witness's confidence and retrospective memory for the event (Neuschatz et al., 2005; Wells & Bradfield, 1998). If a suspect is identified from a showup identification, police should take a statement of confidence before moving the suspect, placing the suspect in handcuffs, or driving the suspect away in a police car, which would undoubtedly serve as confirming feedback.

POLICY RECOMMENDATIONS AND CONCLUSIONS

It is clear that law enforcement, scientists, and the courts all recognize the potential biasing influence showup identifications have on a witness making an identification decision. Many law enforcement agencies realize this and take steps to avoid some of these problems. However, as pointed out in the preceding discussion, factors like expectation, clothing, and mode of presentation have the potential to negatively impact showup identification decisions to a greater extent than lineup identification decisions.

Is a showup a viable procedure compared with a lineup? From our perspective as social scientists, we believe more research is warranted before policy recommendations can be made. Showups have obvious advantages in the field; they are fast and easy to implement and can quickly get criminals off the street or free innocent suspects from suspicion. But if showups are shown to be more suggestive than lineups, then lineup techniques need to be developed for use in the field (see Cutler, Daugherty, Babu, Hodges, & Van Wallendael, 2009, for an example of computerized unbiased lineup procedures). However, what about the role of lineup composition? Gronlund et al. (2009) showed large effects of lineup composition on performance. It is possible that a showup may be more suggestive than a fair lineup, the kind of lineup that could be painstakingly constructed in the lab, but a showup may not be more suggestive than a lineup hastily constructed in the field. Conversely, if showups are shown to be better than lineups at a short delay, or no worse at a long delay, police should be encouraged to use showups given how much easier they are to administer. But more research is needed to make this determination.

Malpass et al. (2008) suggested that to provide policymakers with information regarding potential policy change, a thorough examination of a topic is necessary. In particular, they proposed a systematic exploration of the relevant study space. A study space analysis involves identifying all relevant variables, including those that have been manipulated in existing research, those that have not been, as well as combinations of these variables. Researchers must comprehensively evaluate this study space before making recommendations to policymakers. For example, Malpass and colleagues pointed out that backloading (placing additional photos at the end of a sequential lineup so that the witness does not know how many photos he or she will view) and asking questions about each lineup member is common in sequential lineup presentation but not in the simultaneous procedure. Until variables like these are properly examined (i.e., the study space explored), Malpass et al. argued, one cannot determine the true cause of one lineup format outperforming another, and policy recommendations could be based on an incomplete understanding of the phenomena of interest.

Another prerequisite to policy recommendations involves the role of theory development to support the findings. Often practical questions in the psychology and law domain become the focus of research in lieu of theory development (Bornstein & Meissner, 2008). But Lane and Meissner (2008) argued that eyewitness identification would benefit from incorporating what is known about basic social and cognitive psychological research. This is beginning to happen. For example, Goodsell, Gronlund, and Carlson (2010) made productive use of Clark's (2003) WITNESS computational model to aid understanding of the sequential lineup advantage. Clark et al. (2011) also used the WITNESS computational model to explore relative versus absolute decision processes in simultaneous lineups. A theory-driven approach will prove vital to understanding why one type of identification procedure results in better performance or why one type is better in some circumstances but not others. It may even point to new identification procedures that are an improvement over existing ones.

The importance of understanding eyewitness identification has grown dramatically in the wake of the ever-increasing number of DNA exonerations (see http://www.innocenceproject.org) and with the increase of psychological experts testifying in courts on the reliability of identification evidence (Pezdek, 2007). Eyewitness identification accuracy will never be perfect, but it can be improved. Psychological experts need to determine if showups are part of the solution or part of the problem.

REFERENCES

Beal, C. R., Schmitt, K. L., & Dekle, D. J. (1995). Eyewitness identification of children: Effects of absolute judgments, nonverbal response options, and event encoding. *Law and Human Behavior, 19*, 197–216. doi:10.1007/BF01499325

Behrman, B. W., & Davey, S. L. (2001). Eyewitness identification in actual criminal cases: An archival analysis. *Law and Human Behavior, 25*, 475–491. doi:10.1023/A:1012840831846

Bornstein, B. H., & Meissner, C. A. (2008). Introduction: Basic and applied issues in eyewitness research: A Münsterberg centennial retrospective. *Applied Cognitive Psychology, 22*, 733–736. doi:10.1002/acp.1478

Carmona, A. (2007, July 13). Doing time for no crime: A young man freed after being wrongly imprisoned argues for three remedies. *Los Angeles Times*, p. A21.

Clark, S. E. (2003). A memory and decision model for eyewitness identification. *Applied Cognitive Psychology, 17*, 629–654. doi:10.1002/acp.891

Clark, S. E. (2005). A re-examination of the effects of biased lineup instructions in eyewitness identification. *Law and Human Behavior, 29*, 395–424. doi:10.1007/s10979-005-5690-7

Clark, S. E., Erickson, M. A., & Breneman, J. (2011). Probative value of absolute and relative judgments in eyewitness identification. *Law and Human Behavior*, *35*, 364–380. doi:10.1007/s10979-010-9245-1

Clark, S. E., & Godfrey, R. D. (2009). Eyewitness identification evidence and innocence risk. *Psychonomic Bulletin & Review*, *16*(1), 22–42. doi:10.3758/PBR.16.1.22

Clark, S. E., Howell, R. T., & Davey, S. L. (2008). Regularities in eyewitness identification. *Law and Human Behavior*, *32*, 187–218. doi:10.1007/s10979-006-9082-4

Clark, S. E., Marshall, T. E., & Rosenthal, R. (2009). Lineup administrator influences on eyewitness identification decisions. *Journal of Experimental Psychology: Applied*, *15*, 63–75. doi:10.1037/a0015185

Cutler, B. L., Daugherty, B., Babu, S., Hodges, L., & Van Wallendael, L. (2009). Creating blind photoarrays using virtual human technology: A feasibility test. *Police Quarterly*, *12*, 289–300. doi:10.1177/1098611109339892

Cutler, B. L., & Fisher, R. P. (1990). Live lineups, videotaped lineups, and photoarrays. *Forensic Reports*, *3*, 439–448.

Cutler, B. L., Penrod, S., & Dexter, H. R. (1990). Juror sensitivity to eyewitness identification evidence. *Law and Human Behavior*, *14*, 185–191. doi:10.1007/BF01062972

Dekle, D. J. (1997). Testing delays resulting in increased identification accuracy in line-ups and show-ups. *Journal of Offender Rehabilitation*, *25*(3-4), 35–49. doi:10.1300/J076v25n03_03

Dekle, D. J., Beal, C. R., Elliott, R., & Huneycutt, D. (1996). Children as witnesses: A comparison of lineup versus showup identification methods. *Applied Cognitive Psychology*, *10*, 1–12. doi:10.1002/(SICI)1099-0720(199602)10:1<1::AID-ACP354>3.0.CO;2-Y

Dysart, J. E., & Lindsay, R. C. L. (2007). Show-up identifications: Suggestive technique or reliable method? In R. C. L. Lindsay, D. F. Ross, J. D. Read, & M. P. Toglia (Eds.), *The handbook of eyewitness psychology: Vol II. Memory for people.* (pp. 137–153). Mahwah, NJ: Erlbaum.

Dysart, J. E., Lindsay, R. C. L., & Dupuis, P. R. (2006). Show-ups: The critical issue of clothing bias. *Applied Cognitive Psychology*, *20*, 1009–1023. doi:10.1002/acp.1241

Flowe, H., Ebbesen, E., Burke, C., & Chivabunditt, P. (2001, July). *At the scene of the crime: An examination of the external validity of published studies on line-up identification accuracy.* Paper presented at the meeting of the American Psychological Society, Toronto, Ontario, Canada.

Foster v. California, 394 U.S. 440 (1969).

Fox, S. G., & Walters, H. A. (1986). The impact of general versus specific expert testimony and eyewitness confidence upon mock juror judgment. *Law and Human Behavior*, *10*, 215–228. doi:10.1007/BF01046211

Garrett, B. L. (2011). *Convicting the innocent: Where criminal prosecutions go wrong.* Cambridge, MA: Harvard University Press. doi:10.4159/harvard.9780674060982

Gonzalez, R., Ellsworth, P. C., & Pembroke, M. (1993). Response biases in lineups and showups. *Journal of Personality and Social Psychology, 64,* 525–537. doi:10.1037/0022-3514.64.4.525

Goodsell, C. A., Gronlund, S. D., & Carlson, C. A. (2010). Exploring the sequential lineup advantage using WITNESS. *Law and Human Behavior, 34,* 445–459. doi:10.1007/s10979-009-9215-7

Gronlund, S. D., Carlson, C. A., Dailey, S. B., & Goodsell, C. A. (2009). Robustness of the sequential lineup advantage. *Journal of Experimental Psychology: Applied, 15,* 140–152. doi:10.1037/a0015082

Kassin, S. M., Tubb, V. A., Hosch, H. M., & Memon, A. (2001). On the "general acceptance" of eyewitness testimony research: A new survey of the experts. *American Psychologist, 56,* 405–416. doi:10.1037/0003-066X.56.5.405

Kerstholt, J. H., Koster, E. R., & van Amelsvoort, A. G. (2004). Eyewitnesses: A comparison of live, video, and photo line-ups. *Journal of Police and Criminal Psychology, 19*(2), 15–22. doi:10.1007/BF02813869

Lane, S. M., & Meissner, C. A. (2008). A "middle road" approach to bridging the basic-applied divide in eyewitness identification research. *Applied Cognitive Psychology, 22,* 779–787. doi:10.1002/acp.1482

Light, L. L. (1996) Memory and aging. In E. L. Bjork & R. A. Bjork (Eds.), *Memory: Handbook of perception and cognition* (2nd ed., pp. 444–477). San Diego, CA: Academic Press.

Lindsay, R. C. L., Martin, R., & Webber, L. (1994). Default values in eyewitness descriptions: A problem for the match-to-description lineup foil selection strategy. *Law and Human Behavior, 18,* 527–541. doi:10.1007/BF01499172

Lindsay, R. C. L., Pozzulo, J. D., Craig, W., Lee, K., & Corber, S. (1997). Simultaneous lineups, sequential lineups, and showups: Eyewitness identification decisions of adults and children. *Law and Human Behavior, 21,* 391–404. doi:10.1023/A:1024807202926

Lusted, L. B. (1971). Signal detectability and medical decision-making. *Science, 171,* 1217–1219. doi:10.1126/science.171.3977.1217

Malpass, R. S., & Devine, P. G. (1981). Eyewitness identification: Lineup instructions and the absence of the offender. *Journal of Applied Psychology, 66,* 482–489. doi:10.1037/0021-9010.66.4.482

Malpass, R. S., Tredoux, C. G., Compo, N. S., McQuiston-Surrett, D., MacLin, O. H., Zimmerman, L. A., & Topp, L. D. (2008). Study space analysis for policy development. *Applied Cognitive Psychology, 22,* 789–801. doi:10.1002/acp.1483

Manson v. Brathwaite, 432 U.S. 98 (1977).

McQuiston, D., & Malpass, R. (2001, June). *Eyewitness identifications in criminal cases: An archival study.* Paper presented at the meeting of the Society for Applied Research in Memory and Cognition, Kingston, Ontario, Canada.

Meissner, C. A., Tredoux, C. G., Parker, J. F., & MacLin, O. H. (2005). Eyewitness decisions in simultaneous and sequential lineups: A dual-process signal detection theory analysis. *Memory & Cognition, 33*, 783–792. doi:10.3758/BF03193074

Mid-Atlantic Innocence Project. (2012). *Walter Snyder*. Retrieved from http://www.exonerate.org/other-local-victories/walter-snyder/

Morgan, C. A., Hazlett, G., Doran, A., Garrett, S., Hoyt, G., Thomas, P., . . . Southwick, S. M. (2004). Accuracy of eyewitness memory for persons encountered during exposure to highly intense stress. *International Journal of Law and Psychiatry, 27*, 265–279. doi:10.1016/j.ijlp.2004.03.004

Neil v. Biggers, 409 U.S. 188 (1972).

Neuschatz, J. S., & Cutler, B. L. (2008). Eyewitness identification. In J. Bryne (Series Ed.) & H. L. Roediger III (Vol. Ed.), *Cognitive psychology of memory: Vol. 2. Learning and memory: A comprehensive reference* (pp. 845–865). Oxford, England: Elsevier.

Neuschatz, J. S., Preston, E. L., Burkett, A. D., Toglia, M. P., Lampinen, J. M., Neuschatz, J. S., . . . Goodsell, C. A. (2005). The effects of post-identification feedback and age on retrospective eyewitness memory. *Applied Cognitive Psychology, 19*, 435–453. doi:10.1002/acp.1084

Pezdek, K. (2007). Expert testimony on eyewitness memory and identification. In M. Costanzo, D. Krauss, & K. Pezdek (Eds.), *Expert psychological testimony for the courts* (pp. 99–117). Mahwah, NJ: Erlbaum.

Pisano, E. D., Gatsonis, C., Hendrick, E., Yaffe, M., Baum, J. K., Acharyya, S., . . . Rebner, M. (2005). Diagnostic performance of digital versus film mammography for breast-cancer screening. *The New England Journal of Medicine, 353*, 1773–1783. doi:10.1056/NEJMoa052911

Quinlivan, D. S., Neuschatz, J. S., Cutler, B. L., Wells, G. L., McClung, J., & Harker, D. L. (2012). Do pre-admonition suggestions moderate the effect of unbiased lineup instructions? *Legal and Criminological Psychology*. doi:10.1348/135532510X533554

Smith, S. M. (1988). Environmental context—dependent memory. In G. M. Davies & D. M. Thomson (Eds.), *Memory in context: Context in memory* (pp. 13–34). Oxford, England: Wiley.

Smith, S. M. (1994). Theoretical principles of context-dependent memory. In P. E. Morris & M. Gruneberg (Eds.), *Theoretical aspects of memory* (2nd ed., pp. 168–195). London, England: Routledge.

Steblay, N. (1997). Social influence in eyewitness recall: A meta-analytic review of lineup instruction effects. *Law and Human Behavior, 21*, 283–297. doi:10.1023/A:1024890732059

Steblay, N., Dysart, J., Fulero, S., & Lindsay, R. C. L. (2003). Eyewitness accuracy rates in police showup and lineup presentations: A meta-analytic comparison. *Law and Human Behavior, 27*, 523–540. doi:10.1023/A:1025438223608

Stovall v. Denno, 388 U.S. 293 (1967).

U.S. Department of Justice, Office of Justice Programs, National Institute of Justice. (1999). *Eyewitness evidence: A guide for law enforcement.* Retrieved from http://www.nij.gov/pubs-sum/178240.htm

Valentine, T., & Heaton, P. (1999). An evaluation of the fairness of police line-ups and video identifications. [Special issue]. *Applied Cognitive Psychology: Measuring lineup fairness, 13,* S59–S72. doi:10.1002/(SICI)1099-0720(199911)13:1+<S59:AID-ACP679>3.0.CO;2-Y

Wagenaar, W. A., & Veefkind, N. (1992). Comparison of one-person and many-person lineups: A warning against unsafe practices. In F. Lösel, D. Bender, & T. Bliesener (Eds.), *Psychology and law: International perspectives* (pp. 275–285). Oxford, England: Walter De Gruyter. doi:10.1515/9783110879773.275

Wells, G. L., & Bradfield, A. L. (1998). "Good, you identified the suspect": Feedback to eyewitnesses distorts their reports of the witnessing experience. *Journal of Applied Psychology, 83,* 360–376. doi:10.1037/0021-9010.83.3.360

Wells, G. L., & Quinlivan, D. S. (2009). Suggestive eyewitness identification procedures and the Supreme Court's reliability test in light of eyewitness science: 30 years later. *Law and Human Behavior, 33,* 1–24. doi:10.1007/s10979-008-9130-3

Wells, G. L., Small, M., Penrod, S., Malpass, R. S., Fulero, S. M., & Brimacombe, C. A. E. (1998). Eyewitness identification procedures: Recommendations for lineups and photospreads. *Law and Human Behavior, 22,* 603–647. doi:10.1023/A:1025750605807

Wixted, J. T., & Mickes, L. (2012). *Receiver operating characteristic analysis in the assessment of lineup-based memory.* Manuscript submitted for publication.

Yarmey, A. D., Yarmey, A. L., & Yarmey, M. J. (1994). Face and voice identifications in showups and lineups. *Applied Cognitive Psychology, 8,* 453–464. doi:10.1002/acp.2350080504

Yarmey, A. D., Yarmey, M. J., & Yarmey, A. L. (1996). Accuracy of eyewitness identification in showups and lineups. *Law and Human Behavior, 20,* 459–477. doi:10.1007/BF01498981

3

LINEUP INSTRUCTIONS

NANCY K. STEBLAY

Psychological scientists have amassed hundreds of laboratory experiments on the topic of eyewitness memory for crime events. The research enumerates variables that affect memory accuracy, including eyewitness characteristics, offender attributes, and crime event conditions. In addition, witnesses' attempts to recall the crime and its perpetrator after the event have drawn extensive research attention in part because police procedures that secure eyewitness evidence can be adjusted to reduce the likelihood of recall error. Researchers have described several system-variable reforms (Wells, 1978) that can increase the probative value of identification lineups (Wells, 2006; Wells, Malpass, Lindsay, Turtle, & Fulero, 2000).

The errors that can ensue from police lineups have been highlighted by forensic DNA exoneration cases (see the Innocence Project; http://www.innocenceproject.org). These DNA cases reveal a pattern of mistaken suspect identifications from lineups in which the true culprit was absent. Much research effort has been marshaled to understand this dangerous aspect of

DOI: 10.1037/14094-004
Reform of Eyewitness Identification Procedures, B. L. Cutler (Editor)

eyewitness error—the inability of many witnesses to recognize when the offender is not in the lineup—and to develop revisions to police procedures that may reduce the chance of false identification under such circumstances.

As early as 1975, researchers outlined central questions about effective police strategy for prelineup instruction to eyewitnesses. Eyewitnesses typically approach the lineup task with the intent of pointing to the offender they remember from a crime scene. However, a lineup identification decision is based not only on eyewitness memory but also on witness motivation and expectation. Given that a witness is likely to assume, usually correctly, that the police have placed a viable suspect in the lineup (i.e., a person whom the police believe could be the offender), does this a priori assumption pose a danger to a suspect who is not the culprit? Otherwise stated, can the witness's expectation that the culprit is in the lineup increase the likelihood of a false identification? And could a different strategy—an instruction to inform the witness that the true culprit "may or may not be present in the lineup"—produce more accurate witness decisions? In their conference paper, Hall and Ostrom (1975) reported that this new instruction improved witness decision accuracy by 28% by increasing lineup rejections when the culprit was not in the lineup and yet maintained correct offender identifications from a culprit-present lineup. The comparison instruction in this experiment was the following: "The person is in this lineup. If you recognize him, mark the box . . . if you do not recognize him, mark *none*." The *none-of-the-above* response option was included for both of the tested instruction conditions but framed as a point of memory strength within the *suggestive* instruction—that the witness may not have a strong enough memory to recognize the culprit—rather than that the offender may not be present in the lineup.

The authors of the first published article on suggestive lineup instruction (Malpass & Devine, 1981) were more deliberate about the witness's response options. The *biased* instruction in this study was explicit: "We believe the person who [committed the act] . . . is present in the lineup. Which of these is the person? Circle the number of his position." The *unbiased* lineup instruction allowed that the offender might not be in the lineup and provided the explicit option of rejecting the lineup:

> The person who [committed the act] . . . may be one of the individuals in the lineup. It is also possible that he is not in the lineup. If the person you saw is not in the lineup, circle 0. If the person is present in the lineup, circle the number of his position.

With an unbiased instruction, lineup rejections increased significantly, by 44% when the culprit was not in the lineup and by 17% when the culprit was present. Again, correct culprit identifications were not significantly affected by the unbiased instruction.

With these early reports, a simple and productive revision to police procedure was suggested as a means to reduce identification errors. By 1997, 18 experimental tests were available for a meta-analytic review of the widely accepted claim that police instructions can affect an eyewitness's willingness to make an identification and/or the likelihood that he or she will identify a particular person (Kassin, Ellsworth, & Smith, 1989). More precisely, the hypothesis was that biased instructions pressure the witness to pick someone from the lineup and thereby decrease identification accuracy compared with a more neutral unbiased instruction. The meta-analysis (Steblay, 1997) confirmed that biased instructions produced a significant increase (25%) in identification errors when the lineup did not include the true offender and had minimal impact on correct identifications when the culprit was in the lineup.

The studies of the 1997 meta-analysis included a variety of operational definitions for biased and unbiased instructions because research teams had explored different means to push around witness choosing rates. For example, task-oriented instructions that were encouraging ("We're sure you'll be able to recognize him"), discouraging ("You only saw the man for a short time . . . your memory may play tricks"), or neutral were compared, with no significant differences for culprit-absent lineup decisions (Hilgendorf & Irving, 1978). In another study, the unbiased instruction revealed police uncertainty ("It might be the guy, but we can't be sure"), a manipulation that decreased choosing rates from both culprit-present and culprit-absent lineups compared with an instruction that implied that the police were certain about the suspect (Malpass, Devine, & Bergen, 1980). Warnick and Sanders (1980) reduced the witness choosing rate with an instruction to "not guess" and a response option of "don't know." Explicit response options were tested by O'Rourke, Penrod, Cutler, and Stuve (1989): "Write the number of the suspect" versus "Write the number of the suspect or indicate that the robber is not present by writing *not present*." O'Rourke et al. found that the suggestive instruction reduced identification accuracy to a greater extent with a culprit-absent than with a culprit-present lineup.

As the research developed, the key experimental manipulation coalesced around the intent to disabuse the witness of the notion that the perpetrator had to be in the lineup. This was accomplished either through phrasing that the perpetrator "may or may not be present in the lineup," the explicit provision of a "not there" response option, or both. Thus, the unbiased instruction became more than simply that an eyewitness should not be pressured to choose or should be allowed to say "I don't know." Rather, the instruction clearly provided an additional acceptable option for the witness's consideration: "The culprit is not present."

An explicit lineup instruction was incorporated into the recommendations of the American Psychology–Law Society in 1998 (Wells et al., 1998) and solidified with the 1999 National Institute of Justice report that recommended the following: "Instruct the witness that the person who committed the crime may or may not be in the set of photographs [or the group of individuals] being presented." (U.S. Department of Justice, Office of Justice Programs, National Institute of Justice, 1999, p. 32). The *may-or-may-not* (May/Not) instruction has become a noncontroversial policy reform in many U.S. jurisdictions (see, e.g., the Innocence Project; http://innocenceproject.org). It has been required police procedure in England and Wales since 1986.

As noted previously, the Steblay (1997) review included many types of suggestive prelineup instructions and found an overall significant influence of instructions on identification errors. A subsequent analysis of the literature (Clark, 2005) found some support for the notion that suggestive instructions also may boost witness choosing rates and culprit identifications with culprit-present lineups. The current task is somewhat different: to update and assess the research literature regarding the specific now-prescribed instruction. More than a decade after the Steblay (1997) meta-analysis and publication of the National Institute of Justice guide, the may-or-may-not phrasing is the recommended standard. What might be gained from this admonition? Can one trust the instruction to eliminate most identification errors? Does the instruction come at a cost to correct offender identifications? To differentiate the specific instructional phrasing considered in this chapter from earlier varieties of broadly construed suggestive instructions, the terms May/Not instruction and culprit-present (C/P) instruction rather than unbiased and biased instruction are used. The primary research question: How does a May/Not instruction affect eyewitness decisions?

EFFECT OF THE MAY-OR-MAY-NOT INSTRUCTION

An instruction that the person who committed the crime may or may not be in the lineup is a direct attempt to alert a witness to the possibility that the lineup should be rejected, that the witness may correctly conclude "he's not there." This instruction, therefore, should be most useful when the culprit is not in the lineup, but the May/Not instruction also could reduce filler picks from a culprit-present lineup. In both cases, the benefit is that witnesses avoid a mistaken identification and possibly a dangerous error if an innocent suspect otherwise would be selected from a culprit-absent array. The expectation is that the admonition will significantly increase lineup rejections compared with an instruction that implies or states that the perpetrator is present in the lineup.

Sixteen independently published laboratory tests have examined the impact of the May/Not instruction on eyewitness accuracy with culprit-absent or culprit-present lineups or both (see Appendix 3.1). In each test, half of the witnesses were provided a May/Not instruction before the lineup; the remaining witnesses were provided an instruction that suggested the presence of the culprit in the lineup (C/P instruction).[1] A meta-analytic approach can help determine whether the recommended admonition is useful to enhance eyewitness decision accuracy. The 16 tests included 3,196 adult eyewitnesses who viewed an event and subsequently attempted a memory-based lineup identification of a primary target (culprit). Simultaneous lineups were used in all tests; three studies also ran comparative sequential lineups (Cutler & Penrod, 1988; Greathouse & Kovera, 2009; Lindsay et al., 1991). The time of culprit visibility in the studies ranged from "eye contact" to 5 minutes. Five of the studies (29%) used staged live crimes (Devenport & Fisher, 1996; Hosch, Leippe, Marchioni, & Cooper, 1984; Köhnken & Maass, 1988; Lindsay et al., 1991; Malpass & Devine, 1981); the remainder used video portrayals. Three studies included a delay between crime and lineup of 1 to 3 days (Köhnken & Maass, 1988; Malpass & Devine, 1981; Paley & Geiselman, 1989); the retention period was less than an hour for the remaining tests. Eleven of the tests used lineups of size six; lineups of size five, seven, or eight were used in the remaining tests. The small number of tests in each subset and the multicollinearity of the variables prohibit useful moderator analyses. Nevertheless, the descriptive data provide a picture of the variety and range of experimental designs.

The analyses that follow summarize eyewitness performance across studies. Each experiment contributed one test; thus, the experiments are equally weighted in the cumulative analyses. As presented in Rosenthal (1991), a Z-score indicates the level of statistical significance achieved for the difference in outcomes between the compared May/Not and C/P instruction conditions. An average effect size h (the arc sine transformed difference between two proportions) is reported as in the original Steblay (1997) meta-analysis. The effect size r is also provided because it is a more easily understood statistic, a value that closely approximates the difference between proportions in the two groups. For example, from an r of .20, an approximate difference between the tested groups of 20% can be estimated. Alpha is set at .05, and all confidence intervals are calculated at 95%. A positive sign attached to the reported Z, h, and r values indicates that the May/Not instruction produced a higher score on the tested dependent measure; a negative sign, conversely, indicates that the control condition (C/P instruction) produced a higher score.

---

[1]This group does not include experimental conditions that attempt to moderate the instruction effect, as in the preadmonition suggestion manipulation of Quinlivan et al. (2012).

Culprit-Absent Lineups

When the culprit is not in the lineup, the witness's response can take one of two forms: a lineup rejection (correct) or a pick from the lineup (error). The C/P instruction, of course, is misleading in this case. The culprit is not in the lineup, and therefore any pick from the lineup is an error. Fifteen tests provide a comparison of May/Not and C/P instructions with culprit-absent lineups.

Across studies, the mean rejection rate for a lineup with a C/P instruction is 30%. A May/Not instruction increased the rejection rate to 57%, a significant rise of 27%, $Z = 10.18$, $p < .0001$, $h = .63$, $r = .31$, 95% CI [.19, .43]. Conversely stated, the May/Not instruction significantly reduced identification errors from 70% to 43% (see Table 3.1). Effects are in the predicted direction in all but one test (Fleet, Brigham, & Bothwell, 1987; see Appendix 3.1). In five tests (four studies) a designated innocent suspect, similar looking to the culprit, was placed in the culprit-absent lineup (Greathouse & Kovera, 2009; Leippe, Eisenstadt, & Rauch, 2009; Lindsay et al., 1991; Quinlivan et al., 2012). The risk to that innocent suspect was cut in half by providing a May/Not instruction. The innocent suspect was picked by 40% of culprit-present witnesses compared with a 19% pick rate for witnesses with the May/Not instruction, a significant difference, $Z = 4.85$, $h = .47$, $r = .23$.

TABLE 3.1
Summary Statistics of Witness Decisions for Culprit-Present Versus May-or-May-Not Instructions

Witness decision	Culprit-present instructions M (Mdn)	May-or-may-not instructions M (Mdn)	h	t
Culprit-absent lineup ($k = 15$), all tests				
Rejection	.30 (.25)	.57* (.60)	.63	.31
Filler	.70	.43*		
Culprit-present lineup ($k = 11$), all tests				
Culprit identification	.61 (.63)	.55* (.56)	.12	.06
Culprit-present lineup ($k = 9$), tests that provided breakouts of error type				
Rejection	.15 (.14)	.31* (.31)	.44	.21
Filler	.26 (.25)	.15* (.14)	.33	.14
Culprit identification	.59 (.63)	.54 (.56)	.11	.05
Diagnosticity ($k = 9$), tests with full orthogonal 2 × 2 research design				
Culprit identification	.616	.548		
Culprit-absent lineup filler picks/lineup size	.118	.078		
Diagnosticity ratio	5.22	7.03		

*$p < .05$.

Culprit-Present Lineups

When the offender is present in the lineup, the witness's response can take one of three forms: culprit identification (correct), filler pick (error), or rejection of the lineup (error). A set of nine tests provides this breakout of three witness response categories, which allows analysis of the two types of error that are possible with a culprit-present lineup as well as the overall choosing rate (see Table 3.1, middle panel).

The mean rejection rate of 15% for lineups conducted with a C/P instruction doubled when the May/Not instruction was used to 31%, $Z = 6.08$, $p < .0001$, $h = .44$, $r = .21$, 95% CI [.09, .33]. As with the culprit-absent lineup, witnesses were significantly less likely to choose from the lineup following a May/Not instruction. Again, all but one of the nine tests (Fleet et al., 1987) produced effects in the predicted direction.[2]

In the case of a culprit-present lineup, the C/P instruction may nudge the witness in the correct direction: The culprit *is* in the lineup. One would expect some benefit from this suggestive instruction. In the same nine tests, correct identifications of the culprit were higher with the C/P instruction (59%) than with a May/Not instruction (54%), $Z = 1.80$, $p = .04$, $h = -.11$, $r = -.05$, 95% CI [-.01, .11].[3] Alternatively stated, the May/Not instruction led to an average 5% loss of correct identifications. The confidence interval around this 5% figure includes 0, an indication that the difference was not significant.[4] Also, filler picks dropped significantly with a May/Not instruction by 11% (from 26% to 15%), $Z = 4.29$, $p < .001$, $h = -.33$, $r = -.14$, 95% CI [.04, .24]. In short, a May/Not instruction saved witnesses from making identification errors disproportionately more frequently (2.2 times) than it led them to miss an identification of the culprit.

Summary: Overall Instruction Performance

The May/Not instruction significantly reduces witness choosing rates from both culprit-absent and culprit-present lineups compared with a C/P instruction

---

[2]If Fleet et al. (1987) is considered an anomaly and removed, the pattern of results does not change. Rejection rates for culprit-absent lineups show a somewhat larger difference (30%) between use of a C/P instruction (25%) and those in which a May/Not instruction was used (55%). Rejection rates for culprit-present lineup also show a larger difference (20%) with a rise from 14% to 34% when a May/Not instruction was used.

[3]A slightly larger set of 11 culprit-present tests (including two tests in which fillers and rejections could not be separated with the available data) produces a similar result: Culprit picks at 61% (with no cautionary instruction) and 55% with a cautionary instruction, a statistically significant but small reduction in correct identifications of the culprit, $Z = 2.30$, $p = .01$, $h = -.12$, $r = -.06$ (see Table 3.1, top panel).

[4]The small effect size reflects substantial variability in correct culprit identification rates across studies. No differences due to the May/Not instruction were produced in three tests; one test produced a significant increase in culprit identifications with a May/Not instruction, and the remaining five tests showed drops in culprit identifications when the admonition was used.

and thereby effectively reduces identification errors. The increase in correct rejections from a culprit-absent lineup is greater (27%) than the increase in erroneous lineup rejections from the culprit-present lineup (16%), and there is a smaller reduction from the May/Not instruction in correct culprit identifications (5%) than in filler picks (11%) within the culprit-present lineup. With the admonition, witnesses not only picked from the lineup significantly less frequently, but when they chose, they were more accurate. Of witnesses who picked from a culprit-present lineup, 69% of the C/P instruction group chose the culprit; 78% of the May/Not instruction group picked the culprit.

One way to express the differential outcome between the two lineup instructions is through a diagnosticity ratio calculated for each instruction condition (Wells & Lindsay, 1980; Wells & Olson, 2002). *Diagnosticity* indicates how much more likely one event is in relation to another; in the case of eyewitness identification, this ratio reflects identifications of the culprit to identifications of an innocent suspect. Given any two diagnosticity ratios, the higher of the two is stronger evidence for the proposition that the suspect is the culprit. Nine tests that used a full orthogonal 2 × 2 research design (May/Not vs. C/P Instruction × Culprit Presence vs. Culprit Absence) can provide this analysis. The culprit identification rate dropped by 7% with a May/Not instruction (from 62% to 55%), and mistaken identifications with the culprit-absent lineup dropped by 23% (from 70% to 47%). The risk to any single member of the culprit-absent lineup is used as the denominator in the ratio (filler picks/number of lineup photos). Diagnosticity of a lineup with a May/Not instruction is greater (7.03) than the same lineup with a C/P instruction (5.22). Lineups with a May/Not instruction provide a 1.35 times greater likelihood that a witness's lineup pick is a guilty rather than an innocent suspect. The witness's decision is more probative of guilt when a May/Not admonition is used.

The effect of May/Not instruction was tested with children ages 9 to 14 by Pozzulo and Dempsey (2006). The admonition significantly reduced false positive picks from a culprit-absent lineup, a pattern similar to that obtained with adults. The limited research on older adults (Rose, Bull, & Vrij, 2005) indicated that older witnesses (M = 71 years) are significantly more likely to forget the admonition; those who do not recall the admonition also perform more poorly on the lineup task.

EFFECT OF AN EXPLICIT OPTION TO REJECT THE LINEUP

In four studies, an unbiased instruction was operationalized as the inclusion of an explicit response option for *not present*. In these studies, there was no May/Not instruction for any of the witnesses, nor was there an explicit statement that the culprit was in the lineup for the biased instruction condition. One instruction was suggestive but not explicit ("Write the number of the suspect") and the other instruction provided the not-present option without an explicit may-or-may-not phrasing ("Write the number of the suspect or indicate that the robber is not present by writing NP"). In essence, these were stripped-down versions of the two lineup instructions seen in most studies (see Appendix 3.1).

When the culprit was not in the lineup, the unbiased instruction significantly increased witness rejections of the lineup by 31% (from 20% to 51%). When the culprit was present in the lineup, there was no significant difference in culprit identifications across the four studies, $Z = -.82$, $h = -.02$, $r = -.01$; biased instructions, 51% correct identifications, unbiased instruction, 50% correct identifications. These tests did not separate lineup rejections from filler picks in the culprit-present condition, prohibiting analysis of specific error type.

These four tests all used the same stimulus materials, thereby limiting generalizability of the results (Wells & Windschitl, 1999). Nevertheless, the pattern of results is similar to those obtained with more complete instructions. This is important for two reasons. First, these results underscore the *not-present* provision as a procedural feature to increase lineup rejections, at least under circumstances in which the witness writes his or her response on a printed form that is presented to the witness *prior to the lineup*.[5] Second, these tests show that the suggestiveness of a very simple statement ("Write the number of the suspect") was enough to significantly increase eyewitness decision errors without a consistent gain in correct culprit identifications. To the extent that eyewitnesses implicitly believe the lineup contains the actual culprit, a procedure that does not correct this belief is suggestive by omission.

WHY THE MAY-OR-MAY-NOT INSTRUCTION EFFECT?

The research is clear: An instruction that specifically alerts the witness to the possibility that the true perpetrator may not be in the lineup significantly decreases witness picks from the lineup compared with an instruction that suggests culprit presence in the array. The primary impact of the admonition is to inhibit choosing from witnesses who otherwise would make identification errors.

Some scientists may view these research outcomes through the lens of a signal detection conceptualization: The two instruction conditions

---

[5]Three studies in the larger group of 16 tests used a not-present response option for both instruction conditions. Outcomes from these three tests were similar to those from the other tests.

create differences in witnesses' decision criterion for making an identification (Clark, 2005; Green & Swets, 1966). The reasoning is that a higher criterion is maintained as a result of the May/Not instruction, with concomitant decreases in choosing. With the admonition, the witness needs a stronger match between memory and a lineup photo before making the identification. There is some evidence in these data for a criterion shift because choosing rates decreased with the May/Not instruction for both culprit-present and culprit-absent lineups. However, the admonition does more than merely reduce eyewitnesses' willingness to pick someone from the lineup. The criterion-shift account is not an entirely satisfactory explanation because it does not answer the questions of *how* decisions are made or *why* disproportional increases in correct and misidentifications are produced with the May/Not instruction.

The purpose of the May/Not instruction is to reduce unacceptable suggestiveness of the lineup procedure to secure better eyewitness evidence. The C/P instruction is highly suggestive, as evidenced by high witness choosing rates, approximately 83% when the culprit is present and 70% even when the culprit is not in the lineup. This is the standard, or default, condition against which the impact of the May/Not instruction is measured. There is, necessarily, no *no-instruction* control group that can help to isolate a single feature of the psychological processes involved. Two qualitatively different lineup instructions are pitted against one another. The psychological processes incurred by each instruction may be different and mediated by the quality of witness memory.

Wells (2009) posited a two-process model of eyewitness decision making. A core concept in this model is a witness's *ecphoric* experience, that is, an immediate, fast, automatic recognition of the offender that results in a positive identification. Ecphory is a function of a good memory and a reasonable likeness of the offender in the lineup. The absence of an ecphoric experience—when memory for the culprit is not strong, culprit appearance has changed, or the culprit is not in the lineup—will prompt secondary processes, a slower and more deliberative mode of decision making.[6] One well-documented secondary strategy is *relative judgment,* that is, the comparison of lineup members with one another to select the one who looks most like the offender relative to the other lineup members (Wells, 1984). Other secondary strategies may include attempts to somehow try harder, to spend more time on the task, to imagine each lineup member with a different hairstyle or skin tone, to use a process of elimination, or to otherwise arrive at a lineup decision in the absence of immediate recognition.

---

[6]See also Dunning and Stern (1994), who differentiated between automatic recognition that occurs as a quick and relatively effortless judgment and a process of elimination that tends to be more slow, effortful, and deliberate. Charman and Wells (2007) posited a related notion that the psychological processes operating at the time of the lineup presentation involve a continuum of judgment from automatic to deliberative processes, the latter being less sensitive to the presence of the culprit in the lineup.

The promising aspect of Wells's (1984) conceptualization of ecphoric and secondary processes for understanding lineup instruction lies in the proposition that secondary processes rely less on an eyewitness's memory than on external contextual factors. Eyewitnesses who have a good memory of the offender will not require secondary processes to identify the culprit. Witnesses with weaker memories are more likely to move into secondary processes. It is during this deliberative search to explain and correct for the absence of ecphory that contextual aspects of the lineup matter.

A lineup instruction provides information that cannot improve memory but can drive the secondary decision process. A credible authority provides relevant information about the presence (or possible absence) of the culprit in the lineup and sanctions decision options. In the parlance of social psychology, informational and normative social influences provide a context for the lineup decision (Deutsch & Gerard, 1955; Steblay, 1997).

When ecphory fails, the suggestiveness of a C/P instruction prompts witnesses to use relative judgment, a process of elimination, or other secondary strategies in service to making an assumed-necessary pick from the lineup. On the contrary, the May/Not admonition adds an explanatory possibility for the absence of an ecphoric experience: The criminal is not there! Some witnesses who otherwise would have made an identification error resolve the decision dilemma by rejecting the lineup. The affirmative not-present response of these witnesses probably belies a weak basis of memory for the decision—"not-sure" or "can't remember" may be closer to the truth—but the effect is to pull the witness back from a positive identification.[7]

A witness with a good memory of the culprit is less likely to need or use secondary processes, the strong match between memory and a lineup member overriding contextual factors such as a lineup instruction. Otherwise stated, a lineup instruction will not affect the witness's ability to quickly recognize the culprit when he is present in the lineup. Even when the culprit is not in the lineup, a good memory of the offender may make the reason for failure of ecphoric experience more apparent: "He's not there." The May/Not instruction is a particularly good fit to this witness's memory of whether the culprit is present or absent from the lineup because the admonition matches the witness's immediate reaction to the array.

In sum, the two-process conceptualization explains why the effect of the May/Not instruction is greater for culprit-absent than culprit-present lineups: Only witnesses viewing a culprit-present lineup can have the strong ecphoric experience that can make lineup instruction irrelevant. The two-process conceptualization also explains why a May/Not instruction can inhibit eyewitness

---

[7]The current data do not allow uncoupling of true rejections ("He's not there") from I'm-not-sure responses.

error more than correct identifications: The instruction is more salient to eyewitnesses whose weaker memories have forced them into a deliberative decision process.

LINEUP INSTRUCTION AS PANACEA?

Despite the positive laboratory outcomes cited in this chapter, there are limitations to lineup instruction as a remedy for problems of identification error. Three examples may suffice to make this point. First, relative judgment has the power to severely undercut witness accuracy, as demonstrated by Wells in his 1993 removal-without-replacement experiment. The study compared witnesses who made identifications from a culprit-present lineup with witnesses who attempted the same task with a lineup from which the culprit had been removed. Importantly, *all* witnesses were warned that the offender might not be in the lineup. Even with this explicit warning, removal of the offender from the lineup led a significant number of witnesses to shift to the next best choice of lineup members rather than to correctly reject the lineup.

One effective means of reducing identification errors is the *sequential lineup method*. Briefly stated, the one-at-a-time viewing of lineup members moves witnesses away from relative judgment, instead forcing a comparison of each photo to memory. A recent meta-analysis (Steblay, Dysart, & Wells, 2011; see also Chapter 5, this volume) confirmed the effectiveness of the sequential lineup procedure to reduce identification errors, with a much smaller reduction in culprit identifications. The May/Not instruction was a standard across the majority of these laboratory tests and should be considered an important component of effective sequential or simultaneous lineup procedure. Nevertheless, filler pick rates were at 24% for culprit-present lineups and ranged from 36% to 57% with culprit-absent sequential and simultaneous lineups, respectively.

Finally, recent field tests in four U.S. cities used best lineup practices, including a clear auditory and written instruction that the culprit may or may not be present. Still, these field lineups with real witnesses produced known errors (filler picks) at 18.1% for the simultaneous lineup and 12.2% with a sequential procedure (American Judicature Society, 2011). Even with appropriate lineup instructions, eyewitnesses make mistakes at levels that should be of immense concern.

FUTURE STEPS

The observations that properly instructed simultaneous and sequential lineups produce significantly different levels of protection against eyewitness error and that even current best practices yield identification errors provide a view to the next stage of eyewitness lineup instruction research. Three examples are discussed in the paragraphs that follow.

Greathouse and Kovera (2009) examined lineup instruction effects in the context of double-blind lineup administration with sequential and simultaneous lineups. The lineup instruction outcomes reported in the analyses of this chapter are collapsed across single- and double-blind administrator and lineup format conditions, producing minimal overall instruction effect. However, Greathouse and Kovera's test of their specific research hypotheses indicated that administrator knowledge of the suspect in combination with a simultaneous lineup format and a biased instruction ("We have the suspect") led to higher suspect identifications irrespective of whether the suspect was guilty or innocent. These authors noted that biased instructions and simultaneous lineups increase the likelihood that witnesses will pick from the lineup even in the absence of a clear memory of the offender.

Two additional studies in the current data set included analysis of lineup instruction effects for sequential versus simultaneous lineups. Lindsay et al. (1991) found a significant increase in false identifications of an innocent suspect from a culprit-absent simultaneous lineup when biased instructions were used (20%). Biased instructions increased the rate of false identification for sequential lineups also (10%) but not significantly so. Correct lineup rejections reflected a similar advantage of sequential presentation when the lineup instruction was biased. Cutler and Penrod (1988) found no interaction between lineup presentation format and instruction nor a main effect for the May/Not lineup instruction. However, all subjects in the Cutler and Penrod study had an explicit not-present option, perhaps diminishing differences between the groups.

Finally, Brewer and Wells (2006) found a significant main effect for instructional bias for two different targets and both culprit-present and culprit-absent simultaneous lineups, but they also observed an interaction of instructional bias and foil similarity. Compared with a biased instruction, the May/Not instruction had a greater impact on (reducing) choosing when foil similarity was low than when foil similarity was high; the lowest choosing rate was for lineups of low foil similarity and unbiased instructions. Similarly, Leippe et al. (2009) found more correct rejections of a culprit-absent lineup when the lineup instruction was unbiased and foils were dissimilar to the thief.

The upshot of this group of studies is that future examination of interactions between lineup instructions and other procedural variables such as those reviewed in this volume may illuminate circumstances in which a lineup instruction is more or less likely to prompt and affect witnesses' decision processes, especially deliberative secondary processes. Leach, Cutler, and Van Wallendael (2009) concurred that the boundaries of the May/Not instruction are not well understood. Are there conditions under which the standard instruction loses its protective quality? For example, the broader investigative circumstances in which the lineup instructions are delivered have only recently been examined. If the lineup administrator intimates that the instructions are only a mere formality, might the witness's earlier assumption that the culprit is in the lineup trump the instruction itself? Wells and Quinlivan (2009) posited that informal prelineup information transferred to the witness may elevate the suggestiveness of the identification procedure. This might include police telling the eyewitness that the culprit has been found, that police know who did the crime, or that evidence against the suspect is mounting. Cowitness comments or media reports may provide other sources of prelineup suggestiveness.

Quinlivan and colleagues (2012) tested the impact on witness decisions of a preadmonition suggestion from a credible source. That is, prior to the lineup instruction proper, the witness was led to believe that he or she was poised to perform well at the lineup task ("You were paying close attention . . . surely you can pick the perpetrator"). The hypothesis was that this suggestion of a witness's special ability to identify the culprit would undermine or at least moderate the effectiveness of the recommended lineup instruction. The rationale is sensible: A standard lineup instruction is a formal perfunctory procedure that indicates nothing about the individual witness; on the other hand, a verbal comment comes across as personal and relevant to the specific witness. Quinlivan et al. found a damaging effect from this preadmonition suggestion in the form of increased misidentifications (all lineups were culprit absent, so all identifications were wrong) and in witnesses' subsequently inflated confidence about their identification decision, in their enhanced retrospective evaluation of viewing conditions at the time of the crime and perceived basis for an identification, and in their increased willingness to testify at trial.

WITNESS CONFIDENCE

The Steblay (1997) meta-analysis reported that suggestive (biased) lineup instruction may increase witness confidence when the offender is in the lineup. Effect sizes were reported as significant but very small for culprit-present lineup conditions ($d = -.16$) and minimal for culprit-absent conditions ($d = .02$). The small number of tests available then (and now) does not allow a particularly useful summary analysis. More important, the recommendation for a May/Not admonition is grounded in its effectiveness in protecting against identification error. And suggestive instructions certainly would not be recommended for lineup practice as a means to increase witness confidence.

The investigation of lineup instruction effects on witness confidence has more recently been pulled in a different direction by researchers interested in the broader issue of the eyewitness confidence–accuracy relationship (e.g., Brewer & Wells, 2006). For example, Leippe et al. (2009) found that the recommended instruction helped to protect against the postidentification confidence inflation that weakens the confidence–accuracy relationship. In the Leippe et al. study, a biased instruction combined with positive or neutral prelineup feedback on a recall test significantly increased confidence of witnesses who had chosen an innocent suspect compared with an unbiased instruction. Also, the effect of the biased instruction extended beyond confidence inflation to changes in the witnesses' retrospective assessment of crime-viewing conditions: Witnesses with biased instructions reported a better and longer view of the thief, greater ability to make out the thief's features, and having paid more attention to the thief. The results were not replicated in a second study, however; Leippe et al. found an increase in memory favorability (memory inflation) for unbiased lineup instructions but only with a culprit-absent lineup of high-similarity-to-thief foils. In sum, the findings of recent studies offer an intriguing opening for further consideration of the possible protective function of a prelineup admonition against postidentification confidence and memory inflation as well as the investigation of broader prelineup influences that may undercut the admonition.

OTHER PRELINEUP INSTRUCTIONS

The National Institute of Justice guide recommends that prelineup instructions include a caution that offender features may have changed over time: "Individuals depicted in lineup photos may not appear exactly as they did on the date of the incident because features such as head and facial hair are subject to change" (U.S. Department of Justice, Office of Justice Programs, National Institute of Justice, 1999, p. 32). Two of the tests in this review (Greathouse & Kovera, 2009; Paley & Geiselman, 1989) included the appearance-change-instruction as part of their unbiased (May/Not) instruction manipulation. The appearance-change instruction, alone or in combination with other instruction, has been tested only minimally. Charman and Wells (2007) found that the instruction increased false identifications and filler picks but had only a slight impact on culprit identifications in a condition in which appearance change was greatest (both appearance-change-instruction and the no-appearance-change instruction conditions included a May/Not instruction as well). Steblay (2012) found a small but significant benefit of the appearance-change-instruction but only when the culprit's appearance had changed substantially (again, all conditions included the

May/Not admonition). It might be expected that the appearance-change instruction would influence witnesses who are in a secondary process mode, prompting closer examination of the photos in an attempt to imagine changes in hairstyle, skin tone, or age. This strategy may be productive if the culprit is in the lineup but is potentially dangerous for an innocent suspect. It will be necessary to determine whether the instruction prompts selective picks of the culprit or merely more picks from the lineup.

Finally, Steblay and Phillips (2011) added a salient *I'm-not-sure* option to the witness's response choices, which might be similar to the simple addition of a not-present option. No change in prelineup instruction was part of this manipulation; all witnesses were given a May/Not admonition. The explicit not-sure response option with a sequential lineup reduced picks of both culprits and fillers but led to stronger overall performance; the not-sure option had no significant effect for simultaneous lineups. This response option appears to be a means to reduce suggestiveness of the lineup procedure, at least for sequential lineups, beyond the prelineup admonition by providing a means for witnesses with weaker memories to avoid a definitive answer, an off-ramp for their decision. The recent field tests of the American Judicature Society (2011) used a salient I'm-not-sure response option. As in the lab, the not-sure response was used more frequently by sequential than simultaneous lineup witnesses.

CONCLUSION AND RECOMMENDATIONS

The Steblay (1997) meta-analysis of lineup instruction research established that suggestive instruction wording prompted more witness picks from the lineup and significantly greater risk of identification error compared with a more neutral instruction. The consensus on this topic is evidenced by surveys of eyewitness experts (e.g., see Kassin, Tubb, Hosch, & Memon, 2001), by recommendations for lineup instruction revision in documents of best practices (e.g., U.S. Department of Justice, Office of Justice Programs, National Institute of Justice, 1999; Wells et al., 1998), and by noncontroversial implementation of a cautionary admonition in numerous jurisdictions (see Conclusion, this volume). This current review established the benefit of a specific warning that the offender may not be in the lineup.

The May/Not admonition is sound practice and policy for police identification procedure. Mistaken identifications occur when a lineup does not include the perpetrator, and this instruction reduces the likelihood of decision error when the suspect is not the true offender. The instruction also reduces witness picks from culprit-present lineups, primarily from witnesses who otherwise would have selected fillers. One may speculate that some of the small loss in correct culprit identifications may be witnesses who otherwise may have made the identification through secondary processes. Whatever the case, diagnosticity ratios show the May/Not instruction to produce decisions of greater probative value than an instruction that suggests the presence of the offender in the lineup.

Nevertheless, a warning that the culprit may not be in the lineup does not compensate for having the wrong person in the lineup. The problem that spurred this research—the difficulty for witnesses to recognize when the offender is not in the lineup—remains even with the recommended admonition. Additional safeguards are necessary, as is additional empirical exploration of identification decision making under conditions that strain or exceed witness memory. Future experiments with controlled examination of procedural factors that may interact with lineup instructions will be useful to establish the boundaries of lineup instruction effectiveness and to place instruction effects within developing theories of eyewitness memory and decision making.

APPENDIX 3.1: STUDIES INCLUDED IN ANALYSES, ORDERED BY DATE

Study	Date	Culprit-absent lineup rejections			Culprit-present lineup rejections			Culprit identification	
		n	h	r	n	h	r	h	r
Tests of the may-or-may-not instruction									
*Malpass & Devine	1981	49	.92	.44	51	.85	.31	.20	.10
Hosch et al.	1984				80	.62	.30	.02	.01
*Fleet et al.	1987	49	-.04	-.02	47	-.34	-.18	.04	.02
*Cutler & Penrod, Experiment 1	1988	94	.13	.07	81			.00	.00
Köhnken & Maass, Experiment 2	1988	63	.75	.37					
*Paley & Geiselman	1989	30	1.03	.49	30	.83	.40	-.26	-.13
Lindsay et al.	1991	120	.38	.19					
*Foster, Libkuman, Schooler, & Loftus	1994	179	.46	.22	175	.46	.23	-.34	-.17
*Devenport & Fisher	1996	64	.58	.29	74	.38	.18	-.36	-.18
*Brewer & Wells	2006	599	.30	.14	601			-.12	-.06
Pozzulo & Dempsey, Experiment 1	2006	55	.95	.45					
Pozzulo & Dempsey, Experiment 2	2006	60	.55	.26					
*Greathouse & Kovera	2009	119	.06	.03	115	.32	.14	-.16	-.08
Leippe et al., Experiment 1	2009	98	.56	.27	104	.61	.30	-.11	-.05
*Leippe et al., Experiment 2	2009	92	1.10	.52					
Quinlivan et al.	2011	76	1.77	.69					
Tests of the option-to-reject instruction									
Cutler, Penrod, O'Rourke, & Martens	1986	156	1.05	.49	164			-.42	-.21
Cutler, Penrod, & Martens	1987a	150	.62	.30	140			-.17	-.08
Cutler, Penrod, & Martens	1987b	93	1.07	.50	76			.00	.00
O'Rourke et al.	1989	57	.08	.04	64			.51	.25

Note. An asterisk indicates studies in the diagnosticity calculations.

REFERENCES[8]

American Judicature Society. (2011). *A test of the simultaneous versus sequential Lineup method using double-blind administration with computers: An initial report of the eyewitness identification field experiments in Austin, Charlotte, San Diego and Tucson*. Retrieved from http://www.ajs.org

*Brewer, N., & Wells, G. L. (2006). The confidence-accuracy relationship in eyewitness identification: Effects of lineup instructions, foil similarity, and target-absent base rates. *Journal of Experimental Psychology: Applied, 12*, 11–30. doi:10.1037/1076-898X.12.1.11

Charman, S. D., & Wells, G. L. (2007). Eyewitness lineups: Is the appearance-change instruction a good idea? *Law and Human Behavior, 31*, 3–22. doi:10.1007/s10979-006-9006-3

Clark, S. E. (2005). A re-examination of the effects of biased lineup instructions in eyewitness identification. *Law and Human Behavior, 29*, 575–604. doi:10.1007/s10979-005-7121-1

*Cutler, B. L., & Penrod, S. D. (1988). Improving the reliability of eyewitness identification: Lineup construction and presentation. *Journal of Applied Psychology, 73*, 281–290. doi:10.1037/0021-9010.73.2.281

*Cutler, B. L., Penrod, S. D., & Martens, T. K. (1987a). Improving the reliability of eyewitness identification: Putting context into context. *Journal of Applied Psychology, 72*, 629–637. doi:10.1037/0021-9010.72.4.629

*Cutler, B. L., Penrod, S. D., & Martens, T. K. (1987b). The reliability of eyewitness identification. *Law and Human Behavior, 11*, 233–258. doi:10.1007/BF01044644

*Cutler, B. L., Penrod, S. D., O'Rourke, T. E., & Martens, T. K. (1986). Unconfounding the effects of contextual cues on eyewitness identification accuracy. *Social Behaviour, 1*, 113–134.

Deutsch, M., & Gerard, H. B. (1955). A study of normative and informational social influence upon individual judgment. *The Journal of Abnormal and Social Psychology, 51*, 629–637. doi:10.1037/h0046408

*Devenport, J. L., & Fisher, R. P. (1996). The effect of authority and social influence on eyewitness suggestibility and person recognition. *Journal of Police and Criminal Psychology, 11*, 35–40. doi:10.1007/BF02803685

Dunning, D., & Stern, L. B. (1994). Distinguishing accurate from inaccurate identifications via inquiries about decision processes. *Journal of Personality and Social Psychology, 67*, 818–835. doi:10.1037/0022-3514.67.5.818

*Fleet, M. L., Brigham, J. C., & Bothwell, R. K. (1987). The confidence-accuracy relationship: The effects of confidence assessment and choosing. *Journal of Applied Social Psychology, 17*, 171–187. doi:10.1111/j.1559-1816.1987.tb00308.x

---

[8]Studies marked with an asterisk were included in the data analysis.

*Foster, R. A., Libkuman, T. M., Schooler, J. W., & Loftus, E. F. (1994). Conse-
quentiality and eyewitness person identification. *Applied Cognitive Psychology*,
8, 107–121. doi:10.1002/acp.2350080203

*Greathouse, S. M., & Kovera, M. (2009). Instruction bias and lineup presentation
moderate the effects of administrator knowledge on eyewitness identification.
Law and Human Behavior, *33*, 70–82. doi:10.1007/s10979-008-9136-x

Green, D. M., & Swets, J. A. (1966). *Signal detection theory and psychophysics*. New York,
NY: Wiley.

Hall, D. F., & Ostrom, T. M. (1975, August). *Accuracy of eyewitness identification after
biasing or unbiased instructions*. Paper presented at the meeting of the American
Psychological Association, Chicago, IL.

Hilgendorf, E. L., & Irving, B. L. (1978). False positive identification. *Medicine, Science,
and the Law*, *18*, 255–262.

*Hosch, H. M., Leippe, M. R., Marchioni, P. M., & Cooper, D. S. (1984). Victimiza-
tion, self-monitoring, and eyewitness identification. *Journal of Applied Psychology*,
69, 280–288. doi:10.1037/0021-9010.69.2.280

Kassin, S. M., Ellsworth, P. C., & Smith, N. L. (1989). The "general acceptance" of
psychological research on eyewitness testimony: A survey of the experts. *American Psychologist*, *44*, 1089–1098. doi:10.1037/0003-066X.44.8.1089

Kassin, S. M., Tubb, V. A., Hosch, H. M., & Memon, A. (2001). On the "general
acceptance" of eyewitness testimony research. *American Psychologist*, *56*, 405–416.
doi:10.1037/0003-066X.56.5.405

*Köhnken, G., & Maass, A. (1988). Eyewitness testimony: False alarms on biased
instructions? *Journal of Applied Psychology*, *73*, 363–370. doi:10.1037/0021-
9010.73.3.363

Leach, A., Cutler, B. L., & Van Wallendael, L. (2009). Lineups and eyewitness identification. *Annual Review of Social Science*, *5*, 157–178. doi:10.1146/annurev.
lawsocsci.093008.131529

*Leippe, M. R., Eisenstadt, D., & Rauch, S. M. (2009). Cueing confidence in eyewit-
ness identifications: Influence of biased lineup instructions and pre-identification
memory feedback under varying lineup conditions. *Law and Human Behavior*,
33, 194–212. doi:1007/s10979-008-9135-y

*Lindsay, R. C. L., Lea, J. A., Nosworthy, G. J., Fulford, J. A., Hector, J., LeVan,
V., & Seabrook, C. (1991). Biased lineups: Sequential presentation reduces
the problem. *Journal of Applied Psychology*, *76*, 796–802. doi:10.1037/0021-
9010.76.6.796

*Malpass, R. S., & Devine, P. G. (1981). Eyewitness identification: Lineup instruc-
tions and the absence of the offender. *Journal of Applied Psychology*, *66*, 482–489.
doi:10.1037/0021-9010.66.4.482

Malpass, R. S., Devine, P. G., & Bergen, G. T. (1980). *Eyewitness identification: Real-
ism vs. the laboratory*. Unpublished manuscript, Psychology Department, State
University of New York at Plattsburgh.

*O'Rourke, T. E., Penrod, S. D., Cutler, B. L., & Stuve, T. E. (1989). The external validity of eyewitness identification research: Generalizing across subject populations. *Law and Human Behavior, 13,* 385–395. doi:10.1007/BF01056410

*Paley, B., & Geiselman, R. E. (1989). The effects of alternative photospread instructions on suspect identification performance. *American Journal of Forensic Psychology, 7,* 3–13.

*Pozzulo, J. D., & Dempsey, J. (2006). Biased lineup instructions: Examining the effect of pressure on children's and adults' eyewitness identification accuracy. *Journal of Applied Social Psychology, 36,* 1381–1394. doi:10.1111/j.0021-9029.2006.00064.x

Quinlivan, D. S., Neuschatz, J. S., Cutler, B. L., Wells, G. L., McClung, J., & Harker, D. L. (2012). Do pre-admonition suggestions moderate the effect of unbiased lineup instructions? *Legal and Criminological Psychology, 17,* 165–176.

Rose, R. A., Bull, R., & Vrij, A. (2005). Non-biased lineup instructions do matter—a problem for older witnesses. *Psychology, Crime & Law, 11,* 147–159. doi:10.1080/10683160512331316307

Rosenthal, R. (1991). *Meta-analytic procedures for social research.* Newbury Park, CA: Sage.

Steblay, N. (1997). Social influence in eyewitness recall: A meta-analytic review of lineup instruction effects. *Law and Human Behavior, 21,* 283–297. doi:10.1023/A:1024890732059

Steblay, N. K. (2012). *Reduction of false convictions through improved identification procedures: Further refinements for street practice and public policy* (Final report for National Institute of Justice Grant Award 2007-IJ-CX-0046). Unpublished manuscript, Department of Psychology, Augsburg College, Minneapolis, MN.

Steblay, N. K., Dysart, J. E., & Wells, G. L. (2011). Seventy-two tests of the sequential lineup superiority effect: A meta-analysis and policy discussion. *Psychology, Public Policy, and Law, 17*(1), 99–139. doi:10.1037/a0021650

Steblay, N. K., & Phillips, J. D. (2011). The not-sure response option in sequential lineup practice. *Applied Cognitive Psychology, 25,* 768–774.

U.S. Department of Justice, Office of Justice Programs, National Institute of Justice. (1999). *Eyewitness evidence: A guide for law enforcement.* Retrieved from http://www.nij.gov/pubs-sum/178240.htm

Warnick, D. H., & Sanders, G. S. (1980). Why do eyewitnesses make so many mistakes? *Journal of Applied Social Psychology, 10,* 362–366. doi:10.1111/j.1559-1816.1980.tb00716.x

Wells, G. L. (1978). Applied eyewitness-testimony research: System variables and estimator variables. *Journal of Personality and Social Psychology, 36,* 1546–1557. doi:10.1037/0022-3514.36.12.1546

Wells, G. L. (1984). The psychology of lineup identification. *Journal of Applied Social Psychology, 14,* 89–103. doi:10.1111/j.1559-1816.1984.tb02223.x

Wells, G. L. (1993). What do we know about eyewitness identification? *American Psychologist, 48,* 553–571. doi:10.1037/0003-066X.48.5.553

Wells, G. L. (2006). Eyewitness identification: Systemic reforms. *Wisconsin Law Review, 2,* 615–643.

Wells, G. L. (2009). *When ecphory fails: Secondary processes in eyewitness identification.* National Science Foundation Grant 0850401. Abstract retrieved from http://www.nsf.gov/awardsearch/showAward.do?AwardNumber=0850401

Wells, G. L., & Lindsay, R. C. L. (1980). On estimating the diagnosticity of eyewitness nonidentifications. *Psychological Bulletin, 88,* 776–784. doi:10.1037/0033-2909.88.3.776

Wells, G. L., Malpass, R. S., Lindsay, R. C. L., Turtle, J. W., & Fulero, S. M. (2000). From the lab to the police station: A successful application of eyewitness research. *American Psychologist, 55,* 581–598. doi:10.1037/0003-066X.55.6.581

Wells, G. L., & Olson, E. A. (2002). Eyewitness identification: Information gain from incriminating and exonerating behaviors. *Journal of Experimental Psychology: Applied, 8,* 155–167. doi:10.1037/1076-898X.8.3.155

Wells, G. L., & Quinlivan, D. S. (2009). Suggestive eyewitness identification procedures and the Supreme Court's reliability test in light of eyewitness science: 30 years later. *Law and Human Behavior, 33,* 1–24. doi:10.1007/s10979-008-9130-3

Wells, G. L., Small, M., Penrod, S., Malpass, R. S., Fulero, S. M., & Brimacombe, C. A. E. (1998). Eyewitness identification procedures: Recommendations for lineups and photospreads. *Law and Human Behavior, 22,* 603–647.1doi:10.102 3/A:1025750605807

Wells, G. L., & Windschitl, P. D. (1999). Stimulus sampling and social psychological experimentation. *Personality and Social Psychology Bulletin, 25,* 1115–1125. doi:10.1177/01461672992512005

4

CONSTRUCTING THE LINEUP: LAW, REFORM, THEORY, AND DATA

STEVEN E. CLARK, RYAN A. RUSH, AND MOLLY B. MORELAND

A crime has been committed, and the police have a suspect and an eyewitness. The police have put together a lineup that includes the suspect, of course, along with five fillers who are known to be innocent. If the eyewitness identifies the suspect from the lineup rather than one of the fillers, that person may be arrested, and the case may go to the district attorney for prosecution.

A positive identification provides direct evidence of the suspect's guilt, and yet a positive identification of a suspect does not necessarily mean that the suspect is guilty. Over 100 years of psychological research, tracing back to the early work of Arnold (1906) and Munsterberg (1908), have shown that witnesses can be quite inaccurate. Such inaccurate identifications can lead to false prosecutions and false convictions. Indeed, there is a consensus among eyewitness identification researchers and legal scholars that mistaken identification is a primary cause, if not *the* primary cause, of false convictions of the innocent in the United States (Gross, Jacoby, Matheson, Montgomery, & Patil, 2005).

DOI: 10.1037/14094-005
Reform of Eyewitness Identification Procedures, B. L. Cutler (Editor)

Garrett (2010) analyzed 161 cases in which false convictions were obtained with mistaken eyewitness identification evidence. On the basis of his analyses, Garrett concluded that 55 of those 161 cases involved a suggestive lineup. Consider the following examples. Marvin Anderson was the only person in the lineup whose photograph was in color (the other photographs were black and white). Lonnie Erby was the only person in the lineup who had facial hair. Ronnie Bullock was the only person in the lineup with distinctive markings on his face. Antonio Beaver was the only person in the lineup with a gap between his front teeth.

The common thread in these examples is the phrase *the only person in the lineup*. This phrase can, of course, be attached to any person in any lineup. As the California Supreme Court noted in *People v. Carpenter* (1997), "Because human beings do not look exactly alike, differences are inevitable" (p. 367). Thus, the observation that the defendant was the only person in the lineup who possessed feature *x* does not by itself establish that the lineup was suggestive. A lineup in which all features are common to all lineup members is a lineup of clones.

This raises several questions that form the focus of this chapter: What does make a lineup suggestive? How should a lineup be put together? How should the fillers be selected? Where should the suspect and fillers be placed within the lineup?

The question that has received the most attention in the courts and in the research is the question about how to pick the fillers. On the one hand, if the fillers are not very similar to the suspect, the suspect may stand out in such a way that the lineup almost begs the witness to identify him whether he is guilty or not. But if the fillers are too similar, it may be difficult for even a good witness with a good memory to identify the perpetrator. This fundamental tension—between fillers who are too similar versus not similar enough—is examined next in terms of court decisions, theory, and data.

LINEUP COMPOSITION AND LEGAL DECISIONS IN THE WAKE OF THE WADE TRILOGY

This tension between too similar and not similar enough is reflected in the contrast between the 1969 U.S. Supreme Court decision in *Foster v. California* and two 1975 decisions from the Second Circuit of the U.S. Court of Appeals. *Foster* was decided just 2 years after the U.S. Supreme Court decided three cases that all highlighted problems with eyewitness identification procedures: *U.S. v. Wade, Stovall v. Denno,* and *Gilbert v. California,* all on the same day, June 12, 1967. *Stovall* and *Simmons v. U.S.* (1968), which was decided 1 year later, set a very high bar for the exclusion of eyewitness identification evidence: "Pretrial identification procedure will be set aside on the ground of prejudice only if the pretrial identification was so impermissibly suggestive as to give rise to a very substantial likelihood of irreparable misidentification" (*Simmons v. U.S.*, 1968, p. 384).

Foster met that very high bar. The U.S. Supreme Court reversed the conviction of Walter B. Foster, who had been convicted of robbery in part on the basis of eyewitness identification. The Court noted that Foster was "a tall man—close to six feet in height," whereas the other lineup members "were short—five feet, five or six inches." But just 6 years later, the Second Circuit of the U.S. Court of Appeals, in *U.S. v. Reid and Thomas* (1975), affirmed Reid's conviction on six of seven counts related to the shooting of an FBI agent, noting, "there is no requirement . . . in line-ups that the accused must be surrounded by persons nearly identical in appearance, however desirable that may be" (p. 966). Eight months later the same court borrowed that language in *Pella v. Reid* (1975, p. 384): "The fact that Pella, a short man, was placed in a line-up with mostly taller men, while certainly not the most desirable procedure, does not by itself warrant a finding of unnecessary suggestiveness."[1] Paraphrasing slightly in *Wright v. Smith* (1977, p. 342), the court stated, "there is no requirement that a defendant in a lineup must be surrounded by people nearly identical in appearance, however desirable that may be." The repetition of the phrase regarding the desirability of surrounding the suspect with "nearly identical" fillers raises a question that we come back to often in this chapter: Just how much similarity is desirable?

GUIDELINES AND LEGISLATION

In 1999, the U.S. Department of Justice (DOJ), Office of Justice Programs, National Institute of Justice, in a collaboration of researchers, law enforcement personnel, and both prosecuting and defense attorneys, developed guidelines for law enforcement for interviewing witnesses and for composing, presenting, and documenting the results of eyewitness identification procedures. The guidelines for composing lineups were simple and straightforward: The suspect should not unduly stand out, and the lineup should include a single suspect and a minimum of five fillers who

> generally fit the witness's description of the perpetrator. When there
> is a limited/inadequate description of the perpetrator provided by the

---

[1]Between *Foster* in 1969 and *Pella v. Reid* in 1975, the U.S. Supreme Court in *Neil v. Biggers* (1972) ruled that an identification procedure could be suggestive, but the identification could be admissible nonetheless if other circumstances indicated that the identification was reliable. Thus, a suggestive procedure by itself does not require that the identification be excluded at trial. This point is reflected in the *Pella v. Reid* (1975) opinion.

witness, or when the description of the perpetrator differs significantly from the appearance of the suspect, fillers should resemble the suspect in significant features. (U.S. DOJ, Office of Justice Programs, National Institute of Justice, 1999, p. 29)

The guidelines continued, "complete uniformity of features is not required. Avoid using fillers who so closely resemble the suspect that a person familiar with the suspect might find it difficult to distinguish the suspect from the fillers" (U.S. DOJ, Office of Justice Programs, National Institute of Justice, 1999, p. 29). In 2001, the state of New Jersey adopted the DOJ guidelines (Farmer, 2001), and several states have since adopted similar guidelines.

The DOJ guidelines are consistent with the spirit of the court rulings described previously in stating that the lineup should be composed of fillers who are similar enough so that the suspect does not "unduly" stand out but not so similar as to make the identification unnecessarily difficult. That "just right" degree of similarity is determined by the description of the perpetrator provided by the witness.

The question regarding the "desirable" or optimal level of similarity is to some degree an empirical question that can be informed (although perhaps not completely answered) by empirical data. In the next section, we describe research paradigms for studying eyewitness identification, focusing primarily, but not entirely, on controlled laboratory experiments. We then derive some predictions from a computational model (Clark, 2003), and with those predictions in hand, we present a review of the research literature on the construction of lineups.

EYEWITNESS IDENTIFICATION RESEARCH
AND THE EMPIRICAL BASIS FOR REFORM

There are three paradigms for research on eyewitness identification: field studies, retrospective archival analyses, and experimental studies. Field studies examine eyewitness identification procedures in actual cases but are generally unable to distinguish between correct identifications of the guilty versus false identifications of the innocent. Retrospective archival analyses include those conducted by Garrett (2010) and Gross et al. (2005). Those studies examined well-established wrongful convictions to identify factors that might be associated with the wrongful conviction. The focus in this chapter is on experimental research, which allows one to examine how variations in lineup composition affect correct identifications of the guilty as well as false identifications of the innocent.

Experimental Research Paradigm

In a typical eyewitness identification experiment, participants become witnesses to a staged crime, either live or on video. Later, those witnesses are presented with a lineup that either includes the perpetrator of the staged crime or does not include the perpetrator of the staged crime. The *perpetrator-present* lineup simulates those real-world cases in which the person suspected by the police is indeed guilty, and the *perpetrator-absent* lineup simulates those real-world cases in which the person suspected by the police is innocent. Also, although it is not the focus of this chapter, we note that lineups can be presented simultaneously or sequentially. In a simultaneous lineup all of the lineup members are presented at the same time, and the witness makes a single response, whereas in a sequential lineup, each lineup member is presented one at a time, and the witness makes a response for each lineup member as he or she is presented (see Clark, 2012; Steblay, Dysart, & Wells, 2011; see also Chapter 5, this volume, for recent reviews and analyses).

Witnesses' responses are typically classified as (a) an identification of the suspect, (b) an identification of a filler, or (c) a nonidentification. In some cases, nonidentification responses are further divided into rejections of the lineup or don't know responses. Suspect identifications carry the most severe consequences because they are viewed as direct evidence of the suspect's guilt. For clarity and consistency, we use the term *correct identification* to refer only to the identification of a suspect who is guilty and the term *false identification* to refer only to the identification of suspect who is innocent. It is important to distinguish between false identifications of an innocent suspect versus incorrect identifications of a filler. Fillers are not suspects and are known to be innocent. Thus, except in very unusual circumstances, a filler who is misidentified will not face prosecution. It is the suspect who faces prosecution if identified, and for that reason in this chapter we focus on correct identifications of guilty suspects and false identifications of innocent suspects.

The evaluation of a lineup requires one to consider both the correct and the false identification rates, which together allow one to calculate a measure of the *probative value* of a suspect identification. The identification of the suspect has probative value to the extent that it is likely to occur when the suspect is guilty and unlikely to occur when the suspect is innocent. There are many ways to calculate probative value from correct and false identification rates. It is common to calculate probative value as the ratio of correct and false (C/F) identification rates (see, e.g., Steblay et al., 2011). However, calculation of the C/F ratio is problematic because the ratio will increase if witnesses simply become quite unwilling to make any identification. As the false identification rate approaches zero, the C/F ratio will become quite large, even if the correct identification rate is also very low (see

Clark, 2012; Clark, Erickson, & Breneman, 2011; Clark, Howell, & Davey, 2008). Because of these problems, probative value is measured here in two ways: (a) as the proportion of all suspect identifications that are correct identifications of the suspect, calculated as the correct identification rate divided by the sum of the correct and false identification rates, that is, $C/(C + F)$ and (b) by calculating d' from the correct and false identification rates. Also, following Clark (2012), one can compare two lineup procedures by assessing the proportional decreases in correct and false identification rates by calculating Pearson's r. For present purposes, the question is about the decreases in correct and false identification rates as a result of increases in filler similarity. If the decrease in the false identification rate is proportionally larger than the decrease in the correct identification rate, r is positive, whereas if the decrease in the correct identification rate is proportionally larger than the decrease in the false identification rate, r will be negative. If the decreases in correct and false identification rates are proportional, $r = 0$.

Theories of Eyewitness Identification

The evaluation of eyewitness identification procedures and the development of new procedures require the guidance of a theory regarding the psychological processes that underlie eyewitness identification decisions. Empirical data are informative about what happens under the specific conditions of a specific experiment. To generalize beyond those specific conditions, one must have a theory (Clark, 2008).

How will variation in the similarity of lineup fillers affect correct and false identification rates? To address that question we obtained predictions from the WITNESS model (Clark, 2003; Clark et al., 2011). The model assumes that the witness stores information about the perpetrator in memory and that the memory trace is incomplete and contains some errors. At the time of the lineup, the witness compares each lineup member with his or her memory of the perpetrator. Thus, for a six-person lineup, there will be six comparisons resulting in six match values, each of which represents the match between a given lineup member and the witness's memory of the perpetrator. Our specific question is how the similarity of the fillers affects the correct and false identification rates. Predictions from the model are shown in Figure 4.1. Panels A and B show the decrease in correct and false identification rates, respectively. The x-axis represents the similarity between the fillers and the perpetrator, which can vary from 0, which represents only chance similarity, to 1.0, which represents the case in which the fillers are identical to the perpetrator. The figure shows filler similarity varying from .1 to .8. Panel C plots the correct and false identification rates together as a function of similarity. Given the natural tendency to read effects from left to right,

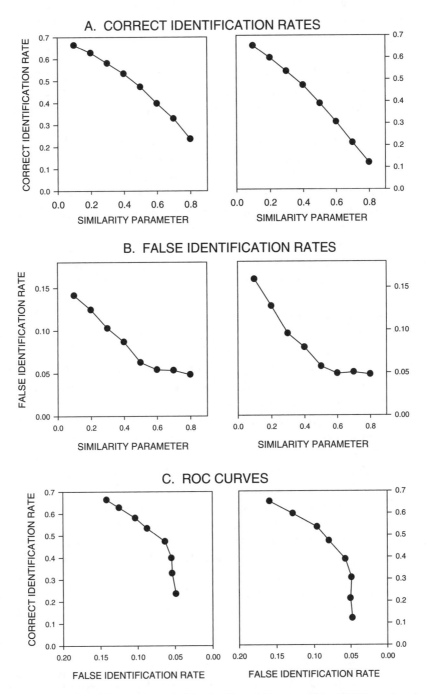

Figure 4.1. WITNESS model predictions for (Panel A) correct identification rates, for (Panel B) false identification rates as a function of similarity, and for (Panel C) backward receiver-operating characteristic (ROC) curves as a function of similarity.

the x-axis for the false identification rates runs from 1 to 0, rather than 0 to 1, to show how correct and false identification rates change with increases in filler similarity. The backward x-axis produces backward receiver-operating characteristic (ROC) curves.

The two sides of the figure show predictions based on different decision rules. The left-hand side of the figure implements a best-above-criterion decision rule, and the right-hand side implements a best-next decision rule. According to a best-above-criterion rule, the witness identifies the best match from the lineup if that best match is above a decision criterion c. According to a best-next rule, the witness identifies the best match if that best match is sufficiently better than any other match. Specifically, the best match is identified if the difference between the best match and the next best match is greater than a criterion c_{DIFF}. The best-above-criterion and best-next models correspond closely with absolute and relative judgment strategies described by Wells (1984).

The two decision models produce similar patterns of results. Correct and false identification rates decrease as the similarity of the fillers is increased. False identifications level off as similarity approaches .8 (where 1.0 represents a lineup of near clones). The specific patterns will vary depending on other parameters, such as the accuracy of the memory trace, the similarity of the innocent suspect to the perpetrator, and the decision criteria c and c_{DIFF}. The main point is that correct and false identification rates both decrease with increases in filler similarity, irrespective of whether identification decisions are based on absolute or relative judgments. Figure 4.1 shows one other salient and important pattern. Beyond a certain point, increases in foil similarity have diminishing returns; this is shown in the ROC curves that bend over steeply as similarity is increased at very high levels.

Filler Similarity, Description Matches, and Mismatches

What do the data show? We begin with a comparison between higher and lower similarity fillers. Filler similarity was operationalized either in terms of the match to a verbal description of the perpetrator or by the rated similarity to the perpetrator. The average correct and false identification rates based on 18 comparisons from eight studies (3,260 participants) from Clark (2012) are shown in Table 4.1.[2] The increase in filler similarity produced a decrease in the false identification rate from .31 to .16 and a decrease in the correct identification rate from .67 to .59. The decrease in the false identification rate

---

[2]Some conditions from Gronlund, Carlson, Dailey, and Goodsell (2009) were excluded from the present analyses on the basis of levels of performance that were below chance. The excluded conditions are those described by Gronlund et al. as "guilty weak" and "innocent strong."

TABLE 4.1
Correct and False Identification Rates and Measures
of Probative Value as a Function of Similarity and Match to
the Perpetrator's Description and Rated Similarity to the Perpetrator

Measure	Similarity		Description		Similarity rating	
	Low	High	Mismatch	Match	Low	High
Correct	.67	.59	.73	.61	.59	.55
False	.31	.16	.39	.16	.15	.13
C/(C × F)	.71	.80	.66	.79	.84	.84
d'	1.09	1.36	.94	1.40	1.52	1.40

Note. Correct = correct identification rate; False = false identification rate; C/(C + F) = correct/ (correct + false) averaged over comparisons; d' is calculated from correct and false identification rates. The two columns under Similarity include data for all 18 filler similarity comparisons. The two columns under Description include only data for 11 comparisons in which similarity was operationalized as description matches and mismatches. The two columns under Similarity rating include data from six comparisons that operationalized similarity in terms of similarity ratings.

was proportionally larger than the decrease in the correct identification rate ($r = .09$). Table 4.1 separates the analyses to show those that operationalized similarity in terms of description matches and mismatches versus those that operationalized similarity on the basis of similarity ratings.[3]

The results of the individual comparisons are shown in Panel A of Figure 4.2. Most studies show the same pattern—decreases in both correct and false identification rates as filler similarity is increased. However, there is considerable variability in that general pattern. Longer, flatter lines indicate larger decreases in false identification rates relative to correct identification rates, and steep lines indicate larger decreases in correct identification rates relative to false identification rates. It is clear from the figure that the functions are flatter to the left side of the figure and tip steeply downward on the right side of the figure as false identification rates converge on zero.

Notably, the effects of filler similarity were different for studies that manipulated similarity in terms of the degree of match to the description of the perpetrator than for studies that manipulated similarity in terms of similarity ratings. Specifically, increasing the degree of match to the description reduced false identification rates proportionally more than correct identification rates ($r = .14$) and increased the probative value of a suspect identification, whereas choosing fillers with higher similarity ratings had very little effect overall.

These results may be interpreted to suggest that increases in filler similarity are fundamentally different when operationalized in terms of description

---

[3]Experiment 3 from Lindsay et al. (1991) does not fall clearly into either category.

A. HIGH SIMILARITY versus LOW SIMILARITY FILLERS

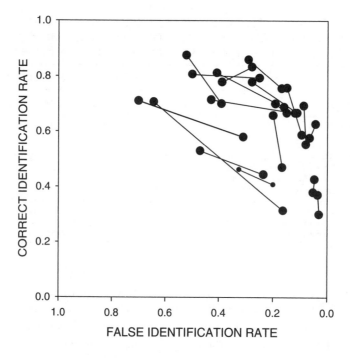

B. DESCRIPTION versus SUSPECT MATCH

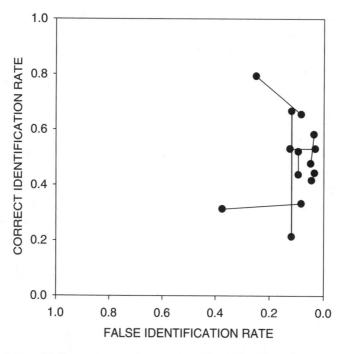

Figure 4.2. Panel A shows changes in correct and false identification rates comparing high- and low-similarity fillers. Panel B shows changes in correct and false identification rates comparing description-matched and suspect-matched fillers.

matches and mismatches than when operationalized in terms of similarity ratings. However, there is another, perhaps simpler explanation. The difference between the description-matching and similarity-rating studies is primarily in the average false identification rate, which was .39 for fillers who mismatched the perpetrator description and .15 for fillers with lower rated similarity to the perpetrator. An increase in similarity, however it is obtained, can lower the false identification rate only to the extent that the false identification rate is high to begin with. As shown in the theoretical analyses in Figure 4.1, if the false identification rate is low to begin with (as was the case for Brewer & Wells, 2006), increasing filler similarity will have very little benefit but very large costs because the false identification rate has very little room to decrease, whereas the correct identification has plenty of room to decrease. By contrast, false identification rates with description-mismatched fillers were very high with plenty of room to decrease with increased filler similarity.

We also considered whether similarity effects followed the same pattern for simultaneous and sequential lineups. The analysis focuses on two studies, one by Carlson, Gronlund, and Clark (2008) and one by Gronlund, Carlson, Dailey, and Goodsell (2009), that varied the similarity of the fillers for both simultaneous and sequential lineups in a full factorial design. Correct and false identification rates were lower for lineups with fillers who more closely matched the description of the perpetrator for both simultaneous and sequential lineups. However, the diagnosticity measures showed different patterns. For simultaneous presentation, better matching fillers increased the probative value of a suspect identification as measured by the conditional probability, C/C+F (from .64 to .76), or by d' (from .97 to 1.21) and Pearson's r was .12. For sequential presentation, C/(C + F) increased only slightly (from .73 to .76); d' decreased slightly (from 1.11 to 1.01); and Pearson's r was .03. These analyses suggest that variation in the similarity of the fillers may have larger effects for simultaneous lineups than for sequential lineups. This pattern of results may be viewed in (at least) two different ways: If the lineup is presented sequentially, increasing the quality of the fillers may produce little or no increase in the probative value of a suspect identification. From a different angle, these results also suggest that sequential presentation may help maintain the probative value of a suspect identification in the event that the composition of the lineup is very biased (see Lindsay et al, 1991).[4] These results and their interpretations should be considered cautiously because they are based on only six comparisons (three simultaneous and three sequential) from two studies.

---

[4]Lindsay et al. (1991) concluded that sequential presentation reduces the impact of a biased lineup over 20 years ago. However, their studies did not examine perpetrator presence, filler similarity, and presentation format in a factorial design in such a way as to calculate and compare measures of probative value.

On the basis of the subset of studies that manipulated the degree of match to the description of the perpetrator, four conclusions seem clear: (a) If the fillers mismatch a general description of the perpetrator, the risk of a false identification may be extremely high. (b) The selection of fillers who are better matches to the description of the perpetrator decreases both the correct and the false identification rate. (c) The decrease in the false identification rate is proportionally larger than the decrease in the correct identification rate, leading to an overall increase in the probative value of a suspect identification. (d) Increases in filler similarity may have diminishing returns. Compared with a case in which the fillers are very dissimilar (i.e., Lindsay & Wells, 1980), the gains due to increased similarity may be quite high. However, beyond a certain point, further increases in similarity may not be desirable. Again, we note that the effects of filler similarity may be smaller for sequential lineups than for simultaneous lineups. Stronger conclusions, however, must wait for additional data.

Suspect-Match Versus Description-Match

The results in Figure 4.2 (Panel A) show that false identification rates can be very high if fillers do not match the perpetrator. Of course, in real criminal investigations the perpetrator does not always make him- or herself available for the purpose of selecting lineup fillers. Rather, the police may have a suspect who may be the perpetrator but who may also be innocent, and they have access to the witness's description of the perpetrator that may vary in its detail and accuracy. Thus, in actual criminal investigations the similarity of the fillers to the perpetrator is moderated through their similarity to the suspect and/or their match to the witness's description of the perpetrator.

The DOJ guidelines are clear in their preference for selecting fillers according to their match to the witness's description of the perpetrator rather than their similarity to the appearance of the suspect. What is the basis of this preference? Description-matched filler selection provides an answer to the "similar enough" question (Luus & Wells, 1991). The lineup fillers may be considered sufficiently similar if they match the description of the perpetrator provided by the witness. Description-matched filler selection not only provides guidance as to how many features should match but also provides guidance as to which features should match—the features described in the witness's description of the perpetrator.

In addition to providing guidance as to how many and which features should be considered in the selection of fillers, the preference for description-matched filler selection is based also on analyses suggesting that description-matched filler selection should increase the correct identification rate (Luus & Wells, 1991; Wells, Rydell, & Seelau, 1993) and decrease the false identification rate (Clark & Tunnicliff, 2001; Navon, 1992; Tunnicliff & Clark, 2000) relative to suspect-matched filler selection.

The higher correct identification rate is predicted because the similarity between the fillers and the perpetrator is limited to only those features that are present in the witness's description (Luus & Wells, 1991). This limit on the number of matching features reduces the chances of selecting fillers who are excessively similar such that a "person familiar with the suspect might find it difficult to distinguish the suspect from the fillers" (U.S. DOJ, Office of Justice Programs, National Institute of Justice, 1999, p. 29).

The prediction regarding lower false identification rates is a bit more complicated (see Clark & Tunnicliff, 2001; Navon, 1992; Tunnicliff & Clark, 2000), but it reduces to a simple point: Fillers can be reasonably similar to the suspect but fail to match key features described by the witness. To illustrate, imagine a lineup with five fillers who are similar to an innocent suspect in every way, except one—the suspect has bigger ears than any of the fillers—and that feature was noted by the witness ("I didn't get a very good look at him, but the one thing I remember was that he had very big ears"). It follows that the big-eared innocent suspect, who is in fact surrounded by fillers who are nearly identical in appearance, would be the person in the lineup who would be most likely to be identified. The selection of lineup fillers on the basis of their match to the witness's description should reduce that problem. If the suspect is in the lineup because he was judged to match the witness's description of the perpetrator, then it makes sense that everyone should be in the lineup because they were judged to match the witness's description of the perpetrator. By equating lineup members in this way, the false identification rate should be reduced, and the innocent suspect should be no more likely to be identified than any of the fillers.

Data from six studies provide seven comparisons (1,186 participants) to evaluate these predictions. Five of these studies were previously reviewed by Clark and Godfrey (2009), and one more study by Darling, Valentine, and Memon (2008) is added here. The correct and false identification rates for each study are shown in Figure 4.2 (Panel B), and the means are given in Table 4.2.

Figure 4.2 (Panel B) looks very different from Figure 4.2 (Panel A). Figure 4.2 (Panel A) shows a fairly consistent pattern of lower correct and lower false identification rates for lineups with better matching fillers. By contrast there is no consistent pattern in the comparison of suspect-matched versus description-matched filler selection. Table 4.2 shows that relative to suspect-matched lineups, description-matched lineups produce a small increase in correct identifications from .46 to .53, $t(6) = 1.07$, $p = .33$ and an increase in false identifications from .07 to .15, $t(6) = 1.95$, $p = .10$.

There is little or no evidence that the description-matched method of filler selection increases the probative value of a suspect identification.

TABLE 4.2
Correct and False Identification Rates and Measures of Probative Value in Suspect-Matched and Description-Matched Lineups

Measure	Suspect matched	Description matched
Correct	.46	.53
False	.07	.15
C/(C + F)	.85	.79
d'	1.42	1.23

Note. Correct = correct identification rate; False = false identification rate; C/(C + F) = correct/(correct + false) averaged over comparisons; d' is calculated from correct and false identification rates.

Quite to the contrary, for five of the seven comparisons, the probative value of a suspect identification was lower for description-matched lineups than for suspect-matched lineups. Selecting fillers on the basis of their match to the witness's description does not appear to reduce the bias of suspect-matched lineups. Rather, for the studies in Table 4.2, the average false identification rate was twice as high for description-matched lineups as for suspect-matched lineups.

These results are inconsistent with predictions (Luus & Wells, 1991; Navon, 1992; Tunnicliff & Clark, 2000) and inconsistent with the guidelines and legislation passed in the last 10 years. This inconsistency begs for an explanation. The principle behind description-matched lineups is intuitively compelling: If the suspect is in the lineup because he was judged to match the witness's description of the perpetrator, then the fillers should also be in the lineup because they were judged to match the witness's description of the perpetrator. This should produce a fair lineup in which lineup members are equated, and the innocent suspect should be identified no more often than anyone else. This pattern was clearly not obtained.

What produces the variability in the results shown in Figure 4.2 (Panel B)? To address that question, Clark (2003) fit the WITNESS model to the data from Wells et al. (1993); Juslin, Olsson, and Winman (1996); and Tunnicliff and Clark (2000). Models can be very useful in revealing the mechanisms that underlie differences across studies. Only one study of all the studies shown in Figure 4.2 (Panel B), the study by Wells et al. (1993), produced a large advantage for description-matched filler selection over suspect-matched filler selection. The correct identification rate was 3 times higher for description-matched lineups (.67) than for suspect-matched lineups (.21), and the false identification rates were equivalent (.12). What was it about that study that produced such a large advantage? The answer is found in the values of the similarity parameters in the model fits. To fit the Wells et al.

data, the filler similarity parameter for suspect-matched lineups had to be set at an extremely high value, much higher than for the Tunnicliff and Clark and Juslin et al. studies. The results of the model fitting suggest that higher correct identification rates for description-matched filler selection over suspect-matched filler selection may be obtained only to the extent that the fillers for suspect-matched lineups are excessively similar to the suspect. To the extent that the police do not select fillers who are excessively similar to the suspect, the selection of foils on the basis of their match to the witness's description, rather than their similarity to the suspect, may address a problem that arises very infrequently.

Relevant to this issue, the lineups used in the Juslin et al. (1996) and Tunnicliff and Clark (2000) studies were created by law enforcement, and the similarity parameters used to fit the WITNESS model to those data were much lower than those used to fit the Wells et al. (1993) data (with lineups created by research assistants), suggesting little evidence of an excessive similarity problem in lineups created by law enforcement. An analysis of lineups from actual criminal investigations, by Valentine and Heaton (1999), suggested that police may select fillers in such a way that lineups are often biased against the suspect rather than against fillers who are too similar to the suspect. However, it is important to recall the example of the big-eared innocent suspect to illustrate an important point: Lineup fillers can be very similar to the suspect and yet the lineup can still be biased.

The issue of lineup bias brings us to the other surprising result from these studies. Contrary to expectations, the selection of fillers on the basis of their match to the description did not reduce the bias in suspect-matched perpetrator-absent lineups but, instead, increased the bias. This is a surprising result because by selecting the suspect and the fillers on the basis of the same description of the perpetrator, suspect and fillers should be equated, and the perpetrator-absent lineups should be fair, that is, the innocent suspect should be identified no more often than the fillers, or about one-sixth of the time in a six-person lineup. The relevant data here are not the false identification rates but rather the false identification rates conditional on witnesses making any identification. These conditional false identification rates were consistently above the fair lineup baseline for description-matched lineups. The simplest explanation of these results is that the standard for what counts as a match to the description of the perpetrator may be higher when considering a person who might be a suspect than when considering a person who might be added to the lineup as a filler.

The bottom line from these analyses is rather mixed. The false identification rate can be extraordinarily high if the fillers do not match a general description of the perpetrator. If fillers are selected who better match the description of the perpetrator, the false identification rate will decrease but so too will the correct identification rate. Thus, there is a trade-off between correct identifications lost in exchange for false identifications avoided. This basic result contradicts earlier suggestions that false identifications are reduced with little or no loss of correct identifications (Lindsay et al., 1987; Lindsay & Wells, 1980; Wells, Memon, & Penrod, 2006). Nonetheless, the trade-off may be viewed favorably as false identifications decrease proportionally more than correct identifications. (There are other factors that policymakers should also consider, including the proportion of police lineups that include innocent or guilty suspects, the downstream consequences of identification outcomes, and the utilities associated with those outcomes; see Clark, 2012.)

However, the preference for description-matched filler selection over suspect-matched filler selection, which is at the heart of the DOJ guidelines as well as recent legislation in many states, is not supported by empirical data. There is no evidence that description-matched filler selection reduces the false identification rate (in fact, in most studies it increased the false identification rate), and the results taken as a whole show that the probative value of a suspect identification is lower with description-matched filler selection than with suspect-matched filler selection. Given the current data, there is no empirical foundation for recommending that foils be selected on the basis of their match to the witness's description of the perpetrator *rather than* their match to the appearance of the suspect. The optimal procedure likely involves some combination of the two procedures such that fillers are both similar to the suspect and consistent with the witness's description of the perpetrator. A recent survey of law enforcement practices by Wise, Safer, and Maro (2011) suggested that many police officers currently use some combination of the two matching procedures to select lineup fillers.

There are a number of additional issues to consider regarding description-matched filler selection: (a) What counts as a match to the description? For example, if the witness described the perpetrator as being "muscular," how muscular must a person be to match that description and be added to the lineup as a filler? (b) Are lineup makers able to maintain a constant standard for what counts as a match to the description? Or will their standard decrease from the first filler selected to the last filler selected? (This question is applicable to suspect-matched foil selection as well.) (c) Can the person who makes the lineup select foils only on the basis of their match to the description of the perpetrator without being influenced by the physical appearance of the suspect? The recommendation, taken at face value, implies that the fillers should be selected without consideration of the suspect's appearance. The best way to achieve that goal would be for the person who selects the fillers to not know what the suspect looks like. (d) What should be done if the suspect does not match the witness's description of the perpetrator? In such circumstances the recommendation is that filler selection be based on individual's similarity to the suspect. This raises a question: How does the lineup maker decide whether the suspect is or is not consistent with the witness's description of the perpetrator? How much deviation between the suspect and witness description is necessary to shift from matching fillers to the description to matching fillers to the suspect?

Other Lineup Composition Issues

Pictorial Similarity Effects

The most basic operating principle regarding the construction of a lineup is that the suspect should not stand out. The suspect can stand out even if all of the lineup members match the witness's description of the perpetrator as a result of pictorial aspects of the suspect's photograph that are different than the other photographs. For example, the suspect's photograph may stand out if it has a different colored background or is larger than the other photographs. Buckhout (1974) and Buckhout, Figueroa, and Hoff (1975) showed that the suspect identification rate was higher when the suspect's photograph was crooked, his head was tilted, and he had a smile on his face (and none of the fillers had tilted heads or smiles). Unfortunately, these studies are uninformative regarding false identifications because there was only a perpetrator-present condition but no perpetrator-absent condition. These studies show that correct identifications of the guilty can increase by making the guilty suspect's photograph distinctive, but one cannot extrapolate from those results to assume that parallel effects will be obtained when the suspect is innocent.

Pictorial standout effects may be quite different from similarity-based or relative similarity effects. They may be driven by attention or deduction rather than relative similarity. A crooked picture may be more likely to be noticed but rejected nonetheless if the person does not bear sufficient resemblance to the perpetrator.

There is anecdotal evidence from our lab to suggest that distinctiveness combined with a reasonable level of similarity can produce very high identification rates. In a study by Clark, Marshall, and Rosenthal (2009) some of the lineups contained a filler who was identified with surprising frequency. This high identification rate was not predicted from the similarity ratings that were used to construct the lineup. Why was this person identified at such a high rate? One can only speculate, but the 20/20 hindsight theory is that in his booking photograph the individual is looking slightly to the left rather than straight at the camera. Indeed, he is *the only person in the lineup who . . .*

Pictorial distinctiveness has not received much attention in the research literature. The lack of interest may be due to a perception that the results are so obvious that research is not needed. Students generally laugh at the crooked Buckhout lineups because the error is so obvious. And yet there are serious questions that need to be addressed: How does pictorial distinctiveness affect correct and false identification rates? Does pictorial distinctiveness interact with similarity such that identification rates of distinctive photos increase only to the extent that the person in the photograph is similar to the perpetrator? What are the psychological mechanisms that underlie pictorial distinctiveness effects (to the extent that they exist)?

Position and Configuration Effects

There is another question the lineup maker must answer: How should one position the lineup members? In a six-person lineup, where should the suspect be positioned? Where should the other lineup members be positioned relative to the suspect? This question has received some attention for sequential lineups but very little attention for simultaneous lineups.

In a survey by Wogalter, Malpass, and McQuiston (2004), police officers indicated that for live lineups they determined the position of the suspect in one of two ways: They would either let the suspect choose his or her place in the lineup or they would place the suspect in the middle of the lineup rather than at the ends. Photographic lineups, of course, are conducted outside the presence of the suspect and counsel, so the suspect can have no input about where he is placed in a photo lineup. Police officers in the Wogalter et al. survey indicated that they typically present photographic lineups in two rows of three photographs and that, again, they usually place the suspect in the middle of the lineup. What this suggests for photographic lineups is that the suspect is typically placed in the top row middle or the bottom row middle.

There is very little research showing what police actually do. One study that does shed some light on the placement of the suspect is the Illinois field study that compared simultaneous and sequential lineups (Mecklenburg, 2006). There are a number of problems in the design and conduct of the Illinois field study (see Schacter et al., 2007; Steblay, 2011) that compromise the comparison between simultaneous and sequential lineups. However, the criticisms do not involve the composition of the lineups (Steblay, 2011), and thus useful data regarding suspect placement are available from the report (see Mecklenburg, 2006, Appendix, Exhibit 17, analyses conducted by Ebbesen and Finklea). The suspect placement data shown in Figure 4.3 are consistent with the "in the middle" responses from the Wogalter et al. (2004) study. For both simultaneous and sequential lineups, the suspect was placed in Positions 3 to 5, and rarely in Positions 1, 2, or 6. Interestingly, suspect placements were different for simultaneous and sequential lineups, χ^2 (5, $N = 393$) = 29.57,

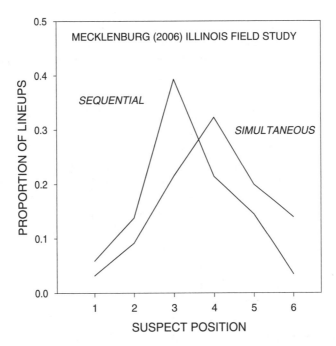

Figure 4.3. Suspect position in the Illinois field study for sequential and simultaneous lineups.

$p < .0001$. It is clear from the figure that suspect position was shifted forward
in sequential lineups relative to simultaneous lineups with a peak at Position
3 compared with a peak at Position 4 for simultaneous lineups.[5] The Illinois
study is, of course, one sample from three jurisdictions in the state (Chicago,
Evanston, and Joliet) for one particular study.

What effect does the position of the suspect have on eyewitness identification? Unfortunately, there is no systematic review of the literature as
to how the position of the suspect affects eyewitness identification decisions
in simultaneous lineups. There has been some research directed at position
effects in sequential lineups; however, those results are inconsistent.

In some studies the suspect is fixed in one (Wells et al. 1993) or two
(Clark & Tunnicliff, 2001) positions. In other studies, the position is rotated
through all six positions (Clark et al., 2009; Parker & Ryan, 1993). In the
latter case, the position of the suspect is not a variable of interest but is
only a nuisance variable to be counterbalanced. Such studies typically report

---

[5]One can only speculate as to the differences in suspect placement in sequential and simultaneous lineups. One possibility is that police may have had some concerns about placing the suspect toward the end
of the sequential lineup such that witnesses might identify a filler before the suspect was shown.

finding no significant differences due to the placement of the suspect. Of course, by slicing the data into the six positions of the lineup, the number of observations for each suspect position may become too small for meaningful analysis.

There are a few interesting exceptions. In the Mecklenburg (2006) field study and in an experimental study by O'Connell and Synnott (2009), witnesses shown simultaneous lineups identified the suspect more often when the suspect was presented in the middle of the lineup than when presented at the ends (first or last position) of the lineup. In another experimental study by Sporer (1993), witnesses shown simultaneous lineups had a clear preference for the bottom middle position, and in a field study by Wells, Steblay, and Dysart (2011), witnesses shown simultaneous lineups showed a very slight preference for Positions 2 and 5 (middle of the top row and middle of the bottom row).[6] These results must be interpreted cautiously. They do not constitute strong evidence for a middle position preference because we do not know how many studies found other patterns or found no differences that were simply not reported.

The issue of the suspect's position has been raised most clearly for sequential lineups. The results fall into three categories: Some studies have reported no effects due to the placement of the suspect's photograph; others have reported that sequential performance may be harmed by late placement in the lineup (Clark & Davey, 2005; Memon & Gabbert, 2003); and others have reported that sequential performance is facilitated by late placement in the lineup (Carlson et al., 2008; Gronlund et al., 2009). The three patterns may be explained as follows.

The position of the suspect in a sequential lineup will have little or no effect if the fillers are easily rejected. To the extent that the filler identification rate is low, they are noncontenders, and it matters little where among those noncontenders the suspect is placed (see Lindsay & Wells, 1985; Wells et al., 2011, Table 1, p. 14). If, on the other hand, a very competitive filler precedes the suspect, the suspect identification rate will be reduced relative to the case in which the same filler follows the suspect later in the lineup (Clark & Davey, 2005). Facilitation due to late placement of the suspect may occur to the extent that witnesses can learn something from the fillers as they are presented prior to the suspect (Carlson et al., 2008; Gronlund et al., 2009).

---

[6]It is hard to overlook the correspondence between the police practice of placing the suspect in the middle positions of the lineup and witnesses' tendency to choose from the middle positions of the lineup. However, the correspondence, to the extent that it exists, is not likely to be viewed as being suggestive. The California Supreme Court wrote in *People v. De Angelis* (1979, p. 841), "the contention of 'strategically' placing defendant's photo toward the center of the display fails of merit. No matter where placed, a like complaint could be made."

Neighborhood Effects

One last issue we discuss with regard to lineup composition concerns what we refer to as *neighborhood effects*. The question was first raised by Gonzalez, Davis, and Ellsworth (1995), who asked, "Who should stand next to the suspect?" They considered how the suspect's neighbors affect the likelihood that nonwitnesses can pick the suspect out of the lineup. For some conditions, the suspect was more likely to be identified when surrounded by low-similarity fillers than when surrounded by high-similarity fillers. The lineup members were constant across conditions; only their arrangement was different in the high- and low-similarity condition. We (Moreland & Clark, 2011) asked the same question regarding the suspect's neighbors in an eyewitness identification task and found a complex interaction between suspect position and the similarity of the suspect's (filler) neighbors. These preliminary results suggest that eyewitness identification decisions may vary not only with the position of the suspect but also with the configuration of fillers near the suspect.

CONCLUSION AND FUTURE RESEARCH DIRECTIONS

Legal decisions from the U.S. Supreme Court and the Second Circuit Court of Appeals suggest a tension between the two ends of a continuum between selecting fillers who are not similar enough and selecting fillers who are too similar. Although the courts suggested that surrounding a suspect with fillers nearly identical in appearance might be desirable, theory and data suggest that there are limitations to that desirability. Without attempting to read the minds of the second circuit justices, one wonders— because the court denied defendants' claims of suggestive lineups—if the justices really did believe in the desirability of creating lineups with very similar fillers.

Theory and data both show a trade-off. As filler similarity increases, false identifications decrease, but correct identifications decrease as well. This trade-off contradicts claims that false identification rates decrease with little or no loss in correct identifications (see Lindsay et al., 1987; Wells et al., 2006). Clearly, correct identifications are lost as the filler similarity is increased. Nonetheless, the results in Figure 4.2 and Table 4.1 suggest that the trade-off may be favorable in that the decrease in false identifications is proportionally larger than the decrease in correct identifications. However, there is an alternative account of this trade-off: The large decrease in false identifications may be restricted to comparisons in which false identification rates are very high due to the selection of fillers who are clearly implausible.

The DOJ guidelines (U.S. DOJ, Office of Justice Programs, National Institute of Justice, 1999; and many eyewitness identification researchers) recommend that fillers be selected on the basis of their match to the witness's description of the perpetrator, rather than their similarity to the suspect. However, there is no evidence that description-matched filler selection reduces the risk of false identification, and indeed, the extant research suggests that the recommended filler selection procedure increases false identification rates rather than decreasing them. Moreover, the results taken as a whole show that the probative value of a suspect identification is lower for description-matched lineups.

At one level the filler-selection issue seems very simple. One cannot select fillers who are so dissimilar as to mismatch even a general description of the perpetrator. Beyond that simple rule, the issues continue to be murky. As similarity increases there may be diminishing returns when false identification rates have very little room to decrease. The recommendation to select fillers on the basis of their match to a description rather than their match to the suspect has little or no empirical support.

There are several additional lineup composition issues for which data are lacking. Perhaps most important, because jurisdictions consider procedural reforms in "packages," that is, sequential presentation *and* recommendations for filler selection, more research is needed to assess filler similarity effects for both simultaneous and sequential lineups. There are other issues as well for which data are lacking. Consider the following examples. There is a lack of systematic research as to how the placement of the suspect affects correct and false identification rates for simultaneous lineups, and there are conflicting findings for sequential lineups. There is no solid empirical evidence to show that pictorial distinctiveness increases the risk of false identification. There is no research on neighborhood or configuration effects. Given the relationship between lineup composition, false identification, and false convictions (Garrett, 2010), there is much more research to be done.

REFERENCES

Arnold, G. F. (1906). *Psychology applied to legal evidence and other constructions of law.* Calcutta, India: Thacker, Spink.

Brewer, N., & Wells, G. L. (2006). The confidence–accuracy relationship in eyewitness identification: Effects of lineup instructions, foil similarity, and target-absent base rates. *Journal of Experimental Psychology: Applied, 12,* 11–30.

Buckhout, R. (1974). Eyewitness testimony. *Scientific American, 231,* 23–31.

Buckhout, R., Figueroa, D., & Hoff, E. (1975). Eyewitness identification: Effects of suggestion and bias in identification from photographs. *Bulletin of the Psychonomic Society, 6,* 71–74.

Carlson, C., Gronlund, S. D., & Clark, S. E. (2008). Lineup composition, suspect position, and the sequential lineup advantage. *Journal of Experimental Psychology: Applied, 14*, 118–128. doi:10.1037/1076-898X.14.2.118

Clark, S. E. (2003). A memory and decision model for eyewitness identification. *Applied Cognitive Psychology, 17*, 629–654. doi:10.1002/acp.891

Clark, S. E. (2008). The importance (necessity) of computational modeling for eyewitness identification research [Special issue]. *Applied Cognitive Psychology, 22*, 803–813. doi:10.1002/acp.1484

Clark, S. E. (2012). Costs and benefits of eyewitness identification reform: Psychological science and public policy. *Perspectives on Psychological Science, 7*, 238–259.

Clark, S. E., & Davey, S. L. (2005). The target-to-fillers shift in simultaneous and sequential lineups. *Law and Human Behavior, 29*, 151–172. doi:10.1007/s10979-005-2418-7

Clark, S. E., Erickson, M. A., & Breneman, J. (2011). Probative value of absolute and relative judgments in eyewitness identification. *Law and Human Behavior, 35*, 364–380. doi:10.1007/s10979-010-9245-1

Clark, S. E., & Godfrey, R. D. (2009). Eyewitness identification evidence and innocence risk. *Psychonomic Bulletin & Review, 16*, 22–42. doi:10.3758/PBR.16.1.22

Clark, S. E., Howell, R. T., & Davey, S. L. (2008). Regularities in eyewitness identification. *Law and Human Behavior, 32*, 187–218. doi:10.1007/s10979-006-9082-4

Clark, S. E., Marshall, T., & Rosenthal, R. (2009). Lineup administrator influence on eyewitness identification decisions. *Journal of Experimental Psychology: Applied, 15*, 63–75. doi:10.1037/a0015185

Clark, S. E., & Tunnicliff, J. T. (2001). Selecting lineup fillers in eyewitness identification experiments: Experimental control and real-world simulation. *Law and Human Behavior, 25*, 199–216. doi:10.1023/A:1010753809988

Darling, S., Valentine, T., & Memon, A. (2008). Selection of lineup fillers in operational contexts. *Applied Cognitive Psychology, 22*, 159–169. doi:10.1002/acp.1366

Farmer, J. J. (2001). *Attorney general guidelines for preparing and conducting photo and live lineup identification procedures.* Retrieved from http://www.state.nj.us/lps/dcj/agguide/photoid.pdf

Foster v. California, 394 U.S. 440 (1969).

Garrett, B. L. (2010). *Convicting the innocent: Where criminal prosecutions go wrong.* Cambridge, MA: Harvard University Press.

Gilbert v. California, 388 U.S. 263 (1967).

Gonzalez, R., Davis, J., & Ellsworth, P. C. (1995). Who should stand next to the suspect? Problems in the assessment of lineup fairness. *Journal of Applied Psychology, 80*, 525–531. doi:10.1037/0021-9010.80.4.525

Gronlund, S. D., Carlson, C. A., Dailey, S. B., & Goodsell, C. A. (2009). Robustness of the sequential lineup advantage. *Journal of Experimental Psychology: Applied, 15*, 140–152. doi:10.1037/a0015082

Gross, S. R., Jacoby, K., Matheson, D. J., Montgomery, N., & Patil, S. (2005). Exonerations in the United States 1989 through 2003. *The Journal of Criminal Law & Criminology, 95*, 523–560.

Juslin, P., Olsson, N., & Winman, A. (1996). Calibration and diagnosticity of confidence in eyewitness identification: Comments on what can be inferred from the low confidence–accuracy correlation. *Journal of Experimental Psychology: Learning, Memory, and Cognition, 22*, 1304–1316. doi:10.1037/0278-7393.22.5.1304

Lindsay, R. C. L., Lea, J. A., Nosworthy, G. J., Fulford, J. A., Hector, J., LeVan, V., & Seebrook, C. (1991). Biased lineups: Sequential presentation reduces the problem. *Journal of Applied Psychology, 76*, 796–802. doi:10.1037/0021-9010.76.6.796

Lindsay, R. C. L., Wallbridge, H., & Drennan, D. (1987). Do the clothes make the man? An exploration of the effect of lineup attire on eyewitness identification accuracy. *Canadian Journal of Behavioural Science, 19*, 463–478.

Lindsay, R. C. L., & Wells, G. L. (1980). What price justice? Exploring the relationship of lineup fairness to identification accuracy. *Law and Human Behavior, 4*, 303–313. doi:10.1007/BF01040622

Lindsay, R. C. L., & Wells, G. L. (1985). Improving eyewitness identifications from lineups: Simultaneous versus sequential lineup presentation. *Journal of Applied Psychology, 70*, 556–564. doi:10.1037/0021-9010.70.3.556

Luus, C. A. E., & Wells, G. L. (1991). Eyewitness identification and the selection of distractors for lineups. *Law and Human Behavior, 15*, 43–57.

Mecklenburg, S. H. (2006). *Report to the legislature of the state of Illinois: The Illinois pilot program on sequential double-blind identification procedures*. Retrieved from http://www.chicagopolice.org/IL%20Pilot%20on%20Eyewitness%20ID.pdf

Memon, A., & Gabbert, F. (2003). Improving the identification accuracy of senior witnesses: Do prelineup questions and sequential testing help? *Journal of Applied Psychology, 88*, 341–347. doi:10.1037/0021-9010.88.2.341

Moreland, M. B., & Clark, S. E. (2012). *Eyewitness identification and the suspect's position and neighborhood*. Manuscript in preparation.

Munsterberg, H. (1908). *On the witness stand*. New York, NY: Clark, Boardman.

Navon, D. (1992). Selection of lineup fillers by similarity to the suspect is likely to misfire. *Law and Human Behavior, 16*, 575–593. doi:10.1007/BF01044624

Neil v. Biggers, 409 U.S. 188, 1972.

O'Connell, M., & Synnott, J. (2009). Position of influence: Variation in offender identification rates by location in a lineup. *Journal of Investigative Psychology and Offender Profiling, 6*, 139–149. doi:10.1002/jip.102

Parker, J. F., & Ryan, V. (1993). An attempt to reduce guessing behavior in children's and adults' eyewitness identifications. *Law and Human Behavior, 17*, 11–26. doi:10.1007/BF01044534

Pella v. Reid, 527 F2d 380 (1975).

People v. De Angelis, 97 Cal. App. 3d 837 (1979).

People v. Carpenter, 15 Cal.4th 312, 366-367 (1997).

Schacter, D. L., Dawes, R., Jacoby, L. L., Kahneman, D., Lempert, R., Roediger, H. L., & Rosenthal, R. (2008). Studying eyewitness investigations in the field. *Law and Human Behavior, 32*, 3–5. doi:10.1007/s10979-007-9093-9

Simmons v. U.S., 390 U.S. 377 (1968).

Sporer, S. L. (1993). Eyewitness identification accuracy, confidence, and decision times in simultaneous and sequential lineups. *Journal of Applied Psychology, 78*, 22–33. doi:10.1037/0021-9010.78.1.22

Steblay, N. K. (2011). What we know now: The Evanston Illinois field lineups. *Law and Human Behavior, 35*, 1–12. doi:10.1007/s10979-009-9207-7

Steblay, N. K., Dysart, J. E., & Wells, G. L. (2011). Seventy-two tests of the sequential lineup superiority effect: A meta-analysis and policy discussion. *Psychology, Public Policy, and Law, 17*(1), 99–139. doi:10.1037/a0021650

Stovall v. Denno, 388 U.S. 293 (1967).

Tunnicliff, J. L., & Clark, S. E. (2000). Matching suspects and descriptions in the selection of distractors for identification lineups. *Law and Human Behavior, 24*, 231–258. doi:10.1023/A:1005463020252

U.S. Department of Justice, Office of Justice Programs, National Institute of Justice. (1999). *Eyewitness evidence: A guide for law enforcement.* Retrieved from Retrieved from http://www.nij.gov/pubs-sum/178240.htm

U.S. v. Reid and Thomas, 517 F.2d 953 (1975).

U.S. v. Wade, 388 U.S. 218 (1967).

Valentine, T., & Heaton, P. (1999). An evaluation of the fairness of police line-ups and video identifications [Special issue]. *Applied Cognitive Psychology: Measuring lineup fairness, 13*, S59–S72. doi:10.1002/(SICI)1099-0720(199911)13:1+<S59:AID-ACP679>3.0.CO;2-Y

Wells, G. L. (1984). The psychology of lineup identifications. *Journal of Applied Social Psychology, 14*, 89–103. doi:10.1111/j.1559-1816.1984.tb02223.x

Wells, G. L., Memon, A., & Penrod, S. D. (2006). Eyewitness evidence: Improving its probative value. *Psychological Science in the Public Interest, 7*(2), 45–75.

Wells, G. L., Rydell, S. M., & Seelau, E. P. (1993). The selection of distractors for eyewitness lineups. *Journal of Applied Psychology, 78*, 835–844. doi:10.1037/0021-9010.78.5.835

Wells, G. L., Steblay, N. K., & Dysart, J. E. (2011). *A test of the simultaneous vs. sequential lineup methods: An initial report of the AJS national eyewitness identification field studies*. Unpublished manuscript, American Judicature Society. Retrieved from http://www.ajs.org/wc/pdfs/EWID_PrintFriendly.pdf

Wise, R. A., Safer, M. A., & Maro, C. M. (2011). What U.S. law enforcement officers know and believe about eyewitness factors, eyewitness interviews and identification procedures. *Applied Cognitive Psychology, 25,* 488–500. doi:10.1002/acp.1717

Wogalter, M. S., Malpass, R. S., & McQuiston, D. E. (2004). A national survey of US police on preparation and conduct of identification lineups. *Psychology, Crime & Law, 10,* 69–82. doi:10.1080/10683160410001641873

Wright v. Smith, 434 F.Supp. 339 (1977).

5

PRESENTATION METHODS

SCOTT D. GRONLUND, SHANNON M. ANDERSEN,
AND COLTON PERRY

The New Jersey Supreme Court recently ordered changes to the way that eyewitness identifications are conducted, stating:

> The current standard for assessing eyewitness identification evidence does not fully meet its goals. It does not offer an adequate measure for reliability or sufficiently deter inappropriate police conduct. It also overstates the jury's inherent ability to evaluate evidence offered by eyewitnesses who honestly believe their testimony is accurate. (*State of New Jersey v. Henderson*, 2011, p. 5)

But the court failed to mandate sequential lineups, stating "there is insufficient, [sic] authoritative evidence accepted by scientific experts for a court to make a finding in favor of either procedure" (p. 68). In this chapter, we

The authors thank the following individuals for improving the ideas presented in an earlier version of this chapter: Neil Brewer, Curt Carlson, Steve Clark, Brian Cutler, Roy Malpass, Jeff Neuschatz, Matt Palmer, and John Wixted.

DOI: 10.1037/14094-006
Reform of Eyewitness Identification Procedures, B. L. Cutler (Editor)

review the evidence involving sequential lineup presentation methods, to understand why it remains a focus of study and controversy.

In the more common *simultaneous lineup* (Wogalter, Malpass, & McQuiston, 2004), a witness views all the lineup members at once and makes one decision—to reject the lineup if the witness believes the perpetrator is not there or to select the lineup member the witness believes is the perpetrator. To date, researchers have focused on comparing simultaneous lineups with what we call the *standard sequential lineup procedure;* variations on the standard sequential procedure are possible and are discussed in the paragraphs that follow. According to the standard sequential procedure, a witness views lineup members one at a time and must make a decision about lineup member i before seeing lineup member $i + 1$. The lineup ends once a witness chooses a lineup member or runs out of options. In contrast to a simultaneous lineup, the witness makes a series of decisions in a sequential lineup (unless the witness selects the first lineup member). Also in contrast to a simultaneous lineup, a witness viewing a sequential lineup does not know how many lineup members will be presented. Malpass et al. (2008) pointed out that these two factors confound comparisons between simultaneous and sequential presentation methods.

Signal detection theory (e.g., Green & Swets, 1966) provides familiar constructs for defining what we mean by a *sequential advantage* and distinguishing it from what we term a *sequential shift* (see Gronlund, Goodsell, & Andersen, 2012). A sequential advantage refers to an increased ability to select the guilty suspect (i.e., the perpetrator) when he or she is present in a lineup and to reject a lineup that contains an innocent suspect when the lineup members are presented sequentially compared with when the lineup members are presented simultaneously (i.e., sequential advantage = sequential d' > simultaneous d'). If the data support a sequential advantage, the policy recommendation is straightforward: Switch to sequential lineups! On the other hand, a sequential shift refers to a conservative shift in response bias. That is, a sequential shift results in an increased unwillingness to make a choice from a sequential lineup, whether it contains a guilty or an innocent suspect, not an enhanced ability to make this discrimination (see also Meissner, Tredoux, Parker, & MacLin, 2005). The innocent are protected but at the cost of reduced identifications of the guilty. If the data support a sequential shift, the policy recommendation might still involve conducting sequential lineups, but the decision is no longer straightforward.

Despite "insufficient, [sic] authoritative evidence" (*State of New Jersey v. Henderson,* 2011, p. 68), the advantage of sequential lineups has diffused into the popular culture. The detectives on *Law and Order: Special Victims Unit* (McCreary, Wolf, & Forney, 2009) have begun conducting sequential lineups. Sequential lineups are featured in Robert Ludlum's (2005) novel *The*

Ambler Warning. One of the characters states, "Now, there's a way to elicit what an eyewitness saw without that distortion: you do it seriatim. Show them photographs of people, not at the same time, but one after another" (pp. 570–571). Even Wikipedia chimes in: "leading researchers suggest that lineups should be conducted sequentially, rather than simultaneously" (http://en.wikipedia.org/wiki/Sequential_lineups).

ESTABLISHING THE SEQUENTIAL ADVANTAGE

We begin with a discussion of the seminal study by Lindsay and Wells (1985) that first demonstrated a sequential lineup advantage. We then review field studies that have compared simultaneous and sequential presentation methods, discuss the decision strategies explanation proposed to explain the sequential advantage, and report the results of two meta-analyses by Steblay, Dysart, Fulero, and Lindsay (2001) and Steblay, Dysart, and Wells (2011), which conclude in favor of a sequential advantage. We conclude this section by discussing research that raises questions about the robustness of the sequential advantage—research that indicates that a sequential advantage may only occur given certain circumstances.

Lindsay and Wells (1985) were the first to compare the performance of sequential and simultaneous lineups. Participants viewed a staged crime and then were asked to identify the perpetrator from either a sequential or simultaneous lineup. Half the lineups contained the guilty suspect (termed *perpetrator present*); in the other half, the guilty suspect was removed from the lineup and replaced with an innocent suspect (termed *perpetrator absent*). They found that sequential lineup presentation produced a marked (and statistically significant) reduction in false identifications of the innocent suspect but only a slight (and nonsignificant) reduction in correct identifications of the guilty suspect: There appeared to be a substantial benefit to conducting lineups in a sequential manner, with little cost in terms of reduced correct identifications.

Other researchers have found similar results (e.g., Lindsay, Lea, & Fulford, 1991; Lindsay, Lea, Nosworthy, et al., 1991). Steblay et al. (2001) summarized the extant data in a meta-analysis. They examined nine published and 14 unpublished studies consisting of 30 tests. They concluded that when moderator variables that approximated real-world conditions were considered, such as between-participants manipulation of presentation method and live or videotaped mock crime videos, the reduction in sequential correct identifications (the cost) was minimal, but the reduction in sequential false identifications (the benefit) remained significant. Since that time, several field studies have been conducted to test Steblay et al.'s (2001) assertion that the sequential advantage becomes more reliable as conditions move out of the lab.

Field Studies

The first field study (Hennepin County, Minnesota) examined the accuracy of sequential double-blind lineups. Klobuchar, Steblay, and Caligiuri (2006) found that sequential identification rates from real police lineups were comparable with what had been achieved in a field study with simultaneous lineups (e.g., Behrman & Davey, 2001). However, because no direct simultaneous–sequential comparisons were conducted, no conclusion could be reached about which presentation method was superior. A direct comparison was the goal of the Illinois Pilot Program. But the conclusion did not favor the sequential advantage: Mecklenburg (2006) reported that "the sequential, double-blind lineups, when compared with the simultaneous method, produced a higher rate of known false picks and a lower rate of 'suspect picks'" (p. *v*). However, the Illinois Pilot Program confounded double-blind sequential lineup administration and nonblind simultaneous lineup presentation. Consequently, no meaningful conclusions could be reached (see Schacter et al., 2008; see also Ross & Malpass, 2008). Moreover, Steblay (2011) reported a breakdown in random assignment in the Illinois Pilot Program that raised further questions about these results.

Preliminary results just released from a field study corrected the problems with the Illinois Pilot Program (Wells, Steblay, & Dysart, 2011). The sequential lineup resulted in 27.3% suspect identifications versus 25.5% suspect identifications from simultaneous lineups. This difference was not significant. Of course, suspect identifications cannot be equated with correct identifications (Malpass, 2006a); in the laboratory the researcher knows which suspect is the guilty one, but the police do not know this. The sequential lineup resulted in fewer filler identifications than from simultaneous lineups (12.2% vs. 18.1%, a significant benefit). Wells et al. (2011) concluded that "the sequential procedure reduces mistaken identifications with little or no reduction in accurate identifications" (p. *x*).

But much remains to be learned from this new field study, including the impact of various procedural changes made to how these sequential lineups were conducted. The research that constituted the aforementioned Steblay et al. (2001) meta-analysis generally followed the standard sequential procedures. But the witnesses in all three of the field studies viewed all faces in the sequential lineup and were allowed to view the faces a second time if they requested it. In addition, witnesses in the Wells et al. (2011) field study used a multistep identification process that required a witness to first indicate whether a lineup member appeared familiar. If the witness made such a designation, it was followed by a question from the computer about why the person was familiar, which was followed by a question from the lineup administrator regarding how the witness knew the identified person. See Chapter 8 of this volume for more details on field studies.

Decision Strategies Explanation

The prevailing explanation offered for the sequential advantage is the decision strategies account (Lindsay & Wells, 1985). This account posits that a simultaneous lineup makes a relative decision strategy more likely: A witness tends to select a lineup member who is the best match to memory relative to the other individuals in the lineup. This is problematic if there is an innocent suspect who resembles the perpetrator. Conversely, a sequential lineup tends to elicit an absolute decision strategy. An absolute decision entails comparing each lineup member to the memory of the perpetrator. Moreover, the best match also must be judged to be a sufficiently good match to the memory of the perpetrator and not just the best available match. For example, in a sequential lineup, a witness might feel that Lineup Member 3 is the best match seen so far but might decide not to choose him or her because the match is not judged to be good enough, and the belief is that a better match might follow. However, that same lineup member might get selected from a simultaneous lineup because he or she is better than any other option.

Gronlund (2004) found support for the decision strategies account, albeit using a nonstandard approach (judgments of individuals' heights). Participants' subjective reports also support the relative–absolute conceptualization (e.g., Dunning & Stern, 1994; Kneller, Memon, & Stevenage, 2001). Clark, Erickson, and Breneman (2011) conducted theoretical analyses in which absolute judgments led to more accurate responding but only under conditions that were different from those of any simultaneous–sequential experiment conducted to date. Carlson and Gronlund (2011) defined an absolute judgment as involving the recollection of distinctive information about the perpetrator (or noticing the absence of this information). Given this definition, they found evidence for a greater likelihood of absolute judgments in sequential lineups, supporting the decision strategies account (although distinctive information also can trigger a strong familiarity response). Taken together, there is some evidence in support of simultaneous and sequential presentation methods eliciting different decision strategies. Researchers are making progress toward meeting McQuiston-Surrett, Malpass, and Tredoux's (2006) challenge to have an explanation for the sequential advantage in support of policy recommendations.

Robustness of the Sequential Advantage

Carlson, Gronlund, and Clark (2008) conducted an experiment that was similar to the Lindsay and Wells (1985) experiment. However, Carlson et al. constructed fairer lineups that contained an innocent suspect who matched the perpetrator much less than did Lindsay and Wells's innocent suspect. Carlson et al. found no sequential advantage, which led them to propose that lineup fairness might be a factor that affects the likelihood of finding a sequential advantage. But the lack of a sequential advantage also could have been the result of floor effects in the rate at which the innocent suspect was chosen. Carlson et al. conducted a second experiment in which they manipulated lineup fairness and changed the innocent suspect to increase this choosing rate. Two of the three performance measures favored the sequential lineup when the lineups were biased; one measure favored the sequential for the intermediate lineups; and there was little difference among any of the measures for the fair lineups. In sum, there was moderate support for the idea that lineup fairness plays a role in producing a sequential advantage.

Carlson et al. (2008, Figure 3) subsequently assessed performance by reporting the conditional probability that a suspect identification (ID) was of the guilty suspect (correct ID) rather than the innocent (false ID) suspect [correct ID/(correct ID + false ID)]. They reported the conditional probability as a function of the positioning of the guilty or innocent suspect in the sequential lineup (collapsing over lineup fairness). If the guilty or innocent suspect was placed in the first two positions in the sequential lineup, the simultaneous lineup resulted in better performance (.56 vs. .46). However, if the guilty or innocent suspect was placed in the fifth or sixth positions, a sequential advantage resulted (.56 vs. .66). Gronlund, Carlson, Dailey, and Goodsell (2009) explicitly manipulated suspect position, comparing an early (second) and late (fifth) position. This study had a number of independent variables and 24 comparisons contrasting sequential lineups to simultaneous lineups. Despite the large number of comparisons, they only found two significant sequential advantages (based on the conditional probability performance measure) and three significant simultaneous advantages. But both of the sequential advantages were found when the guilty or innocent suspect was in the fifth position within the sequential lineup, replicating the findings of Carlson et al. (2008); all three simultaneous advantages were found with the guilty or innocent suspect in the second position. It appears that late suspect placement contributes to producing a sequential advantage. See Perfect, Dennis, and Snell (2007, Experiment 4) for a similar result (for Position 4 relative to Position 1) for correct identifications only.

Gronlund et al. (2009) proposed two possible explanations for why performance might improve as the sequential lineup unfolds. One possibility related to the aforementioned decision strategies explanation: After viewing several fillers in the sequential lineup, a witness might shift from making absolute comparisons with memory to making relative comparisons among lineup members. But without additional assumptions, that explanation only predicts a greater likelihood of choosing as the lineup unfolded. However, participants make better choices, not more choices; that is, participants are better able to discriminate between the guilty and the innocent suspect when the suspect is in Position 5. The second possibility was that participants develop a better memory probe as the lineup unfolds. For example, on seeing the first lineup member, a witness might decide that the eyes are right, but the perpetrator's nose was narrower. On rejecting this first lineup member and viewing the next, the witness might develop a better representation of the nose or learn something about face shape and so on. Goodsell, Gronlund, and Carlson (2010) instantiated this explanation in a computational memory model (WITNESS; Clark, 2003) and showed that it could produce a sequential advantage.

In sum, there exist several studies that demonstrate evidence for a sequential advantage (e.g., Lindsay & Wells, 1985). A sequential advantage also was the conclusion reached by a meta-analysis by Steblay et al. (2001). This conclusion was confirmed by a recent meta-analysis by Steblay, Dysart, and Wells (2011). A recent field study (Wells et al., 2011) also concluded in favor of sequential presentation methods but did not use standard sequential procedures. Explanations have been proposed and tested regarding how sequential advantages are produced. But concerns remain regarding how robust the sequential advantage is. This is important because if researchers advocate a switch to sequential presentation methods it should be because sequential presentation is superior across a wide range of conditions that potentially vary in real lineups (e.g., lineup fairness, degree to which the guilty suspect photo matches the perpetrator, similarity of the innocent suspect to the perpetrator, positioning of the suspect in the sequential lineup). Moreover, a differential effect of the positioning of a suspect in the sequential lineup might be problematic: "For sequential lineup presentation to be a viable alternative, it is important that the results of the procedure not be unduly influenced by order effects" (Lindsay & Wells, 1985, p. 561).

In addition to the policy implications, a lack of robustness raises concerns about the extant data. How is it that the two meta-analyses by Steblay et al. (2001) and Steblay, Dysart, and Wells (2011) found support for a sequential advantage if Gronlund et al. (2009) found only two significant sequential advantages out of 24? In the next section, we examine the evidence for the sequential shift, beginning with a meta-analysis by Clark (2012) that reexamines the conclusions reached by the Steblay et al. (2011) meta-analysis.

CHALLENGING THE SEQUENTIAL ADVANTAGE

Steblay, Dysart, and Wells (2011) recently updated the Steblay et al. (2001) meta-analysis. It is worth reiterating that the preponderance of the studies included in both these meta-analyses followed the standard sequential procedures described previously. The count is now at 72 tests comparing simultaneous and sequential presentation methods. Steblay, Dysart, and Wells (2011, p. 99) reported: "The results are very similar to the 2001 results in showing that the sequential lineup is less likely to result in an identification of the suspect, but also more diagnostic of guilt than is the simultaneous lineup." For a subset of the 27 tests that included both simultaneous and sequential presentation methods and perpetrator-present and perpetrator-absent lineups, they reported an 8% decrease in correct identifications from perpetrator-present sequential lineups but 22% fewer errors from perpetrator-absent sequential lineups. This appears to be compelling proof of a sequential advantage. But policymakers might misinterpret the errors from perpetrator-absent lineups because they combine two different types of errors.

Eyewitness identification researchers have long appreciated the distinction between these two types of errors (Wells & Turtle, 1986). One type of error involves the selection of a designated innocent suspect from the perpetrator-absent lineup. In this situation, a perpetrator-absent lineup was created by replacing the guilty suspect (the perpetrator) with an innocent suspect (who typically resembles him or her). The rate of falsely identifying the one-and-only designated innocent suspect can be directly compared with the rate of correctly identifying the one-and-only guilty suspect. However, studies that do not designate an innocent suspect report a second type of error—a *total* identification rate—the proportion of witnesses who identified *any* lineup member from the perpetrator-absent lineup. In this situation, a perpetrator-absent lineup was created by replacing the guilty suspect with a filler who was not distinguished from the other fillers. But before designated innocent suspect errors and total identification errors can be combined into a single quantity that reflects false identification errors, an estimated innocent suspect rate must be computed by taking the total identification rate divided by the number of fillers in the lineups. Once this adjustment is made, these two types of errors can be combined and compared with the correct identification rate of a single guilty suspect. And once this is done, the resulting false identification rate is 7.5%, not 22%—almost identical to the 8% decrease in the correct identification rate (see Clark, 2012).

Conflicting Meta-Analysis

Clark (2012) raised other questions regarding the Steblay, Dysart, and Wells (2011) meta-analysis. He raised questions about the data that were included. For example, Clark argued that Lindsay, Lea, Nosworthy, et al. (1991, Experiment 1) should not have been included because it confounded simultaneous lineups with biased instructions and fillers who were "not the best available" with sequential lineups presented with unbiased instructions and "the best available" fillers. Clark also raised questions about some of the data that Steblay, Dysart, and Wells (2011) excluded, which involved data deemed not above chance levels of performance. Steblay, Dysart, and Wells (2011) adopted an inclusion criterion such that the difference between the correct and false identification rates or the correct versus false rejection rates must exceed .10. Clark showed that tests from Douglass and McQuiston-Surrett (2006), many from Gronlund et al. (2009), and from Steblay, Dietrich, Ryan, Raczynski, and James (2011) did in fact exceed the .10 criterion and should be included.

Clark (2012) examined 51 tests, all of which involved a 2 × 2 fully randomized factorial design (Sequential/Simultaneous × Perpetrator Present/Absent), were published, and had adult witnesses and participants. The majority of these tests overlapped the 27 tests considered by Steblay, Dysart, and Wells (2011), although Clark disaggregated those tests over which Steblay et al. had collapsed. We report parts of Clark's (2012) Table 1 in Table 5.1, including correct/false (C/F), C/(C + F), correct and false identification rates,

TABLE 5.1
Means, t, and p Values for Correct and False Identification Rates,
Criterion $\log(\beta)$, and Measures of Probative Value for 51 Tests
Taken From Clark (2012)

Presentation method	M correct	M false	d'	$\log(\beta)$	C/F	CP
Simultaneous	.54	.15	1.27	.70	7.27	.79
Sequential	.43	.09	1.25	.98	8.17	.82
$t(50)$	4.48	4.41	0.30	−3.84	−0.73	−1.68
p	<.001	<.001	.76	<.001	.47	.10

Note. C/F = correct/false; CP stands for conditional probability and is equal to C/(C + F). CP gives the probability that the suspect was guilty given that a suspect was chosen. Six tests were included from Gronlund et al. (2009). These six involved pairing Guiltystrong (the photo of the guilty suspect that was chosen frequently) with Innocentweak (the photo of an innocent suspect that was chosen infrequently).

and d' and response bias $[\log(\beta)]$ from signal detection theory. Table 5.1 also includes the results of paired-sample t-tests comparing simultaneous and sequential performance for each measure. Both C/F and C/(C + F) favored the sequential lineup, but neither was significant; there was no difference in d'. In contrast, both the correct and false identification rates were significantly reduced by sequential presentation, consistent with a conservative sequential shift. Also consistent with a sequential shift, $\log(\beta)$ was significantly more conservative for the sequential lineup.

A policymaker might misconstrue the fact that sequential lineups generally result in a greater probative value as evidence for a sequential advantage. But the fact that the sequential advantage is not statistically significant is important. It means that the sequential advantage is neither large enough nor consistent enough to be reliable. Granted, reasonable people disagree about which tests should be included or excluded; however, the fact remains that irrespective of these inclusions and exclusions, correct and false identifications consistently exhibit a greater decline as a result of sequential presentation, but the evidence in favor of a sequential advantage wavers and never overwhelms. One reason that the magnitude of the sequential advantage wavers across experiments is because probative value measures such as C/F and C/(C + F) are affected by response biases (see also Clark et al., 2011; Wixted & Mickes, 2012).

Problem With Probative Value Measures

It is misleading to compare the performance of simultaneous and sequential presentation methods using C/F and C/(C + F) because a higher value for an identification procedure could signal that one procedure is superior to another or that one procedure has a more conservative rate of choosing than the other. Because sequential presentation results in more conservative choosing, the evidence that does exist for a sequential advantage arises to some degree from this factor. Hence, the magnitude of the sequential advantage as assessed by C/F and C/(C + F) not only varies across experiments as a result of differences in stimuli, lineup composition, instructions, and procedures but also as a function of how these factors interact to influence a participant's response bias. If memory for a perpetrator is held constant and only a participant's willingness to respond changes, performance should be unaffected. For example, a student taking a multiple-choice test does not know more if he or she answers 20 questions when he or she earns 1 point for each correct answer and loses 0 points for each incorrect answer or answers only 15 questions when he or she earns 1 point for each correct answer and loses 1 point for each incorrect answer.

He or she is just being more conservative in the latter case, requiring more evidence before endorsing a choice.

To illustrate this problem, we fit the WITNESS model (Clark, 2003) to the data from Table 5 in Clark, Howell, and Davey (2008). The C/F values appear to illustrate a strong sequential advantage (simultaneous = 2.29 vs. sequential = 4.83). We then simulated four alternative experiments, two in which participants were more willing to choose and two in which participants were less willing to choose. We accomplished this by adjusting the response criteria in WITNESS but holding memory (the remaining parameters) constant. As is apparent in the bottom panel of Figure 5.1, C/F changes

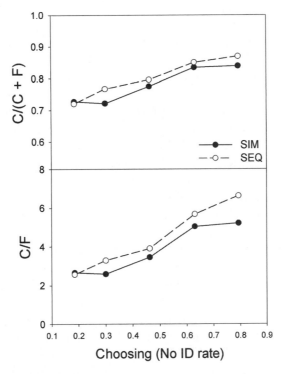

Figure 5.1. We fit the WITNESS model (Clark, 2003) to the data from Clark et al. (2008, Table 5). The best-fitting parameters values were as follows: Encoding of the perpetrator in memory was .22; similarity of the innocent suspect to the perpetrator was .5; and similarity of the fillers to the perpetrator was .33. The simultaneous criterion was .038, and the sequential criterion was .079. The attention weights were both set to .5. We then simulated four alternative experiments, two in which participants were more willing to choose and two in which participants were less willing to choose. We accomplished this by adjusting the criteria in the WITNESS model but holding memory (the remaining parameters) constant. The bottom panel shows how correct/false (C/F) varies as the willingness to choose varies; the top panel gives the same information for C/(C + F). SIM = simultaneous; SEQ = sequential; ID = identification.

drastically. It ranges from 2.6 to 6.6 as the willingness to choose decreases despite memory not changing. Consequently, a simultaneous advantage, a sequential advantage, or no difference could arise as a result of the adoption of particular combinations of response biases between simultaneous and sequential lineups. For example, if conservative choosing from a simultaneous lineup is paired with standard sequential lineup data, the purported sequential advantage in C/F is eliminated (simultaneous C/F = 5.21 vs. sequential C/F = 4.83). In other words, if witnesses viewing simultaneous lineups were instructed to make a selection only if they were absolutely certain and that was compared with the standard sequential lineup, researchers would have concluded that presentation method did not matter. The top panel of Figure 5.1 shows that the same problem arises for C/(C + F), although it is reduced in magnitude.

Obviously, the use of measures like C/F and C/(C + F) obfuscates researchers' ability to determine which identification procedure is superior. Wixted and Mickes (2012) argued that the solution to this problem is to compare performance using receiver-operating characteristic curves (Egan, 1958) to determine which testing procedure is more accurate. This is standard procedure in the medical literature when comparing different diagnostic procedures (e.g., Lusted, 1971; Metz, 1978; Pisano et al., 2005, compared digital vs. film mammography for breast cancer screening).

In sum, there was strong evidence in support of sequential lineups decreasing both correct and false identifications. With the evidence favoring the sequential criterion shift represented by log(b) and the fact that the probative measures used to assess lineup performance favor sequential lineups in part because they induce more conservative rates of choosing, we reach the following conclusion: Sequential lineups tested using standard procedures produce more conservative choosing—a trade-off between correct and false identifications that favors neither lineup presentation method. Palmer and Brewer (2012) supported these results using an alternative formulation of d' that is more appropriate for eyewitness experiments than the traditional measure reported by Clark (2012).

Applying the Compound Signal Detection Model

Palmer and Brewer (2012) applied Duncan's (2006) compound signal detection model to most of the 27 tests from the Steblay, Dysart, and Wells (2011) meta-analysis. Palmer and Brewer excluded the same Lindsay, Lea, Nosworthy, et al. (1991) study that Clark (2012) did as well as three other studies for which they could not compute response frequencies. The compound signal detection model was designed for eyewitness tasks because it allows separate detection (is a perpetrator present?) and identification (which one is the perpetrator?) decisions. As a result, estimates of discriminability (d') and response bias (criterion) can be extracted. Palmer and Brewer found no significant difference in d' between sequential and simultaneous lineups, and hence, no evidence for a sequential advantage. However, they did find evidence for a conservative sequential shift because the criterion position for the sequential lineup was significantly more conservative. These conclusions matched the conclusions reached by Clark (2012) and are summarized in Table 5.1.

Palmer and Brewer (2012) stated:

> the results demonstrate that it is quite appropriate to claim that the sequential advantage is due to a conservative shift in responding rather than to improved discriminability . . . it is this conservative shift in responding that is responsible for the higher accuracy rates observed for sequential (cf. simultaneous) presentation in experimental settings. (p. 253)

We have two issues regarding these statements. First, Palmer and Brewer continued to refer to a sequential advantage when, according to our definition, the lack of any d' difference signals a sequential shift, not a sequential advantage. However, we acknowledge that not everyone agrees with our definition of a sequential advantage, referring instead to a sequential advantage defined by the proportion of correct decisions (i.e., correct identifications from perpetrator-present lineups + correct rejections from perpetrator-absent lineups).

Second, Palmer and Brewer (2012) indicated that a conservative shift in responding produces "higher accuracy rates" for sequential presentation. In the compound signal detection model, accuracy is assessed by d', which Palmer and Brewer showed was unaffected by presentation method. Also, as we showed previously, alternative accuracy measures like C/F and C/(C + F) are inflated by the more conservative sequential procedure and therefore are not solely a reflection of superior performance. But Palmer and Brewer were referring to sequential presentation producing a greater proportion of correct decisions, a conclusion that is dependent on assumptions that Palmer and Brewer acknowledged likely do not hold in the real world.

Signal detection allows researchers to estimate the criterion position that maximizes the proportion of correct decisions (see Wickens, 2002, Equation 2.16, p. 35). Indeed, the more conservative criterion position engendered by sequential presentation moves a criterion closer to that optimal position and thereby increases the proportion of correct decisions relative to simultaneous presentation. But the criterion position that maximizes the proportion of correct decisions is dependent on the base rates of perpetrator-present versus perpetrator-absent lineups. Police experts queried by Brewer, Keast, and Rishworth (2002) estimated that 90% of lineups contain guilty suspects. If that estimate holds generally, a more liberal criterion position engendered by simultaneous presentation actually would produce more correct decisions: If most lineups have guilty suspects, witnesses should choose from lineups.

Our analysis of the literature, informed by the meta-analyses of Clark (2012) and Palmer and Brewer (2012), indicates that the extant data favor the sequential shift. Although a sequential advantage clearly can happen, it does not appear to be robust. In the next section, we take up the policy implications of this view of sequential presentation methods. As the procedures for how to conduct sequential lineups change, as in the recent field study by Wells et al. (2011), more research must be undertaken that examines the performance of sequential lineups conducted in this manner. This research must be guided by theory, in a manner that we briefly overview. In a final section, we turn to a review of alternative eyewitness identification procedures.

IMPLICATIONS FOR PRACTICE, POLICY, AND FUTURE RESEARCH

What are the policy implications of a sequential shift? The two factors to be considered are the base rates that guilty suspects are included in lineups and the utilities assigned to the different responses that a witness can make (see Clark, 2012; Malpass, 2006b). Policymakers must take both these factors into account, and there are well-established procedures for how to do so (for a review, see Swets, Dawes, & Monahan, 2000). We begin with base rates.

Clark (2012) described two examples involving 1,000 lineups in which the base rate of guilty suspects is low (.6 or 600 out of 1,000) versus high (.9 or 900 out of 1,000). Let the correct identification rates equal .5 and .4 for Identification Procedures A and B, and let the false identification rates equal .2 and .12 for Procedures A and B, respectively. That means that if the guilty suspect rate is low (.6), Procedure B results in 60 fewer correct identifications ($[600 \times .5] - [600 \times .4] = 300 - 240$) and 32 fewer false identifications ($[400 \times .2] - [400 \times .12] = 80 - 48$). Policymakers might view this favorably, given that for every innocent suspect not implicated, slightly fewer than two guilty ones are not chosen (60:32 or 1.88 to 1). And just because a suspect is not chosen from a lineup does not mean that he or she will be freed. It is the factually guilty suspects for whom the police likely have additional evidence, which would lead the police to infer that a witness who fails to choose is unreliable rather than inferring that the suspect is innocent. But if the guilty suspect rate is high, Procedure B results in 90 fewer correct identifications ($[900 \times .5] - [900 \times .4] = 450 - 360$) but only eight fewer false identifications ($[100 \times .2] - [100 \times .12] = 20 - 12$). Policymakers might balk if every innocent suspect not implicated resulted in more than 11 guilty ones not being identified (90:8 or 11.25 to 1).

A sequential shift also means that policymakers must weigh the utilities of the errors that a witness can make. If we assume that fillers are known to be innocent if a lineup contains the guilty suspect, an error involves not making a choice or picking a filler, and if a lineup contains an innocent suspect, an error involves falsely identifying the innocent suspect. Policymakers must decide on the relative utility of correct identifications lost and false identifications gained. A straightforward application of expected utility theory (von Neumann & Morgenstern, 1944) dictates that the preferred identification procedure would be the one that maximizes utility—the sum of the utilities of the responses weighted by their probability of occurrence. But Ceci and Friedman (2000) showed that the decision rule regarding which ID procedure should be preferred could be determined by the following inequality:

$$\frac{Correct\ IDs\ lost}{False\ IDs\ avoided} < \frac{Cost\ of\ innocent\ suspect\ ID}{Cost\ of\ failing\ to\ ID\ guilty\ suspect} \tag{1}$$

Clark (2012, Appendix B) provided a description of the derivation of this inequality.

Take the two aforementioned Identification Procedures A and B in which the correct and false identification rates are lower for Procedure B. According to the examples provided earlier, if the proportion of lineups with guilty suspects is low (.6), the left-hand side of the inequality is 60/32 or 1.88. However, if the proportion of lineups with guilty suspects is high (.9), the left-hand side of the inequality is 90/8 or 11.25. One commonly cited value for the right-hand side of the inequality is 10/1 (Blackstone, 1769/1979). If one follows Blackstone's ratio, Procedure B is preferred if the guilty suspect rate is low, but Procedure A is preferred if the guilty suspect rate is high.

Given that sequential lineups are becoming the norm in jurisdictions around the country, it appears that many policymakers already have decided that the evidence favors sequential presentation. But those decisions were reached presuming the existence and robustness of a sequential advantage. Policymakers might still reach the same conclusion given a sequential shift, but the decision is more complex because it depends on the rates at which guilty suspects are put into lineups and the relative importance of false identifications versus missed correct identifications. These are the factors that policymakers must consider as they contemplate the results from the laboratory and field experiments proffered by eyewitness researchers. Eyewitness researchers should not be involved in setting these utilities. Although researchers can try to estimate the base rates and provide the machinery for properly weighing the base rates and the utilities (see Swets et al., 2000), their contribution should remain the conduct of experiments that provide the foundation from which policymakers make recommendations.

Right now there is a growing disconnect between the standard procedures for conducting sequential lineups and the procedures being adopted in the field studies, which include, among other modifications, the provision of more than one lap through the sequential lineup. Unfortunately, most of the data summarized in the meta-analyses involve data collected using the standard sequential procedure. How applicable are those data to alternative procedures for conducting sequential lineups? What is the impact of informing a witness in advance that he or she will see all the lineup members even after he or she makes a choice? What about allowing a witness to make more than one choice? What is the impact of allowing a witness to take another lap through the sequential lineup? Should the witness know when the lineup starts that another lap is optional or required?

These are important practical questions for which we currently have limited empirical answers. McQuiston-Surrett et al. (2006) found that a strict stopping rule (i.e., one choice, lineup terminates) resulted in no sequential advantage but a more lax rule (view the entire lineup, can make more than one selection) produced a sequential advantage. Valentine, Darling, and Memon (2007) found that a more lax stopping rule with multiple laps, like those in the British Police and Criminal Evidence Act (1984) standards, resulted in more correct identifications with no change in false identifications. But Horry, Memon, Wright, and Milne (2012) conducted a field study in England using video sequential lineups in which witnesses were allowed multiple laps. They found that witnesses who opted for repeated viewings of the lineup were more than twice as likely to identify fillers compared with those who did not request additional viewing. Similarly, Steblay, Dietrich, et al. (2011) found that sequential lineups with either an optional or required second lap resulted in higher choosing (more correct and incorrect decisions), especially in perpetrator-absent lineups.

More research is needed to determine what combination of these alternative sequential procedures will be most effective. But researchers can make better and quicker progress toward making this determination if their choices are guided by theory. In 2008, *Applied Cognitive Psychology* devoted an entire issue to the discussion of eyewitness identification, arguing that there has been an "overemphasis on practical questions, accompanied by a lack of theoretical relevance" (Bornstein & Meissner, 2008, p. 734). In that volume, Lane and Meissner (2008) argued that the field of eyewitness identification had failed to capitalize on basic cognitive and social psychological research and theory, relying instead on an ecological or practical perspective. Although real-world application is the goal of most eyewitness research, Lane and Meissner argued that it should be the setting for which theories are tested, not the foundation of research. Moreover, we agree with

Clark (2008) that formal computational models like WITNESS (Clark, 2003; Goodsell, Gronlund, & Carlson, 2010) should play a central role in this endeavor.

What other theories might help guide our research? There are many, but we highlight a few. Criterion placement will be affected by whether a witness is expecting to make a second lap and whether the witness expects the lineup to terminate once a choice is made. Benjamin, Diaz, and Wee (2009) proposed a theory of criterion placement that can provide guidance. The secretary problem (e.g., Hill, 2009) might be a source of information regarding the best stopping rule to adopt in a sequential lineup. In the secretary problem, you wish to hire the best secretary out of N applicants. The applicants are interviewed one by one; a decision must be made after each interview; and once rejected, an applicant cannot be recalled. Mathematicians have proven that the optimal strategy for maximizing the probability of selecting the best applicant is to reject the first N/e applicants (where e is the base of the natural logarithm) and then choose the first applicant who is better than every applicant interviewed so far. Does this optimal decision strategy contribute to why the sequential advantage tends to occur when a suspect is placed later in a sequential lineup (see Gronlund et al., 2009)? Koriat and Goldsmith (1996; see also Benjamin, 2007) proposed a theory for the strategic control of memory, and Weber and Perfect (2012) demonstrated the benefit of allowing witnesses to monitor and control their memory by providing witnesses with the option to say "I don't know" during a showup task. This resulted in the elimination of a high number of low-confidence and low-accuracy decisions but still maintained correct identifications. Perhaps control over the conduct of the sequential lineup should be given to the witness, allowing him or her to decide whether to terminate after making a selection or to continue, whether to select more than one individual from the lineup, and whether to view a second lap.

ALTERNATIVES TO CURRENT PRESENTATION METHODS

Sequential and simultaneous lineups with binary decisions are not the only way to test the memory of an eyewitness. In the concluding section of this chapter, we turn our attention to variations on the conduct of simultaneous and sequential lineups as well as alternative methods for collecting eyewitness identification evidence. Any alternative should increase correct identifications while minimizing false identifications. Furthermore, new alternatives should be tested and found robust, meaning that they outperform an alternative procedure in most circumstances. Finally, we must understand how they work.

One such alternative presentation method involves modifying the size of a lineup. Levi (2011) compared three different lineup sizes consisting of 12, 24, or 120 photos. The lineups contained no innocent suspects, so we estimated that rate by dividing the total identification rate in perpetrator-absent lineups by the number of fillers. We then computed the conditional probability of a guilty suspect identification. Those values were very high: .89, .85, and .96 for the 12-, 24-, and 120-person lineups, respectively, making it difficult to assess the impact of lineup size. At the other extreme are showup identifications, which are akin to a one-person lineup. The police make extensive use of showups, which constitute 30% to 77% of all identification procedures (Gonzalez, Ellsworth, & Pembroke, 1993; McQuiston & Malpass, 2001). Showups have been criticized for leading to more innocent suspect identifications than traditional lineup presentations (Clark & Godfrey, 2009), but this conclusion may be premature (see Chapter 2, this volume). In sum, more work needs to be done to determine the effect of lineup size on the performance of eyewitnesses.

An alternative presentation method called the *elimination lineup* was developed to aid children with lineup identifications (Pozzulo & Lindsay, 1999). In an elimination lineup, witnesses view a simultaneous lineup and are asked to select one lineup member that most closely resembles their memory for the perpetrator. Following their selection, witnesses are presented with this individual and asked if he is the perpetrator. Pozzulo et al. (2008) compared simultaneous, sequential, and elimination lineups but did not find significant differences in correct identification rates. Correct rejection rates were significantly lower for the simultaneous lineup, but the elimination and sequential lineup did not differ. An estimate of the conditional probability of choosing the guilty suspect showed little difference among the three types of lineups, consistent with a criterion shift across conditions.

Pryke, Lindsay, Dysart, and Dupuis (2004) developed a lineup presentation technique in which different features of the perpetrator should be tested in separate lineups. For example, there could be separate lineups for the suspect's face, body, and voice. The more times a witness selects the suspect out of these independent lineups, the more likely the suspect is guilty. A witness with a poor memory would have a 1 in 6 chance of selecting the suspect's face when guessing; however, there would be a 1 in 36 chance ($\frac{1}{6} \times \frac{1}{6}$) that the witness would select the same person's voice from a voice lineup. However, other research shows that people are more likely to retrieve a memory if we use the available cues in a multiplicative manner to focus the search (Nairne, 2002) rather than in an additive manner.

It is common to assess confidence after an eyewitness's binary (identifying someone as the perpetrator or not) decision, and recent studies have shown that confidence can be a reasonable indicator of accuracy for eyewitnesses who choose a lineup member (Sauer, Brewer, Zweck, & Weber, 2010; Sauerland & Sporer, 2009; Sporer, 1992; Sporer, Penrod, Read, & Cutler, 1995). On the basis of this work, a confidence-based means of assessing eyewitness accuracy recently has arisen. Brewer, Weber, Wootton, and Lindsay (in press; see also Sauer, Brewer, & Weber, 2008) asked participants to provide a quick confidence assessment (0%–100%) for each of the sequentially presented lineup members. Both group- and participant-level analyses showed that the probative value obtained from these confidence judgments outweighed that of binary eyewitness identification decisions.

The final alternative approach we detail focuses on improving lineup performance through the use of intervening tasks prior to the actual lineup (see also Goodsell, Gronlund, & Buttaccio, 2010). Macrae and Lewis (2002) presented participants in the experimental conditions with arrays of Navon (1977) stimuli (a large letter consisting of many small letters, such as a large H formed by small Ts) and asked them to make either global judgments (responding with the large letter, e.g., "H") or local judgments (responding with the small letters, e.g., "T"). Participants were then presented with a target-present eight-person simultaneous lineup. Whereas the control condition yielded 60% correct identifications, oddly, the global processing condition produced an increase to 83% correct. Conversely, the local processing condition fell to only 30% correct. Perfect et al. (2007) had participants interact with a female confederate and then later attempt to identify the target from six-person perpetrator-present or perpetrator-absent simultaneous lineups. As with Macrae and Lewis (2002), participants completed a global or local orientation task prior to the lineup procedure. This task either involved similar Navon stimuli judgments or qualitative judgments of faces (rating each face for honesty—global processing—or eye distinctiveness—local processing). They found increased correct decisions— correct identifications in perpetrator-present lineups plus correct rejections in perpetrator-absent lineups—after global processing in comparison to a control group. See Perfect, Weston, Dennis, and Snell (2008) for further explorations of this effect.

In sum, a variety of alternative approaches to the standard lineup procedures exist. Researchers and policymakers should give consideration to these possibilities, both the alternatives discussed in this chapter as well as other yet-to-be-developed ideas. Witnesses seem to hold more information than the standard binary choice decision can extract, and in many cases, it seems the information they hold is worth extracting. Although many of these techniques and measures require additional testing and evaluation, we recommend they be part of any discussion of policy change regarding eyewitness identification evidence.

CONCLUSION

In this chapter, we outlined the evidence for the existence of a sequential advantage and a sequential shift. On the basis of the use of the standard sequential procedure, the laboratory evidence supports that sequential presentation produces a conservative sequential shift. A sequential advantage is possible using the standard procedure, but it tends to occur only in certain circumstances. We also reviewed the policy implications of a sequential shift. But as researchers explore variations on the standard sequential procedure, as was done in the recent field study (Wells et al., 2011), additional research is needed to evaluate these alternative procedures to determine if the sequential lineup continues to produce more conservative choosing or if a more robust sequential advantage can be achieved. Theory should guide this research as well as promote the development and evaluation of explanations for the findings.

It was not our intention in this chapter to disparage sequential presentation methods and the resulting sequential shift they produce. The sequential shift, and the resulting increased protection for the innocent, is a laudable accomplishment given that faulty eyewitness evidence played a role in over 75% of the 292 DNA exoneration cases to date (http://www.innocence project.org; see Introduction, this volume, more details on the role of mistaken identification in exoneration cases). False convictions take a heavy financial toll. An investigation by the Better Government Association and the Center on Wrongful Convictions at Northwestern University School of Law showed that wrongful convictions for violent crimes have cost Illinois taxpayers $214 million ("Editorial: Better laws", 2011). More important, they take a heavy human toll not only on the falsely imprisoned but also on the new victims arising from the 14 murders, 11 sexual assaults, 10 kidnappings, and at least 62 other felonies committed by the actual Illinois perpetrators, while innocent men or women served time for their crimes. Sequential presentation methods may be the answer to this profound social problem; but as we have reviewed in light of the evidence favoring a sequential shift and the impact of various sequential procedural variations, that answer remains complex and multifaceted.

Human memory is ill equipped to make the kind of decisions that professionals ask it to make when viewing a lineup. This is a recipe for trouble when coupled with the fact that jurors believe eyewitnesses far beyond what the reliability of memory evidence merits (e.g., Cutler, Penrod, & Dexter, 1990; Lindsay, Wells, & O'Connor, 1989). The trouble is confirmed by the fact that faulty eyewitness identification is the leading contributor to wrongful conviction. However, more important than a determination of which lineup presentation method is the best is the overreliance on memory evidence by the criminal justice system. No matter how a witness's memory is queried and no matter which procedure is used, memory evidence is and will remain problematic and unreliable.

REFERENCES

Behrman, B. W., & Davey, S. L. (2001). Eyewitness identification in actual criminal cases: An archival analysis. *Law and Human Behavior, 25*, 475–491. doi:10.1023/A:1012840831846

Benjamin, A. S. (2007). Memory is more than just remembering: Strategic control of encoding, accessing memory, and making decisions. In A. S. Benjamin & B. H. Ross (Eds.), *The Psychology of learning and motivation: Skill and strategy in memory use* (Vol. 48, pp. 175–223). London, England: Academic Press. doi:10.1016/S0079-7421(07)48005-7

Benjamin, A. S., Diaz, M., & Wee, S. (2009). Signal detection with criterion noise: Applications to recognition memory. *Psychological Review, 116*, 84–115. doi:10.1037/a0014351

Blackstone, W. (1979). *Commentaries on the laws of England* (Vol. 2, Book 4). Chicago, IL: University of Chicago Press. (Original work published 1769)

Bornstein, B. H., & Meissner, C. A. (2008). Introduction: Basic and applied issues in eyewitness research: A Münsterberg centennial retrospective. *Applied Cognitive Psychology, 22*, 733–736. doi:10.1002/acp.1478

Brewer, N., Keast, A., & Rishworth, A. (2002). The confidence–accuracy relationship in eyewitness identification: The effects of reflection and disconfirmation on correlation and calibration. *Journal of Experimental Psychology: Applied, 8*, 44–56. doi:10.1037/1076-898X.8.1.44

Brewer, N., Weber, N., Wootton, D., & Lindsay, D. S. (in press). Identifying the bad guy in a lineup using deadlined confidence judgments. *Psychological Science*.

Carlson, C. A., & Gronlund, S. D. (2011). Searching for the sequential lineup advantage: A distinctiveness explanation. *Memory, 19*, 916–929. doi:10.1080/09658211.2011.613846

Carlson, C. A., Gronlund, S. D., & Clark, S. E. (2008). Lineup composition, suspect position, and the sequential lineup advantage. *Journal of Experimental Psychology: Applied, 14*, 118–128. doi:10.1037/1076-898X.14.2.118

Ceci, S. J., & Friedman, R. D. (2000). Suggestibility of children: Scientific research and legal implications. *Cornell Law Review, 86*, 33–108.

Clark, S. E. (2003). A memory and decision model for eyewitness identification. *Applied Cognitive Psychology, 17*, 629–654. doi:10.1002/acp.891

Clark, S. E. (2008). The importance (necessity) of computational modeling for eyewitness identification research. *Applied Cognitive Psychology, 22*, 803–813. doi:10.1002/acp.1484

Clark, S. E. (2012). Costs and benefits of eyewitness identification reform: Psychological science and public policy. *Perspectives on Psychological Science, 7*, 238–259. doi:10.1177/1745691612439584

Clark, S. E., Erickson, M. A., & Breneman, J. (2011). Probative value of absolute and relative judgments in eyewitness identification. *Law and Human Behavior, 35*, 364–380. doi:10.1007/s10979-010-9245-1

Clark, S. E., & Godfrey, R. D. (2009). Eyewitness identification evidence and innocence risk. *Psychonomic Bulletin & Review, 16*, 22–42. doi:10.3758/PBR.16.1.22

Clark, S. E., Howell, R. T., & Davey, S. L. (2008). Regularities in eyewitness identification. *Law and Human Behavior, 32*, 187–218. doi:10.1007/s10979-006-9082-4

Cutler, B. L., Penrod, S. D., & Dexter, H. R. (1990). Juror sensitivity to eyewitness identification evidence. *Law and Human Behavior, 14*, 185–191. doi:10.1007/BF01062972

Douglass, A. B., & McQuiston-Surrett, D. (2006). Post-identification feedback: Exploring the effects of sequential photospreads and eyewitnesses' awareness of the identification task. *Applied Cognitive Psychology, 20*, 991–1007. doi:10.1002/acp.1253

Duncan, M. J. (2006). *A signal detection model of compound decision tasks* (Technical Report No. TR2006-256). Retrieved from http://www.dtic.mil/cgi-bin/GetTRDoc?AD=ADA473015

Dunning, D., & Stern, L. B. (1994). Distinguishing accurate from inaccurate eyewitness identifications via inquiries about decision processes. *Journal of Personality and Social Psychology, 67*, 818–835. doi:10.1037/0022-3514.67.5.818

Editorial: Better laws can help keep the innocent from prison. [Editorial]. (2011, October 5). *Chicago Sun-Times*. Retrieved from http://www.suntimes.com/opinions/8029679-474/editorial-better-laws-can-help-keep-the-innocent-from-prison.html

Egan, J. P. (1958). *Recognition memory and the operating characteristic*. (Technical Note AFCRC-TN-58-51, AO-152650). Bloomington: Indiana University Hearing and Communication Laboratory.

Gonzalez, R., Ellsworth, P. C., & Pembroke, M. (1993). Response biases in lineups and showups. *Journal of Personality and Social Psychology, 64*, 525–537. doi:10.1037/0022-3514.64.4.525

Goodsell, C., Gronlund, S., & Buttaccio, D. R. (2010, March). *A test of the better memory probe hypothesis: Improving eyewitness identification accuracy*. Paper presented at the meeting of the American Psychology–Law Society, Vancouver, BC, Canada.

Goodsell, C. A., Gronlund, S. D., & Carlson, C. A. (2010). Exploring the sequential lineup advantage using WITNESS. *Law and Human Behavior, 34*, 445–459. doi:10.1007/s10979-009-9215-7

Green, D., & Swets, J. (1966). *Signal detection theory and psychophysics*. New York, NY: Wiley.

Gronlund, S. D. (2004). Sequential lineups: Shift in criterion or decision strategy? *Journal of Applied Psychology, 89*, 362–368. doi:10.1037/0021-9010.89.2.362

Gronlund, S. D., Carlson, C. A., Dailey, S. B., & Goodsell, C. A. (2009). Robustness of the sequential lineup advantage. *Journal of Experimental Psychology: Applied, 15*, 140–152. doi:10.1037/a0015082

Gronlund, S. D., Goodsell, C. A., & Andersen, S. M. (2012). Lineup procedures in eyewitness identification. In L. Nadel & W. Sinnott-Armstrong (Eds.), *Law and Neuroscience* (pp. 59–83). New York, NY: Oxford University Press.

Hill, T. (2009). Knowing when to stop: How to gamble if you must—the mathematics of optimal stopping. *American Scientist, 97*, 126–133.

Horry, R., Memon, A., Wright, D. B., & Milne, R. (2012). Predictors of eyewitness identification decisions from video lineups in England: A field study. *Law and Human Behavior, 36*, 257–265.

Klobuchar, A., Steblay, N. K. M., & Caligiuri, H. L. (2006). Improving eyewitness identifications: Hennepin County's blind sequential lineup pilot project. *Cardozo Public Law, Policy, and Ethics Journal, 4*, 381–414.

Kneller, W., Memon, A., & Stevenage, S. (2001). Simultaneous and sequential lineups: decision processes of accurate and inaccurate eyewitnesses. *Applied Cognitive Psychology, 15*, 659–671. doi:10.1002/acp.739

Koriat, A., & Goldsmith, M. (1996). Monitoring and control processes in the strategic regulation of memory accuracy. *Psychological Review, 103*, 490–517. doi:10.1037/0033-295X.103.3.490

Lane, S. M., & Meissner, C. A. (2008). A "middle road" approach to bridging the basic–applied divide in eyewitness identification research. *Applied Cognitive Psychology, 22*, 779–787. doi:10.1002/acp.1482

Levi, A. M. (2011). Much better than the sequential lineup: A 120-person lineup. *Psychology, Crime & Law, 18*, 631–640. doi:10.1080/1068316X.2010.526120

Lindsay, R. C. L., Lea, J. A., & Fulford, J. A. (1991). Sequential lineup presentation: Technique matters. *Journal of Applied Psychology, 76*, 741–745. doi:10.1037/0021-9010.76.5.741

Lindsay, R. C. L., Lea, J. A., Nosworthy, G. J., Fulford, J. A., Hector, J., LeVan, V., & Seabrook, C. (1991). Biased lineups: Sequential presentation reduces the problem. *Journal of Applied Psychology, 76*, 796–802. doi:10.1037/0021-9010.76.6.796

Lindsay, R. C. L., & Wells, G. L. (1985). Improving eyewitness identifications from lineups: Simultaneous versus sequential lineup presentation. *Journal of Applied Psychology, 70*, 556–564. doi:10.1037/0021-9010.70.3.556

Lindsay, R. C. L., Wells, G. L., & O'Connor, F. J. (1989). Mock-juror belief of accurate and inaccurate eyewitnesses. *Law and Human Behavior, 13*, 333–339. doi:10.1007/BF01067033

Ludlum, R. (2005). *The Ambler warning.* New York, NY: St. Martins Press.

Lusted, L. B. (1971, March 26). Signal detectability and medical decision-making. *Science, 171*, 1217–1219. doi:10.1126/science.171.3977.1217

Macrae, C. N., & Lewis, H. L. (2002). Do I know you? Processing orientation and face recognition. *Psychological Science, 13*, 194–196. doi:10.1111/1467-9280.00436

Malpass, R. S. (2006a). Notes on the Illinois pilot program on sequential double-blind identification procedures. *Public Interest Law Reporter, 11*(2), 5–47.

Malpass, R. S. (2006b). A policy evaluation of simultaneous and sequential line-ups. *Psychology, Public Policy, and Law, 12*, 394–418. doi:10.1037/1076-8971.12.4.394

Malpass, R. S., Tredoux, C. G., Schreiber Compo, N., McQuiston-Surrett, D. E., MacLin, O. H., Zimmerman, L. A., & Topp, L. D. (2008). Study space analysis for policy development. *Applied Cognitive Psychology, 22*, 789–801. doi:10.1002/acp.1483

McCreary, J., Wolf, D., & Forney, A. W. (2009). Unstable. In Wolf Films, *Law & order: Special victims unit*. Universal City, CA: National Broadcasting Company.

McQuiston, D., & Malpass, R. (2001, June). *Eyewitness identifications in criminal cases: An archival study*. Paper presented at the meeting of the Society for Applied Research in Memory and Cognition, Kingston, Ontario, Canada.

McQuiston-Surrett, D., Malpass, R. S., & Tredoux, C. G. (2006). Sequential vs. simultaneous lineups: A review of methods, data, and theory. *Psychology, Public Policy, and Law, 12*, 137–169. doi:10.1037/1076-8971.12.2.137

Mecklenburg, S. (2006). *Report to the legislature of the state of Illinois: The Illinois pilot program on double-blind, sequential lineup procedures*. Retrieved from http://www.chicagopolice.org/IL%20Pilot%20on%20Eyewitness%20ID.pdf

Meissner, C. A., Tredoux, C. G., Parker, J. F., & MacLin, O. H. (2005). Eyewitness decisions in simultaneous and sequential lineups: A dual-process signal detection theory analysis. *Memory & Cognition, 33*, 783–792. doi:10.3758/BF03193074

Metz, C. E. (1978). Basic principles of ROC analysis. *Seminars in Nuclear Medicine, 8*, 283–298. doi:10.1016/S0001-2998(78)80014-2

Nairne, J. S. (2002). Remembering over the short-term: The case against the standard model. *Annual Review of Psychology, 53*, 53–81. doi:10.1146/annurev.psych.53.100901.135131

Navon, D. (1977). Forest before trees: The precedence of global features in visual perception. *Cognitive Psychology, 9*, 353–383. doi:10.1016/0010-0285(77)90012-3

Palmer, M. A., & Brewer, N. (2012). Sequential lineup presentation promotes less biased criterion setting but does not improve discriminability. *Law and Human Behavior, 36*, 247–255. doi:10.1037/h0093923

Perfect, T. J., Dennis, I., & Snell, A. (2007). The effects of local and global processing orientation on eyewitness identification performance. *Memory, 15*, 784–798. doi:10.1080/09658210701654627

Perfect, T. J., Weston, N. J., Dennis, I., & Snell, A. (2008). The effects of precedence on Navon-induced processing bias in face recognition. *The Quarterly Journal of Experimental Psychology: Human Experimental Psychology, 61,* 1479–1486. doi:10.1080/17470210802034678

Pisano, E. D., Gatsonis, C., Hendrick, E., Yaffe, M., Baum, J. K., Acharyya, S., . . . Rebner, M. (2005, October 27). Diagnostic performance of digital versus film mammography for breast-cancer screening. *The New England Journal of Medicine, 353,* 1773–1783. doi:10.1056/NEJMoa052911

Police and Criminal Evidence Act (1984). Retrieved from http://www.legislation. gov.uk/ukpga/1984/60

Pozzulo, J. D., Dempsey, J., Corey, S., Girardi, A., Lawandi, A., & Aston, C. (2008). Can a lineup procedure designed for child witnesses work for adults? Comparing simultaneous, sequential, and elimination lineup procedures. *Journal of Applied Social Psychology, 38,* 2195–2209. doi:10.1111/j.1559-1816.2008.00387.x

Pozzulo, J. D., & Lindsay, R. C. L. (1999). Elimination lineups: An improved identification procedure for child eyewitnesses. *Journal of Applied Psychology, 84,* 167–176. doi:10.1037/0021-9010.84.2.167

Pryke, S., Lindsay, R., Dysart, J. E., & Dupuis, P. (2004). Multiple independent identification decisions: A method of calibrating eyewitness identifications. *Journal of Applied Psychology, 89,* 73–84. doi:10.1037/0021-9010.89.1.73

Ross, S. J., & Malpass, R. S. (2008). Moving forward: Response to "Studying eyewitness investigations in the field." *Law and Human Behavior, 32,* 16–21. doi:10.1007/ s10979-007-9104-x

Sauer, J. D., Brewer, N., & Weber, N. (2008). Multiple confidence estimates as indices of eyewitness memory. *Journal of Experimental Psychology: General, 137,* 528–547. doi:10.1037/a0012712

Sauer, J. D., Brewer, N., Zweck, T., & Weber, N. (2010). The effect of retention interval on the confidence–accuracy relationship for eyewitness identification. *Law and Human Behavior, 34,* 337–347. doi:10.1007/s10979-009-9192-x

Sauerland, M., & Sporer, S. L. (2009). Fast and confident: Postdicting eyewitness identification accuracy in a field study. *Journal of Experimental Psychology: Applied, 15,* 46–62. doi:10.1037/a0014560

Schacter, D. L., Dawes, R., Jacoby, L. L., Kahneman, D., Lempert, R., Roediger, H. L., & Rosenthal, R. (2008). Policy forum: Studying eyewitness investigations in the field. *Law and Human Behavior, 32,* 3–5. doi:10.1007/s10979-007-9093-9

Sporer, S. L. (1992). Post-dicting eyewitness accuracy: Confidence, decision-times and person descriptions of choosers and non-choosers. *European Journal of Social Psychology, 22,* 157–180. doi:10.1002/ejsp.2420220205

Sporer, S. L., Penrod, S., Read, D., & Cutler, B. (1995). Choosing, confidence, and accuracy: A meta-analysis of the confidence-accuracy relation in eyewitness identification studies. *Psychological Bulletin, 118,* 315–327. doi:10.1037/0033-2909.118.3.315

State of New Jersey v. Henderson, 27A.3d 872 (N.J. 2011).

Steblay, N. K. (2011). What we know now: The Evanston Illinois field lineups. *Law and Human Behavior, 35*, 1–12. doi:10.1007/s10979-009-9207-7

Steblay, N. K., Dietrich, H. L., Ryan, S. L., Raczynski, J. L., & James, K. A. (2011). Sequential lineup laps and eyewitness accuracy. *Law and Human Behavior, 35*, 262–274. doi:10.1007/s10979-010-9236-2

Steblay, N. K., Dysart, J., Fulero, S., & Lindsay, R. C. L. (2001). Eyewitness accuracy rates in sequential and simultaneous lineup presentations: A meta-analytic comparison. *Law and Human Behavior, 25*, 459–473. doi:10.1023/A:1012888715007

Steblay, N. K., Dysart, J. E., & Wells, G. L. (2011). Seventy-two tests of the sequential lineup superiority effect: A meta-analysis and policy discussion. *Psychology, Public Policy, and Law, 17*, 99–139. doi:10.1037/a0021650

Swets, J. A., Dawes, R. M., & Monahan, J. (2000). Psychological science can improve diagnostic decisions. *Psychological Science in the Public Interest, 1*, 1–26. doi:10.1111/1529-1006.001

Valentine, T., Darling, S., & Memon, A. (2007). Do strict rules and moving images increase the reliability of sequential identification procedures? *Applied Cognitive Psychology, 21*, 933–949. doi:10.1002/acp.1306

von Neumann, J., & Morgenstern, O. (1944). *Theory of games and economic behavior.* Princeton, NJ: Princeton University Press.

Weber, N., & Perfect, T. J. (2012). Improving eyewitness identification accuracy by screening out those who say they don't know. *Law and Human Behavior, 36*, 28–36. doi:10.1037/h0093976

Wells, G. L., Steblay, N. M., & Dysart, J. E. (2011). *A test of the simultaneous vs. sequential lineup methods: An initial report of the AJS national eyewitness identification field studies.* Unpublished manuscript, American Judicature Society. Retrieved from http://www.ajs.org/wc/pdfs/EWID_PrintFriendly.pdf

Wells, G. L., & Turtle, J. W. (1986). Eyewitness identification: The importance of lineup models. *Psychological Bulletin, 99*, 320–329. doi:10.1037/0033-2909.99.3.320

Wickens, T. D. (2002). *Elementary signal detection theory.* New York, NY: Oxford University Press.

Wixted, J. T., & Mickes, L. (2012). The field of eyewitness memory should abandon probative value and embrace receiver operating characteristic analysis. *Perspectives on Psychological Science, 7*, 275–278. doi:10.1177/1745691612442906

Wogalter, M. S., Malpass, R. S., & McQuiston, D. E. (2004). A national survey of US police on preparation and conduct of identification lineups. *Psychology, Crime & Law, 10*, 69–82. doi:10.1080/10683160410001641873

6

DOUBLE-BLIND LINEUP ADMINISTRATION: EFFECTS OF ADMINISTRATOR KNOWLEDGE ON EYEWITNESS DECISIONS

JACQUELINE L. AUSTIN, DAVID M. ZIMMERMAN, LINDSEY RHEAD, AND MARGARET BULL KOVERA

Over 100 years ago, the horse Clever Hans captivated the public's attention with his apparent ability to provide correct numerical answers to mathematical questions. If the answer to the question was five, Hans tapped his hoof five times to indicate the correct answer. The psychologist Oskar Pfungst (1911/1965) examined this phenomenon and discovered that Hans could no longer answer the questions accurately when the questioner stood farther away from him, when the questioner was blocked from his view, or when the questioner did not know the correct answer to the question. Hans's accuracy depended on having a clear, close view of the person with the right answer. Upon this discovery, Pfungst shifted his focus from studying the horse to studying the people who questioned the horse and observed that

Portions of this material are based in part on work supported by National Science Foundation Grants SES-0922314 and SES-9986240. Any opinions, findings, and conclusions or recommendations expressed in this material are those of the authors and do not necessarily reflect the views of the National Science Foundation.

DOI: 10.1037/14094-007
Reform of Eyewitness Identification Procedures, B. L. Cutler (Editor)

the questioners involuntarily and unknowingly changed postures and facial expressions when Hans had provided the correct number of taps. Indeed, the questioners provided the correct answer to Hans through subtle nonverbal cues. Thus, Hans's cleverness became the first documented evidence of an interpersonal expectancy effect.

Interpersonal expectancy effects have been documented in a variety of settings, including laboratories (Rosenthal & Fode, 1963), classrooms (Rosenthal & Jacobson, 1966), and even courtrooms (Blanck, Rosenthal, & Cordell, 1985; Halverson, Hallahan, Hart, & Rosenthal, 1997; Hart, 1995). Do interpersonal expectancies operate in other legal settings, including those in which police officers administer lineups or photo arrays to eyewitnesses? When administrators show witnesses a lineup or an array of photos, they typically have a hypothesis that one of the lineup members is or one of the photos depicts the perpetrator of a crime. Do police officers communicate their hypotheses—consciously or unconsciously—to witnesses through their behavior? If so, do these behaviors influence witnesses to identify the suspect more frequently than they would if the police administrator did not know which lineup member was the suspect? To examine these questions, we review psychological research on expectancy effects more generally and then discuss evidence for the operation of interpersonal expectancies in legal settings, including lineup administrations.

PSYCHOLOGICAL RESEARCH ON EXPECTANCY EFFECTS

More than 5 decades of research has documented the influence of interpersonal expectancies on both animal and human behavior (Rosenthal, 2002). In one of the first experiments to demonstrate this effect, experimenters were randomly assigned to receive an expectation about the ability of particular rats to learn how to navigate a maze to find food, with some rats expected to be maze-smart and others to be maze-dumb. After receiving the expectations, experimenters trained their rats to maneuver a maze. Although no intellectual differences between the two groups of rats existed (e.g., they were bred to be highly similar genetically), when experimenters expected the rats to be maze-smart, the rats learned to discriminate which arm of a maze held a reward faster than when experimenters expected their rats to be maze-dumb (Rosenthal & Fode, 1963). Thus, the expectancy of the experimenters influenced the rats' behavior.

Experimenters' expectancies also affect people's behavior. For example, in one study, the researchers instructed experimenters to collect participants' ratings of the physical attractiveness of 10 faces. The researchers led half of the experimenters to expect that participants would rate the target faces to be very physically attractive. The researchers led the other experimenters to expect low ratings of physical attractiveness. Although a separate group of participants had previously rated these faces to be relatively average in attractiveness, participants gave higher ratings of attractiveness to experimenters who expected high ratings than to those who expected low ratings (Rosenthal, 1976).

Perhaps one of the best-known examples of research on expectancy effects investigated the effects of manipulating teachers' expectations about student achievement. At the beginning of the school year, researchers administered intelligence tests to students. The researchers randomly selected some students (regardless of their test scores) and informed their teacher that they should expect intellectual gains from these children over the course of the year. When teachers expected a student to excel, the student demonstrated superior achievement at the end of the year. When teachers did not expect the student to excel, the student demonstrated average achievement (Rosenthal & Jacobson, 1966, 1992).

On the basis of this research on experimenter expectancy effects, it is clear that to ensure valid conclusions about the effects of experimental manipulations, experimenters should be blind to which conditions participants are assigned. If the experimenter is unaware of the participant's condition during data collection, the experimenter cannot possess prior hypotheses about how a particular participant will behave on the basis of their randomly assigned condition. This precaution prevents experimenters from systematically biasing participants' responses in the direction of the experimental hypothesis (Rosenthal & Rubin, 1978).

EXPECTANCY EFFECTS IN THE LEGAL SETTING

Experimenter expectancy effects have also been documented in legal settings. For example, judges' beliefs about a defendant's guilt influenced juror judgments because the judges' beliefs influenced the manner in which the judge delivered the judicial instructions (Blanck et al., 1985; Halverson et al., 1997; Hart, 1995). More recently, researchers began to articulate concerns that experimenter-expectancy effects may also occur during eyewitness identification tasks. If lineup administrators know which lineup members are the suspects, they may communicate this knowledge to the witness through their verbal or nonverbal behavior. Moreover, witnesses are likely unaware of this influence from the lineup administrator (Clark, Marshall, & Rosenthal, 2009; Greathouse & Kovera, 2009).

Administering a lineup shares many features with the process of conducting an experiment (Wells & Luus, 1990). Within this analogy, police officers are akin to experimenters, witnesses to study participants, lineup members to stimulus materials, and eyewitness behaviors to dependent variables. The factors that introduce bias into experiments may also introduce bias into lineup procedures (Wells et al., 1998). To prevent lineup administrators from communicating the suspect's identity to the witness, lineup administrators should use procedures that are similar to those that scientists use when conducting experiments (e.g., blindness to condition) to obtain valid data. This form of lineup administration is referred to as a *double-blind procedure*. Identifications should be based purely on a witness's memory (i.e., the identification should not be based on the verbal and nonverbal cues from the lineup administrator); therefore, double-blind lineup administration, which prevents administrators from intentionally or unintentionally communicating the suspect's identity to the witness, should be the preferred method of administration. When the administrator knows the suspect's identity (i.e. a single-blind lineup procedure), the witness may be more likely to choose the suspect regardless of the suspect's guilt.

SUPPORT FOR THE IMPLEMENTATION OF DOUBLE-BLIND LINEUP PROCEDURES

The American Psychology–Law Society supported the use of double-blind lineup procedures when it endorsed the recommendations made by a panel of experts for best practices to follow when designing and administering lineups (Wells et al., 1998). The panel made four recommendations to improve eyewitness lineup procedures. The first of these recommendations was that the police should conduct lineups using double-blind procedures in which neither the administrator nor the witness knows the identity of the suspect. The panel also recommended that lineups be accompanied by unbiased instructions that inform the witness that the perpetrator may not be present in the lineup, that lineups be created fairly so that the suspect does not stand out in the context of the other lineup members, and that the officer conducting the lineup obtain a statement of confidence from the witness at the time of the identification before the witness receives any feedback about his or her identification choice (Wells et al., 1998).

The U.S. Department of Justice, Office of Justice Programs, National Institute of Justice (1999) also issued guidelines for police departments to follow when designing and administering lineups. These guidelines address the selection of foils, the instructions given to witnesses, how confidence should be recorded, and methods for the presentation of lineup photos. These guidelines did not fully sanction the use of double-blind lineup administration, but they did advocate that law enforcement personnel not leak any information about the suspect or the case to the witness. The introduction to the guidelines did mention double-blind lineup administration as a potential future reform. Some scholars regard the absence of double-blind procedures from the guidelines as a major deficiency (Haw & Fisher, 2004; Phillips, McAuliff, Kovera, & Cutler, 1999; Wells et al., 2000). Even without the support of double-blind lineup administration from the National Institute of Justice, nine states and many cities (e.g., Boston, Dallas, Denver, Minneapolis) have passed reforms for lineup procedures that include the implementation of double-blind lineup administration procedures (see Conclusion, this volume). Some states (New Jersey and North Carolina) even dictate that officers must use double-blind lineup methods.

Courts are beginning to recognize the importance of double-blind lineup administration in the protection of defendants from mistaken identification and wrongful conviction. For example, in a recent New Jersey Supreme Court ruling (*State of New Jersey v. Henderson*, 2011), the court held that it was necessary to revise the legal standard used to judge the reliability of eyewitness identification evidence because the current standard does not provide a sufficient basis for evaluating identifications, nor does it serve as a deterrent for police misconduct in obtaining identifications. In addition to these failings, the standard places too much faith in the ability of jurors to recognize when identifications are made under unreliable conditions. The court noted that extensive psychological research on eyewitness identification decisions had been conducted since earlier courts had established the standard for evaluating identification reliability (e.g., *Manson v. Brathwaite*, 1977), including research on double-blind administration (Greathouse & Kovera, 2009). This holding may influence policy in many other states as they also begin to acknowledge that the body of scientific research on eyewitness identifications supports methods for improving lineup procedures.

The implementation of double-blind lineup procedures has met with resistance from some police officers and prosecutors who believe that there may be drawbacks to double-blind administration (Mecklenburg, 2006). Some are concerned that prohibitive costs may be associated with the implementation of double-blind lineup procedures, particularly for those jurisdictions with few officers. In these smaller jurisdictions, it may be unlikely that there will be an officer who is unaware of the suspect's identity. Police have also expressed concern that an officer who is unaware of the suspect's identity may miss pertinent information provided by the witness during the identification procedure that may be helpful for the investigation. Finally, a highly publicized case may also restrict the practice of conducting a double-blind lineup procedure because much like in smaller jurisdictions it may be impossible to locate an officer who is unaware of the suspect's identity. However, police do admit that double-blind procedures protect them from appeals and lawsuits when witnesses allege that the administrator influenced their decision (Mecklenburg, 2006).

Effects of Administrator Knowledge on Eyewitness Identification Accuracy

Although scholars have expressed concern about the possibility of experimenter expectancy effects during eyewitness identification tasks when the person who is administering the lineup knows which lineup member is the suspect (Wells et al., 1998), there is relatively little research that directly tests the effects of administrator knowledge of the suspect on the accuracy of witnesses' identifications. Research on experimenter expectancy effects suggests that when administrators know which lineup member is the suspect, they may communicate this knowledge to the witness. The end result is an increase in the rate at which witnesses identify suspects from lineups that is independent of the guilt of the suspect, with an increase in the rates of both guilty and innocent suspects. To prevent an increase in mistaken identifications, scholars have argued for the implementation of double-blind lineup administration (Wells et al., 1998). Not only is there little published research on how administrator knowledge may impact eyewitness identification accuracy, early studies produced mixed results, sometimes showing a damaging influence of administrator knowledge, with other studies showing no impact of administrator knowledge.

The first study to investigate the effects of administrator knowledge of the suspect's identity on eyewitness identification decisions manipulated administrator knowledge (single- vs. double-blind), lineup presentation (simultaneous vs. sequential), and the presence of a silent third party observer (present vs. absent; Phillips et al., 1999). One purpose of the study was to assess whether witnesses make more false identifications from target-absent lineups (i.e., a lineup in which the actual perpetrator is not present) when the investigator knows which lineup member is the suspect than when the investigator does not know the identity of the suspect. Another purpose was to assess whether different methods of lineup presentation moderated the effects of administrator knowledge of the suspect's identity. Thus, half of the administrators conducted a sequential lineup (e.g., showed the photos of the lineup members one at a time and elicited an identification decision from the witness after each photo), and half conducted a simultaneous lineup (e.g., showed all the photos of the lineup members at the same time). Finally, to test whether the presence of a defense attorney at the identification procedure might discourage administrators with knowledge of the suspect's identity from exhibiting behaviors that would influence witnesses' identification decisions, the researchers examined whether the presence of a silent third-party observer moderated the effects of administrator knowledge on identification decisions (Phillips et al., 1999).

During an introductory psychology class, two confederates (one male, one female) entered a classroom, interrupted the lecture, and removed media equipment from the classroom (Phillips et al., 1999). The professor stated that the equipment was needed for a class demonstration and expressed anger at both the interruption and removal of the media equipment. The entire interaction between the confederates and the teacher lasted approximately two minutes. During the two minutes, the experimenters ensured that witnesses saw a complete view of the each confederate's front, profile, and back. After a delay, the researchers brought the student witnesses back to participate in two photographic lineup identification tasks—one for each confederate.

The researchers trained participant administrators to present lineups in either a sequential or a simultaneous manner. Administrators learned of the suspect's identity for one lineup (single-blind administration) but not for the other lineup (double-blind administration; Phillips et al., 1999). To emulate a police officer's motivation to obtain an identification of the suspect, the researchers offered the participant administrators a monetary reward if the participant witness identified the suspect.

The participant administrator first told the participant witnesses that they would be viewing two photographic lineups, one for the male perpetrator and one for the female perpetrator. Participant administrators instructed participant witnesses that the perpetrator may or may not be present in the lineup, the appearance of the perpetrator may or may not have changed, and to examine each photograph carefully while thinking of the perpetrators who removed the media equipment from their classroom. During the lineup administration, the experimenter either remained present or left the room. On completion of the lineup administration, both participant witnesses and administrators completed questionnaires assessing lineup administration fairness, pressure to make an identification, and confidence in the identification decision (Phillips et al., 1999).

Sequential lineups produced more identifications of the suspect than did simultaneous lineups (Phillips et al., 1999). Additionally, when the third-party observer was present during a sequential lineup presentation, participant witnesses made significantly more suspect identifications in the single-blind than in the double-blind conditions. Suspect identifications in the simultaneous lineup presentation did not differ as a function of third-party observer presence or administrator knowledge. Both participant administrators and participant witnesses reported fair lineup presentation, irrespective of conditions. Additionally, participant witnesses did not report pressure to make identifications by the administrator. Participant witnesses in single-blind conditions reported feeling slightly less confident about their identification than did participant witnesses in double-blind conditions (Phillips et al., 1999). Taken together, these results demonstrate how administrator knowledge can bias eyewitness decisions when lineups are presented sequentially.

In two follow-up studies, investigators examined the influence of administrator knowledge of the suspect's identity on eyewitness identification accuracy by varying administrator knowledge (single- vs. double-blind), lineup presentation (sequential vs. simultaneous), and perpetrator presence in the photo array (present vs. absent; Russano, Dickinson, Greathouse, & Kovera, 2006). While participants were completing a personality inventory for an ostensibly unrelated study, a young man entered the room, took a purse from a table, and fled. After this interaction, the researchers informed the participants that they would be asked to be an eyewitness and identify the man who stole the purse from a photographic lineup. The researchers trained participant administrators to administer either a sequential or a simultaneous lineup procedure and provided the administrators with a set of unbiased instructions to read to the participant witnesses. Additionally, the researchers told half of the participant administrators which lineup member was the suspect but did not inform the other half of the administrators. Again, to emulate a police officer's motivation to obtain a suspect identification, the researchers offered participant administrators a monetary reward if they obtained an identification of the suspect from the participant witness. All lineup procedures were videotaped for analysis and coding.

In accordance with previous research, sequential lineups reduced the rate of false identifications (Russano et al., 2006). Administrator knowledge did not affect the rate of suspect identity in either sequential or simultaneous lineups. Data from the videotaped lineup procedures showed that lineup administrators did little to actually bias their witnesses during administration, which was likely the reason for the null results obtained (Russano et al., 2006). To address the lack of administrator bias during lineup administration, the researchers conducted a second study that allowed for more flexibility in the lineup procedure by the participant administrator (Russano et al., 2006). Making changes to only the procedure and keeping all other variables identical to those in the first study, the researchers again manipulated administrator knowledge (single- vs. double-blind), lineup presentation (sequential vs. simultaneous) and perpetrator presence (present vs. absent).

Students in an introductory psychology class witnessed a young man enter the classroom, steal a purse, and flee. After a delay, the students reported to the laboratory and participated in a memory experiment (i.e., these students became participant witnesses). The researchers trained participant administrators to administer either a sequential or simultaneous lineup procedure and provided the administrators with a set of instructions to read to the participant witnesses. These instructions consisted of a warning that the perpetrator may or may not be present; however, this time the administrators were not provided with specific instructions to read to the participant witness in an attempt to allow the administrators more latitude for inadvertently communicating the suspect's identity to the participant witness. Despite the change in procedure allowing for greater flexibility in lineup administration, there was again no evidence that the administrators' knowledge of the suspect's identity influenced witnesses' decisions perhaps because the overall choosing rates were low and did not provide enough variability to demonstrate the effects of administrator cuing (Russano et al., 2006).

The most recently published research on the effects of double-blind administration on witness identification accuracy manipulated administrator knowledge (single- vs. double-blind), lineup presentation (sequential vs. simultaneous), lineup instructions (biased vs. unbiased), and perpetrator presence in the photo array (present vs. absent; Greathouse & Kovera, 2009). The goal of this research was to provide a context for understanding the inconsistent findings of past research. The researchers hypothesized that when conditions encourage witnesses to adopt a lower threshold of confidence for making an identification decision, as is the case for simultaneous lineup presentation and biased instructions that fail to warn the witness that the perpetrator may not be in the lineup, single-blind administrators would be able steer witnesses from identifying a filler in the lineup to identifying the suspect in the lineup (Greathouse & Kovera, 2009).

Participant witnesses watched a videotaped speech used in previous research (Haw & Fisher, 2004) in which a young man interrupted the speaker and asked to remove media equipment from the room. After a delay, researchers informed participant witnesses that the equipment was now missing and that as eyewitnesses to the theft they were being asked to identify the man who removed the media equipment from a photographic lineup. Researchers trained another group of participants to administer either a sequential or a simultaneous lineup and provided each participant administrator with instructions (biased or unbiased) to provide the participant witness, dependent on condition. For the biased instructions, administrators told the participant witnesses that a suspect was in custody and that the witness was being asked to view a photo array to see whether the witness could identify him. For the unbiased instructions, administrators told the participant witness the suspect may or may not be present in the lineup. Half of the administrators learned the identity of the suspect before administering the lineup procedure (single-blind administration) and the other half did not (double-blind administration). As in previous research, to emulate a police officer's motivation to obtain a suspect identification, participant administrators received a monetary reward if the participant witnesses identified the suspect (Greathouse & Kovera, 2009). Participant administrators then administered the photographic lineup to the participant witness and recorded the witness's identification decision and confidence in that identification decision. All lineup administrations were surreptitiously videotaped for later coding and analysis. After the lineup administration, witnesses and administrators completed postidentification questionnaires assessing their perceptions of lineup procedure fairness and administrator bias (Greathouse & Kovera, 2009).

When presented with a target-present photo array, participant witnesses identified the suspect 10 times more often than when presented when presented with a target-absent photo array (Greathouse & Kovera, 2009). When the administrator presented a simultaneous photo array and biased instructions, single-blind administrations of the photo array elicited greater identifications of the suspect from participant witnesses than did double-blind administrations. As predicted, the manipulations did not affect the rate at which witnesses rejected the photo array (e.g., stated that the perpetrator was not present in the photo array). Similar to findings from previous research, witnesses reported feeling more confident in their identifications when the lineup administrator was unaware of the suspect's identity, although this finding was not statistically significant at conventional levels. Despite the significant influence of administrator knowledge of the suspect's identity on witnesses' identification decisions, witnesses did not report that the administration of the photo array was biased in anyway, regardless of whether the conditions contained bias. Participant administrators reported that they had encouraged the witness to make an identification more in simultaneous than sequential lineup procedures. Additionally, participant administrators reported that they were more biased during lineup administration when they had knowledge of the suspect's identity and had presented biased instructions, but only in target absent lineup conditions (Greathouse & Kovera, 2009).

Two research assistants who were unaware of the conditions under which the identifications were obtained coded whether administrators engaged in specific behaviors and provided an overall rating of administrator pressure to choose a photo (Greathouse & Kovera, 2009). On the basis of these ratings, single-blind administrators exerted greater pressure on witnesses to choose a photograph. Moreover, administrators who knew which lineup member was the suspect were more likely to encourage witnesses to examine the lineup carefully, to ask witnesses to take another look at the photo array if they did not make an identification, and to remove rejected photographs slowly than were administrators who did not know which photo in the array represented the suspect (Greathouse & Kovera, 2009). This research is the most comprehensive investigation of double-blind lineup administration and provides behavioral evidence for the biasing impact administrator knowledge can have on eyewitness identification decisions.

Additional Moderators of Administrator Knowledge Effects

Researchers are beginning to investigate the factors that may reduce, exacerbate, or ameliorate bias that may be introduced into an identification procedure when the administrator has knowledge of the suspect's identity.

Administrator–Witness Contact

One potential exacerbating factor of investigator bias could be contact between lineup administrators and witnesses (Haw & Fisher, 2004). To examine whether reducing administrator–witness contact would similarly reduce mistaken identifications, researchers manipulated lineup presentation (sequential vs. simultaneous), administrator–witness contact (high vs. low), and perpetrator presence in the photo array (present vs. absent; Haw & Fisher, 2004). The researchers hypothesized that witnesses would make more accurate identification decisions when the administrators had restricted contact with the witness than when they had opportunities for greater contact with the witness because administrators who had with limited contact with the witness would not have an opportunity to inadvertently leak information about the suspect's identity to the witness (Haw & Fisher, 2004). Restricting contact would provide an additional method for reforming lineup procedures to reduce administrator influence on witnesses.

Witnesses watched one of several versions of a videotaped speech, which was interrupted by a man asking to borrow media equipment (Haw & Fisher, 2004). Each version of the video depicted a different person interrupting the speech. The man was visible for 20 seconds with full frontal and side views. After a short delay, the researcher informed the witnesses that they would be asked identify the man who took the equipment during the speech from a photographic lineup. One of eight experimenters with training to administer both sequential and simultaneous photo arrays presented one of several photo arrays to each witness; half the photo arrays were target present and half were target absent. The administrator who obtained the most identifications of the suspect throughout the course of the study received a monetary reward (Haw & Fisher, 2004). For every lineup, the administrator knew which lineup member was the suspect, regardless of whether the perpetrator or an innocent person was the suspect. Although administrators were not allowed to tell the witness which photo to choose, they could conduct the lineup procedure any way necessary to obtain an identification of the suspect.

At the beginning of the lineup administration, witnesses listened to tape-recorded instructions. Administrators confirmed that the witnesses understood the instructions and administered the lineup procedure. In the high administrator–witness contact condition, administrators sat across from the witness, presented the photographic lineup, and recorded the witness's identification decision and confidence. In the low administrator–witness contact condition, administrators sat out of view of the witness and watched while witnesses presented their lineups to themselves, correcting the witnesses when they presented their lineup incorrectly. Witnesses recorded their own identification decisions and confidence (Haw & Fisher, 2004).

Witnesses were significantly more likely to make an identification when administrator–witness contact was high. Specifically, witnesses in high administrator–witness contact conditions identified the suspect more often than in the low administrator–witness conditions (Haw & Fisher, 2004). However, this main effect of administrator contact was moderated by the method used to present the photo array. When presented with simultaneous target-absent photo arrays, witnesses made more false identifications when administrator–witness contact was high than when it was low. Level of administrator–witness contact did not influence false identification rates in target-absent sequential photo arrays (Haw & Fisher, 2004).

In target-present lineups, witnesses rejected the lineup more frequently when there was low administrator–witness contact than when there was high administrator–witness contact, which also suggests that administrator expectancy effects may be at play when administrator–witness contact is high (Haw & Fisher, 2004). Although this research is suggestive of administrator expectancy effects, unlike research that manipulates whether the administrator has an expectation about which lineup member is the suspect (Greathouse & Kovera, 2009; Phillips et al., 1999; Russano et al., 2006), all the administrators in this study had an expectancy about the perpetrator's identity, and what was manipulated was the opportunity that any behavioral manifestation of the administrators' expectancies had to influence the witnesses' decisions. This research provides additional evidence that administrator knowledge can bias eyewitness identification decisions and shows that limiting contact between lineup administrators and witnesses is another method for reducing the biasing effects of administrator knowledge. Moreover these results provide additional support for the conclusion that administrator knowledge is most biasing when photo arrays are presented simultaneously.

Witnesses' Motivation to Make an Identification

Another factor that may exacerbate investigator bias is the motivation of witnesses; when a witness is highly motivated to make an identification, he or she may be more susceptible to administrator influence (Greathouse & Kovera, 2009). Terror management theory provides a framework for exploring the role of witness motivation in eyewitness identification behavior (Arndt, Greenberg, Solomon, Pyszczynski, & Simon, 1997). Terror management theory posits that thoughts of one's own death (i.e., mortality salience) produce anxiety. The mortality salience hypothesis contends that there is a psychological structure acting as a protection against the anxiety that people feel when thinking of their death. Being reminded of their mortality increases people's need to believe that the world is just and increases their support of cultural worldviews, ultimately leading to a positive evaluation of individuals who support those worldviews and a negative evaluation of individuals who threaten those worldviews, including criminals (Pyszczynski, Greenberg, & Solomon, 1999).

Laboratory studies have successfully induced participants to experience a state of mortality salience and demonstrated that people are more likely to make punitive judgments when their mortality is salient (e.g., Florian & Mikulincer, 1997; Rosenblatt, Greenberg, Solomon, Pyszczynski, & Lyon, 1989). When an individual has been a victim of a violent crime, the victimization may produce death-related anxiety. Participating in an identification task provides the victim an opportunity to affirm his or her notion of justice in an attempt to reduce the death-related anxiety because identifying the perpetrator will result in the punishment of a guilty person—a person who has threatened the witness's belief in a just world (Rhead, Rodriguez, Korobeynikov, Yip, & Kovera, 2011). Thus, mortality salient witnesses may be more motivated to make a choice of a lineup member during an identification task. This motivation to make a choice from the lineup may make mortality salient witnesses more susceptible to administrator influence than non-mortality-salient witnesses because if they are uncertain about which lineup member to choose, they may look to the administrator for clues to the suspect's identity (Rhead et al., 2011).

To examine whether witness motivation might moderate the influence of administrator expectancies on witness identification accuracy, in a recent study we manipulated whether the administrator steered the witness toward a particular lineup member using behaviors exhibited by lineup administrators who know which lineup member is the suspect, perpetrator presence in a photo array (target present vs. target absent), and mortality salience (present vs. absent; Rhead et al., 2011). We hypothesized that mortality salient witnesses would be more likely to make a lineup identification of a suspect or a filler than witnesses who were not mortality salient would be. We also hypothesized that mortality salient witnesses would be more susceptible to the influence of a single-blind administrator, which would result in a larger simple main effect of administrator steering on the likelihood that the witness would identify the suspect when the witnesses were mortality salient than when they were not.

Participants viewed a videotaped crime in which a man entered an office, looked around, and stole an iPod from a backpack. The video appeared to have been captured by a surveillance camera. After the participants viewed the video, the researchers told them that they had witnessed an actual crime that was being prosecuted but that the lineup procedure that the police had used to gain an identification of the defendant was in question. Therefore, a judge asked a professor within the department to conduct an investigation on the identification procedure used. The researchers told the witnesses that a New York City detective would be administering their lineup and the results of this study would determine whether the actual eyewitness identification evidence could be used at trial. The researcher asked whether the participants would be willing to participate in an unrelated study for a graduate student in the department while they waited for the detective to arrive. If they agreed, the participants participated in a standard mortality salience induction procedure to induce a mortality salient state or a state of comparable anxiety (Pyszczynski et al., 1999). Specifically, witnesses wrote a detailed story describing what would happen to them physically and emotionally when they die (mortality salient) or wrote a detailed story describing their physical and emotional reactions to dental pain (control).

After completing a measure of experienced positive and negative emotions (the PANAS–X; Watson & Clark, 1994) and the word-stem completion task measuring the accessibility of death thoughts (Pyszczynski et al., 1999), participants were brought into a room where the lineup administrator was waiting. One of two trained experimenters presented a simultaneous lineup to the participants, steering the participants toward the suspect for half of the arrays administered. To standardize the steering, administrators followed a script when steering the witnesses to make a suspect identification; the script instructed the administrators to run through a series of behaviors that previous research showed single-blind administrators used when administering lineups (e.g., if witnesses identify someone other than the suspect, ask them if they are sure and to look again). Administrators conducted the lineup and recorded the identification decision and witness confidence. All administrations were videotaped. On completion of the lineup, witnesses completed postidentification forms assessing their perceptions of lineup procedure fairness and administrator bias.

Although our mortality salience induction was successful, with participants in the mortality salience condition providing more death-related words on the word-stem completion task than did control participants, identifications of the suspect did not vary as a function of mortality salience. However, administrator steering did influence witness accuracy. When the administrator did not steer the witness, there was no difference in identification accuracy as a function of target presence. In steering conditions, however, identification accuracy was higher for target-present (61.8%) than for target-absent lineups (29.4%). These results provide support for previous findings of investigator bias but suggest that mortality salience may not differentially increase the rate of mistaken identifications due to administrator influence.

In sum, administrator knowledge of a suspect's identity appears to influence the rate at which witnesses identify the suspect irrespective of whether the suspect is the perpetrator. Although early research suggested that administrator influence would be strongest when the lineup members are presented sequentially (Phillips et al., 1999), theory and more recent research supports the hypothesis that administrator influence will be greatest in simultaneous lineups (Greathouse & Kovera, 2009; Haw & Fisher, 2004). Similarly, biased instructions, which decrease witnesses' criterion for choosing as simultaneous lineups do, also increase the influence of administrator expectancies (Greathouse & Kovera, 2009). The current data do not support the operation of other theoretically derived moderators like mortality salience (Rhead et al., 2011). Despite the extensive research on experimenter expectancy effects in other settings (e.g., education), the investigation of the operation of administrator expectancy effects on eyewitness tasks is in its infancy, and there are many more moderators of the effect that could be tested to establish the robustness of the phenomenon in this context.

Despite the problems associated with single-blind lineup administration, mock jurors do not assign double- and single-blind lineups differential probative values in criminal cases (Wright, Carlucci, Evans, & Compo, 2010). Across a series of four studies, mock jurors read synopses and rendered verdicts in mock criminal cases that described lineup procedures that were either single-blind or double-blind, and the experimenters also varied whether the witness made a suspect or filler identification or a nonidentification. Across all four studies, participants consistently interpreted eyewitness evidence similarly, regardless of whether the lineups were reported to have been single-blind or double-blind. Small verdict differences arose as a function of lineup administration method only when the experimenters used a within-participants design or heavy-handed manipulations. Thus, legal decision makers must receive explicit instructions that single-blind lineups are less reliable than double-blind lineups; otherwise jurors are likely to assign the two methods similar probative value.

Limitations of the Double-Blind Lineup Reform

Despite evidence that double-blind lineup administration reduces the frequency of false identifications of innocent suspects (e.g., Greathouse & Kovera, 2009; Haw & Fisher, 2004; Phillips et al., 1999), the presence of certain conditions, such as when a lineup administrator is asked to administer a lineup more than once, may still introduce bias in double-blind lineups. In one study, suspect-blind participant administrators presented confederate witnesses with target-absent photo arrays (Douglass, Smith, & Fraser-Thill, 2005). The confederate witnesses identified a photo from the array with either high or low confidence. Following the administration of the lineup with the confederate witness, administrators presented the same target-absent photo array to an actual participant witness who had watched a videotaped crime. When the confederate witness had reported low confidence in his or her identification to the administrator, actual participant witnesses were more likely to pick the same photo in the second photo array than were witnesses paired with an administrator who had previously administered to a confederate witness who made a highly confident identification. Administrators in the low-confidence condition may have believed that the identification task was more difficult than administrators in the high-confidence condition, leading administrators in the low-confidence condition to provide cues to assist the witness. The experimenters did not collect any evidence to support the interpretation that administrators' perceptions of task difficulty affected the number of cues they emitted, but this study nevertheless suggests that double-blind administrators should not conduct multiple lineups in the same investigation.

Lineup administrators may also introduce bias in a double-blind administration after providing unbiased lineup instructions. In another study, lineup administrators who were blind to the suspect's identity remained silent during the lineup administration (no influence control), prompted witnesses to "take your time" and "look at each photograph carefully" (subtle influence condition), or prompted witnesses to consider the person from the lineup that looked most similar to the perpetrator (similarity influence condition; Clark et al., 2009). Witnesses viewed both target-absent and target-present lineups, and all witnesses received standard unbiased instructions. In spite of being blind to the identity and position of the suspect, administrators elicited more designated innocent suspect identifications in the subtle influence condition than in the no influence control condition without any relative increase in correct identifications of the *guilty* suspect. Furthermore, administrators in the similarity influence condition elicited more identifications of the most commonly picked foil than administrators in the control condition, a result the authors suggested would be analogous to the worst-case scenario in which the innocent suspect is the most commonly picked lineup member (i.e. unfair lineup composition). Despite uncertainty regarding how to interpret the cognitive mechanisms underlying shifts in choosing rates across experimental conditions (specifically the subtle influence condition), this study unambiguously indicates that suspect-blind administrators can still bias lineup administration through simple communication with the witness. Further, unbiased instructions do not appear to eliminate administrator influence, suggesting that minimal interaction with the witness is the only surefire way to prevent administrator bias.

FUTURE DIRECTIONS

Despite mounting evidence that administrator expectancy effects operate in the eyewitness context and evidence of the ability of double-blind lineup administration to reduce the effects, many jurisdictions continue to resist the adoption of this particular lineup reform. Thus, continued research is needed to determine when administrator expectancy effects are most likely to operate and double-blind lineup administration is most needed. We are conducting a series of three studies to examine the effects of a number of variables that may moderate the influence of administrator expectancy on eyewitness identification accuracy. In each study, only target-absent lineups are used. We are first examining whether system variables that are thought to lower a witness's criterion for picking somebody from a lineup increase the effects of administrator expectancy. As suggested by previous research (Greathouse & Kovera, 2009), we expect that biased instructions (versus unbiased) and simultaneous lineups (versus sequential) will increase the likelihood that single-blind administrators will elicit innocent suspect identifications from mock witnesses. Additionally, we are testing whether *change-of-appearance* instructions indicating that the perpetrator may now look different in some respect (U.S. Department of Justice, Office of Justice Programs, National Institute of Justice, 1999) may also increase the likelihood that single-blind administrators will elicit innocent suspect identifications from mock witnesses. Change-of-appearance instructions appear to lower the criterion for picking in the same way as biased instructions, so we expect single-blind administrators to elicit more innocent suspect identifications when using these instructions (Charman & Wells, 2007).

Additionally, one study directly manipulates witness motivation as a moderator of administrator expectancy effects. Individual witnesses might be internally motivated to either pick the correct person from the lineup (i.e. the suspect) or to avoid picking the wrong person, but no research to date has directly manipulated these motivations; all studies to date have manipulated witness motivation indirectly (e.g. using biased instructions). Using monetary incentives, we are manipulating witness motivation to correctly identify the suspect or correctly reject the lineup. We expect that single-blind administration will elicit more innocent suspect identifications when witnesses are motivated to pick the suspect, but single-blind administration should produce less of an effect on innocent suspect identifications when witnesses are motivated to correctly reject the lineup.

The final study also measures the magnitude of the effect on the basis of the participant administrator sample—students versus police officers. Most studies use students to play the role of the lineup administrator (Greathouse & Kovera, 2009; Haw & Fisher, 2004; Phillips et al., 1999). The assumption underlying these studies is that experimenter expectancies will affect the behavior of police officers in the same way that they affect the behavior of student administrators. However, police officers may develop skills over time, rendering them more successful at obtaining witness identifications of suspects during lineup administration (Russano et al., 2006). Thus, in one study we are examining the impact of administrator knowledge and sample (student vs. police officer) to see whether we are underestimating the effects of investigator knowledge with student samples.

Along with the previous criterion related variables, we are testing whether suspect–perpetrator similarity moderates administrator expectancy effects. The dominant model for eyewitness decision making (Clark's, 2003, WITNESS model) asserts that witnesses will always pick the lineup member who best matches the perpetrator's appearance, assuming that (a) the match exceeds the witness's criterion for rejection and (b) there is an adequate difference between the chosen lineup member and the next best match to the perpetrator. However, an innocent suspect in a lineup may not be the best match to the perpetrator. In these cases administrator expectancy might work against the basic assumption that witnesses will always choose the best match. Thus, we are manipulating suspect–perpetrator similarity in our current research to test whether single-blind administration is more detrimental to innocent suspects who are not the best match to the perpetrator because the WITNESS model suggests that single-blind administration should not have much influence when suspects are the best match to the perpetrator. In cases of high suspect–perpetrator similarity, single-blind administration should simply reinforce the suspect identifications that a witness is already likely to make, whereas in cases of low suspect–perpetrator similarity, single-blind administrators may shift a witness's attention to the less similar suspect and lead the witness to pick that suspect.

Finally, we are examining witness memory as a possible moderator of administrator expectancy. Using manipulations of both retention interval (time between crime and lineup) and exposure duration (time viewing perpetrator's face), we are exploring whether the strength of a witness's memory determines the relative influence of single-blind administration on picking the innocent suspect. We expect that witnesses with a weaker memory for the perpetrator will be more likely to turn to the administrator for cues, leading to more innocent suspect identifications in single-blind lineups. Witnesses with stronger memories for the perpetrator should make fewer innocent suspect identifications in single-blind lineups because they will more easily recognize that the perpetrator is absent.

These ongoing studies aim to clearly identify moderators of administrator expectancy effects observed in previous studies. Additionally, we are exploring new variables (suspect–perpetrator similarity and witness memory) that may determine the viability of administrators' cues during single-blind lineups. Our ultimate goal with the current research is to create a more complete theoretical model of witness decision making that includes administrator expectancy as a key variable because no model to date has done so. However, these studies are not exhaustive. We are not manipulating other variables that are known or suspected to affect the accuracy of eyewitness identification decisions such as cross-race identifications or clothing bias, and future research should continue to explore other moderators of investigator knowledge.

CONCLUSION

Since 1907, when Oskar Pfungst (1911/1965) launched his formal investigation into the purported abilities of Clever Hans, people have been aware that experimenter expectancies can have a profound effect on both human and animal behavior. The existing research regarding the effects of administrator knowledge on witness decision making generally demonstrates that when lineup administrators are made aware of a suspect's identity, they may intentionally or unintentionally influence witness identifications and subsequent decisions (e.g. Greathouse & Kovera, 2009; Haw & Fisher, 2004; Phillips et al., 1999). In target-absent lineups, the presence of administrator knowledge increases the rate of mistaken eyewitness identifications. In target-present lineups, we observe an increase in the rate of correct suspect identifications, but this increase is a function of administrator influence, not more accurate witnesses. Police cannot guarantee that the perpetrator is present in the lineup; after all, the purpose of the lineup is to test the hypothesis that the suspect is the perpetrator. Further, identifications based on the presence of cues emitted by the administrator reduce the value of any identification.

Until the use of double-blind lineups is mandated, courts should take extra precautions to educate jurors about the issues surrounding expectancy effects, administrator knowledge, and eyewitness decisions. Jurors are simply unaware of how administrator knowledge affects the validity of eyewitness identifications (Wright et al., 2010). Although expert testimony and judicial instructions may be able to educate jurors about the effects of administrator knowledge, research must continue to examine the effectiveness of these educational methods. In addition, because the existing research does not always demonstrate a robust effect of administrator knowledge, researchers should continue to clarify the variables that may moderate the influence of administrator expectancy on eyewitness identification accuracy (Russano et al., 2006).

Keeping lineup administrators blind to the suspect's identity during the identification procedure is one solution to maintaining the validity of eyewitness identifications. However, even double-blind lineups will not protect from administrator influence when lineup administrators administer the same lineup more than once. Research show that when the initial witnesses expresses low confidence in the identification, administrators engage in more steering behaviors to assist the witness with the identification procedure than when witnesses express high confidence in their identification (Douglass et al., 2005). In situations such as this, perhaps other feasible solutions to double-blind lineups exist. For example, computer administered lineups would reduce contact between the investigator and the witness and may be a sustainable solution when finding a blind lineup administrator is not. Alternatively, if a nonblind procedure must occur, perhaps videotaping the lineup may help judges, attorneys, and jurors determine whether bias was present during the administration (Russano et al., 2006; Wells et al., 1998).

Double-blind lineup administration will likely become a core component of valid lineup administration. As noted, some, but not nearly enough, police stations already embrace this recommendation because the benefits of reducing future mistaken eyewitness identifications seem to outweigh any costs associated with the reform. In light of New Jersey's recent State Supreme Court case, *State of New Jersey v. Henderson* (2011), however, many states may adopt policies that follow from the extensive psychological research on lineup reforms. Although double-blind lineup administration may be one safeguard to reduce the frequency of false identifications for innocent suspects, additional eyewitness reform is needed. Double-blind lineup administration is merely one safeguard on which to build a foundation for proper police procedures (see also Chapters 3, 4, and 5, this volume for other recommendations).

REFERENCES

Arndt, J., Greenberg, J., Solomon, S., Pyszczynski, T., & Simon, L. (1997). Suppression, accessibility of death-related thoughts, and cultural worldview defense: Exploring the psychodynamics of terror management. *Journal of Personality and Social Psychology, 73,* 5–18. doi:10.1037/0022-3514.73.1.5

Blanck, P. D., Rosenthal, R., & Cordell, L. H. (1985). The appearance of justice: Judges' verbal and nonverbal behavior in criminal trials. *Stanford Law Review, 38,* 89–164. doi:10.2307/1228603

Charman, S. D., & Wells, G. L. (2007). Eyewitness lineups: Is the appearance change instruction a good idea? *Law and Human Behavior, 31,* 3–22. doi:10.1007/s10979-006-9006-3

Clark, S. E. (2003). A memory and decision model for eyewitness identification. *Applied Cognitive Psychology, 17,* 629–654. doi:10.1002/acp.891

Clark, S. E., Marshall, T. E., & Rosenthal, R. (2009). Lineup administrator influences on eyewitness identification decisions. *Journal of Experimental Psychology: Applied, 15*, 63–75. doi:10.1037/a0015185

Douglass, A. B., Smith, C., & Fraser-Thill, R. (2005). A problem with double-blind photospread procedures: Photospread administrators use one eyewitness's confidence to influence the identification of another eyewitness. *Law and Human Behavior, 29*, 543–562. doi:10.1007/s10979-005-6830-9

Florian, V., & Mikulincer, M. (1997). Fear of death and the judgment of social transgressions: A multidimensional test of terror management theory. *Journal of Personality and Social Psychology, 73*, 369–380. doi:10.1037/0022-3514.73.2.369

Greathouse, S. M., & Kovera, M. (2009). Instruction bias and lineup presentation moderate the effects of administrator knowledge on eyewitness identification. *Law and Human Behavior, 33*, 70–82. doi:10.1007/s10979-008-9136-x

Halverson, A. M., Hallahan, M., Hart, A. J., & Rosenthal, R. (1997). Reducing the biasing effects of judges' nonverbal behavior with simplified jury instruction. *Journal of Applied Psychology, 82*, 590–598. doi:10.1037/0021-9010.82.4.590

Hart, A. J. (1995). Naturally occurring expectation effects. *Journal of Personality and Social Psychology, 68*, 109–115. doi:10.1037/0022-3514.68.1.109

Haw, R. M., & Fisher, R. P. (2004). Effects of administrator–witness contact on eyewitness identification accuracy. *Journal of Applied Psychology, 89*, 1106–1112. doi:10.1037/0021-9010.89.6.1106

Manson v. Brathwaite, 432 U.S. 98 (1977).

Mecklenburg, S. (2006). *Addendum to the report to the legislature of the state of Illinois: The Illinois pilot program on sequential double-blind identification procedures.* Retrieved from http://eyewitness.utep.edu/Documents/IllinoisPilotStudyOnEyewitness IDAddendum.pdf

Pfungst, O. (1965). *Clever Hans* (C. L. Rahn, Trans.). New York, NY: Holt, Rinehart & Winston. (Original work published 1911)

Phillips, M. R., McAuliff, B. D., Kovera, M., & Cutler, B. L. (1999). Double-blind photoarray administration as a safeguard against investigator bias. *Journal of Applied Psychology, 84*, 940–951. doi:10.1037/0021-9010.84.6.940

Pyszczynski, T., Greenberg, J., & Solomon, S. (1999). A dual-process model of defense against conscious and unconscious death-related thoughts: An extension of terror management theory. *Psychological Review, 106*, 835–845. doi:10.1037/0033-295X.106.4.835

Rhead, L. M., Rodriguez, D. N., Korobeynikov, V., Yip, J. H., & Kovera, M. B. (2011, June). *The effects of administrator influence and mortality salience on witness identification accuracy.* Poster session presented at the meeting of the Society of Applied Research in Memory and Cognition, New York, NY.

Rosenblatt, A., Greenberg, J., Solomon, S., Pyszczynski, T., & Lyon, D. (1989). Evidence for terror management theory: I. The effects of mortality salience on reactions to those who violate or uphold cultural values. *Journal of Personality and Social Psychology, 57,* 681–690. doi:10.1037/0022-3514.57.4.681

Rosenthal, R. (1976). *Experimenter effects in behavioral research* (Rev. ed.). New York, NY: Appleton-Century-Crofts.

Rosenthal, R. (2002). Covert communication in classrooms, clinics, courtrooms, and cubicles. *American Psychologist, 57,* 839–849. doi:10.1037/0003-066X.57.11.839

Rosenthal, R., & Fode, K. L. (1963). The effect of experimenter bias on the performance of the albino rat. *Behavioral Science, 8,* 183–189. doi:10.1002/bs.3830080302

Rosenthal, R., & Jacobson, L. (1966). Teachers' expectancies: Determinants of pupils' IQ gains. *Psychological Reports, 19,* 115–118. doi:10.2466/pr0.1966.19.1.115

Rosenthal, R., & Jacobson, L. (1992). *Pygmalion in the classroom: Teacher expectation and pupils' intellectual development* (Rev. ed.). New York, NY: Irvington.

Rosenthal, R., & Rubin, D. B. (1978). Interpersonal expectancy effects: The first 345 studies. *Behavioral and Brain Sciences, 1,* 377–415. doi:10.1017/S0140525X00075506

Russano, M. B., Dickinson, J. J., Greathouse, S. M., & Kovera, M. B. (2006). Why don't you take another look at number three: Investigator knowledge and its effects on eyewitness confidence and identification decisions. *Cardozo Public Law, Policy, and Ethics Journal, 4,* 355–379.

State of New Jersey v. Henderson, 27 A.3d 872 (N.J. 2011).

U.S. Department of Justice, Office of Justice Programs, National Institute of Justice. (1999). *Eyewitness evidence: A guide for law enforcement.* Retrieved from http://www.nij.gov/pubs-sum/178240.htm

Watson, D., & Clark, L. A. (1994). *The PANAS–X: Manual for the positive and negative affect schedule—Expanded form.* Iowa City: University of Iowa.

Wells, G. L., & Luus, C. A. E. (1990). Police lineups as experiments: Social methodology as a framework for properly conducted lineups. *Personality and Social Psychology Bulletin, 16,* 106–117. doi:10.1177/0146167290161008

Wells, G. L., Malpass, R. S., Lindsay, R. C. L., Fisher, R. P., Turtle, J. W., & Fulero, S. M. (2000). From the lab to the police station: A successful application of eyewitness research. *American Psychologist, 55,* 581–598. doi:10.1037/0003-066X.55.6.581

Wells, G. L., Small, M., Penrod, S., Malpass, R. S., Fulero, S. M., & Brimacombe, C. A. E. (1998). Eyewitness identification procedures: Recommendations for lineups and photospreads. *Law and Human Behavior, 22,* 603–647. doi:10.1023/A:1025750605807

Wright, D. B., Carlucci, M. E., Evans, J. R., & Compo, N. (2010). Turning a blind eye to double-blind lineups. *Applied Cognitive Psychology, 24,* 849–867. doi:10.1002/acp.1592

7

EYEWITNESS CERTAINTY
AS A SYSTEM VARIABLE

LAURA SMALARZ AND GARY L. WELLS

Eyewitness certainty plays a critical role in the evaluation of eyewitness identification evidence in the criminal justice system. The certainty expressed by eyewitnesses is a primary determinant of whether prosecutors proceed with prosecution, whether judges will admit the testimony into trial when faced with reliability concerns, and whether juries will ultimately judge the identification as probative evidence of guilt. Even the U.S. Supreme Court has explicitly endorsed the use of witness certainty when making determinations about the likely accuracy of a witness's identification (*Neil v. Biggers*, 1972). The justice system's heavy reliance on eyewitness certainty as a measure of the validity of identification evidence has led eyewitness scientists to devote considerable attention to studying the relation between eyewitness certainty and identification accuracy and the factors that affect the certainty–accuracy relation. A large body of psychological literature has developed that has important implications for the use of certainty as an indicator of accuracy,

DOI: 10.1037/14094-008
Reform of Eyewitness Identification Procedures, B. L. Cutler (Editor)

particularly with respect to increasing the understanding of the factors that can compromise the integrity of the certainty–accuracy relation. On the basis of this work, eyewitness researchers have recommended a number of best practices for use by law enforcement for the collection and preservation of eyewitness identification evidence. In this chapter, we review some of the key scientific findings on eyewitness certainty and discuss the importance of the recommended procedural reforms in maximizing the utility of witness certainty as an indicator of accuracy.

THE IMPORTANCE OF EYEWITNESS CERTAINTY

The first question that tends to be asked of witnesses after they make identifications is something to the effect of "Are you sure?" The certainty expressed by eyewitnesses in their identifications plays a crucial role in determining the trajectory of criminal cases. For example, in the initial stages of an investigation, a suspect identified by an uncertain witness is much less likely to be indicted than a suspect identified by a highly certain witness. During pretrial evidentiary hearings, identification testimony from an uncertain witness is unlikely to be admitted into evidence, whereas identifications from certain witnesses are rarely excluded. Finally, jurors' decisions to convict are heavily influenced by the certainty expressed by witnesses; in fact, eyewitness certainty is the primary determinant of whether a jury will accept an identification as reliable (Wells, Ferguson, & Lindsay, 1981).

The implicit trust placed by the legal system in eyewitness certainty stems from a couple of sources. First, the use of witness certainty is built directly into the legal architecture that determines which identifications should be included and which excluded from evidence at trial. In *Neil v. Biggers* (1972), the U.S. Supreme Court listed eyewitness certainty as a variable that should be considered in the evaluation of the reliability of identification evidence along with the witness's opportunity to view the assailant, the degree of attention paid by the witness, the quality of the witness's description, and the passage of time between the witnessed event and the identification. Although the certainty of the witness is only one of five factors that judges are instructed to consider, eyewitness scholars have pointed out that the courts seem to accept identification testimony that falls short on some or all of the other criteria provided that the witness is certain (Wells & Quinlivan, 2009). For example, in 1977 a man was convicted of murder on the basis of the highly certain identification testimony of a witness who was 450 feet away, which exceeds the capability of the human visual system (Loftus & Harley, 2005). And in *State of Connecticut v. Ledbetter* (1981), the court said that even a "fleeting glance" might be sufficient to infer reliability and cited the witness's high degree of certainty as justification for admitting the identification evidence. Hence, even identifications that display clear signs of unreliability are unlikely to be excluded from trial when the eyewitness expresses a high level of certainty (Wells, Greathouse, & Smalarz, 2011).

Second, in addition to the explicit focus placed by the legal system on eyewitness certainty, people are psychologically predisposed to use certainty to gauge accuracy. There is a general belief that certainty in a memory is strongly related to the accuracy of that memory (Wells, 1984; Yarmey & Jones, 1983). Therefore, people tend to assume that a certain witness is an accurate witness. Research examining laypeople's evaluations of eyewitness testimony supports this idea—people are generally willing to accept an eyewitness's testimony as long as the eyewitness appears to be certain (e.g. Cutler, Penrod, & Dexter, 1990; Fox & Walters, 1986). In jury simulation studies, mock-jurors have even been shown to overlook other predictors of accuracy when a witness expresses a high degree of certainty. For example, in one study, witnesses observed a staged crime under poor, moderate, or strong viewing conditions (i.e., witnesses had a poor, partial, or full view of the perpetrator's face, and the perpetrator was in view for 12 or 20 seconds). Witnesses were then asked to identify the perpetrator from a photo lineup and to indicate their level of certainty. The witnesses failed to give proper weight to the quality of the witnessing conditions when they rendered their certainty statements. Also, when the videotaped testimony of these witnesses was shown to mock-jurors, the mock-jurors failed to sufficiently account for the effects of witnessing condition quality on identification accuracy (Lindsay, Wells, & Rumpel, 1981). Instead, the mock-jurors were disproportionately influenced by the witnesses' expressions of certainty, leading them to overestimate the accuracy of the witnesses' identifications.

The general failure of witnesses and jurors to appropriately consider the effects of witnessing conditions on identification accuracy stems from a deeper problem involving limitations to laypeople's understanding of human memory. Although psychological science has made great strides in elucidating the workings of human memory, research suggests that many people are still unfamiliar with the factors that influence memory and, in particular, those that influence eyewitness memory. In a series of studies illustrating this, mock-jurors viewed a videotape of a criminal trial that contained varying levels of eyewitness identification evidence. Specifically, the researchers manipulated 10 different variables that have been shown to have a substantial impact on eyewitness memory (e.g., perpetrator disguise, presence of a weapon, retention interval), and the impact of each of these manipulations on jurors' verdicts and judgments of the identification testimony was measured. The results of these studies indicated a serious underutilization of virtually every other indicator of accuracy; witness certainty was the only variable that had a strong and consistent impact on jurors' perceptions of the identification evidence and their verdict decisions (Cutler et al., 1990; Cutler, Penrod, & Stuve, 1988).

To the extent that fact finders such as judges and jurors lack a full appreciation of the many factors that affect eyewitness accuracy, they naturally direct their attention toward eyewitness certainty to make inferences about the reliability of identification evidence. And, in fact, there is little other information about the witness's identification that could provide such information in real cases. For example, the amount of time spent making an identification has been found to be a reliable postdictor of accuracy in the context of scientific eyewitness experiments, but response latency data are almost never available in real-world instances of eyewitness identification. Another promising postdictor of identification accuracy is the behavior of other eyewitnesses who do not identify the suspect from a lineup. This information can be used to assess the likely accuracy of the eyewitnesses who do identify the suspect (Clark & Wells, 2008; Wells & Olson, 2002). But information regarding the behavior of other eyewitnesses is limited to instances in which there were multiple eyewitnesses to the crime and in which the defense attorney is aware of and able to present into evidence these other nonidentifications. A measure of witness certainty, on the other hand, is available every time a witness gives testimony at a pretrial hearing or at trial. As a consequence, witness certainty has become perhaps the most commonly used postdictor of identification accuracy in real-world eyewitness cases.

CAN CERTAINTY POSTDICT ACCURACY?

Much of the initial research examining eyewitness certainty suggested that certainty was unrelated to identification accuracy (e.g., Clifford & Scott, 1978; Deffenbacher, Brown, & Sturgill, 1978; Leippe, Wells, & Ostrom, 1978). In fact, this idea is still endorsed by members of the legal system who have not followed closely the development of the empirical literature. But our appreciation of the value of certainty for postdicting accuracy has grown considerably as a result in part of methodological changes in the way that researchers study eyewitness identification. During the early days of the research, the prevailing methodology for manipulating identification accuracy was to replace the photo of the culprit in the culprit-present lineup with a photo of an individual who closely resembled the culprit in the culprit-absent lineup. Studies using this methodology were characterized by low accuracy rates, which had the unintended effect of masking the certainty–accuracy correlation. Specifically, as accuracy rates approach chance levels, it becomes increasingly difficult to detect a certainty–accuracy correlation because, by definition, nothing can correlate with chance. To illustrate this idea, we offer an extreme case in which the perpetrator's photo in the culprit-present lineup is replaced with a photo of the culprit's identical twin in the culprit-absent lineup. Every identification of the identical twin from the target-absent lineup would be made with very high certainty, but it would be inaccurate. In this extreme case, accuracy would be at chance levels, and the certainty–accuracy correlation would be zero. Studies using this methodology would lead researchers to incorrectly conclude that there is no correlation between certainty and accuracy. Although none of the original studies were quite this extreme, the net effect of using the *similar-replacement* method was the same: It decreased accuracy and thus undermined the ability to detect a certainty–accuracy relation. As a result, researchers tended to report that certainty was unrelated to accuracy.

With time, however, researchers gradually recognized the limitations of the similar-replacement strategy, and they began to use other methods for selecting a replacement for the culprit in the culprit-absent lineup, such as using someone who fits the description of the culprit but who is not chosen specifically to resemble the culprit. Along with the higher accuracy rates secured by these new methods came a more optimistic view of the certainty–accuracy relation. It is now widely accepted that there is a moderate but reliable positive correlation between eyewitness certainty and identification accuracy. In a comprehensive meta-analysis including 35 simulated-crime studies, Bothwell, Deffenbacher, and Brigham (1987) found that the average certainty–accuracy correlation was $r = .25$ (with a 95% confidence interval of .08–.42). A more recent meta-analysis that combined the results of 30 empirical studies found an impressive correlation of .41 when the analysis was restricted to those who made identifications (Sporer, Penrod, Read, & Cutler, 1995). A certainty–accuracy correlation of around .40 could be rather diagnostic. For instance, if overall accuracy were around 50%, then a correlation of .40 would mean that 70% of the highly certain witnesses are accurate and only 30% of the uncertain witnesses are accurate. However, in many cases, the certainty–accuracy correlation is likely to be considerably lower than .40. As mentioned previously, a low accuracy rate resulting from replacing the culprit's photo with a photo of an innocent suspect who closely resembles the culprit stacks the deck against accuracy, consequently sabotaging the certainty–accuracy relation. Similarly, poor witnessing conditions can lead to low identification accuracy, causing the certainty–accuracy relation to suffer (Bothwell et al., 1987). In general, any variable that pushes accuracy rates closer to chance levels (e.g., poor witnessing conditions, low distinctiveness of culprit, large disparities in culprit's appearance at encoding vs. retrieval) will likely muddle the certainty–accuracy correlation in a manner similar to what was observed with the similar-replacement strategy.

Another variable that has been shown to drastically influence estimates of the certainty–accuracy relation is whether witnesses who did not make an identification (nonchoosers) are included in the analyses. Specifically, the inclusion of nonchoosers in analyses causes a drop in the certainty–accuracy correlation. We take a moment in the next section to give a closer look to research on the certainty–accuracy relation among nonchoosers.

CHOOSERS VERSUS NONCHOOSERS

The inclusion or exclusion of nonchoosers from analyses of the certainty–accuracy relation hinges on both theoretical and practical considerations. Theoretically, it can be argued that witnesses' certainty in a nonidentification is a qualitatively different variable than the certainty of witnesses who have made an identification. Practically speaking, there has been limited forensic interest in the certainty of nonchoosers because nonidentifications do not run the risk of leading to wrongful conviction. Furthermore, researchers have generally argued that the certainty–accuracy relation exists only among choosers (Sporer et al., 1995). We argue, however, that a critical examination of the literature is needed before dismissing altogether the postdictive utility of certainty statements from nonchoosers.

Much like the way in which methodological differences between earlier and later eyewitness studies led to discrepant estimates of the certainty–accuracy correlation, the apparent lack of a certainty–accuracy correlation among nonidentifying eyewitnesses might, too, be a methodological artifact. The vast majority of eyewitness studies that have measured identification accuracy and witness certainty have unknowingly introduced a conceptual confound that has important implications for estimates of the certainty–accuracy relation among nonchoosers. Specifically, the literature has failed to distinguish between two types of nonchoosers: those who do not make an identification because they are uncertain (i.e., *not-sure* witnesses) and those who do not make an identification because they are confident that the culprit is not in the lineup (i.e., *not-there* witnesses). A nonidentification from a not-sure witness might occur because the witness's memory was weak to begin with or because the identification task is too difficult (i.e., there is a high degree of similarity between the photos). Certainty is unlikely to be correlated with accuracy in these cases. On the other hand, the certainty expressed by not-there witnesses who reject the lineup outright would likely provide useful information about the absence of the culprit in the lineup. Until these two types of nonidentifying witnesses are parsed out and examined independently, the conclusion that there is no certainty–accuracy relation among nonchoosers might be a misleading one.

Although the distinction between not-sure nonchoosers and not-there nonchoosers has been largely overlooked in the literature, it is of critical importance in the real world. Witnesses in the lab are often constrained to one of two options: to make an identification or not to make an identification. However, the not-sure and not-there options are both legitimate and used categories among real-world eyewitnesses. Investigators interacting with a witness can get a sense for, if not discover overtly, whether a nonidentification has resulted from uncertainty or because the witness is confident that the perpetrator is not present in the lineup. Furthermore, determining which one of these alternatives was at play largely guides the subsequent steps of the investigation. We suggest that the explicit inclusion of both of these categories as options for real eyewitnesses might be a useful consideration for procedural reforms. In a recent experiment involving actual witnesses to serious crimes, 19% of those who made no identification from simultaneous lineups and 47% of those who made no identification from sequential lineups indicated that they were not sure rather than actually rejecting the lineup (Wells, Steblay, & Dysart, 2011). The failure of lab studies to separate these two types of nonidentifiers could be clouding the certainty–accuracy relation. After all, those whose nonidentifications were actually not-sure responses would be unlikely to show a certainty–accuracy relation. Additional lab studies are needed to determine whether a certainty–accuracy correlation exists among lineup rejecters.

CERTAINTY AS A SYSTEM VARIABLE

Specific estimates of the certainty–accuracy relation change depending on a complex set of factors, making certainty a more or less useful indicator of accuracy in any given case. For example, the strength of the certainty–accuracy relation has been shown to vary as a function of the eyewitness's level of self-awareness (Kassin, 1985), the timing of the certainty judgment (Cutler & Penrod, 1989), the physical distinctiveness of the perpetrator (Brigham, Ready, & Spier, 1990), and the extent to which the perpetrator looks the same or different from the time of the witnessed event (Read, Vokey, & Hammersley, 1990). Nevertheless, eyewitness researchers generally endorse the utility of witness certainty because under the right conditions, certainty has some diagnostic value. As research in the domain of eyewitness certainty has progressed, the focus has shifted from trying to estimate a single value of the certainty–accuracy correlation to trying to understand the conditions under which certainty is a strong indicator and under which it is a weak indicator of identification accuracy. When the conditions are right, accurate witnesses do tend to be more certain than inaccurate witnesses (Bradfield,

Wells, & Olson, 2002). Under nonoptimal conditions, however, inaccurate witnesses can display certainty levels that are as high as and sometimes even higher than the certainty displayed by witnesses who made accurate identifications. In such cases, certainty loses its utility as a reliable indicator of accuracy.

Researchers interested in applying their research to procedural reform efforts have found it useful to categorize variables that compromise the certainty–accuracy relation according to a well-known distinction in the eyewitness literature—the system-variable versus estimator-variable distinction (Wells, 1978; see also Chapter 1, this volume). According to this distinction, two types of variables exist: system variables, which are under the control of the criminal justice system, and estimator variables, which are outside of the control of the justice system, and thus, their impact on any given case can only be estimated. Estimator variables, although important, are less relevant to the issue of lineup reform because it is not possible to control these variables in the real world. For example, whether the perpetrator was wearing a hat or a disguise may lead to a weaker memory and, thus, decreased identification accuracy, without causing a corresponding drop in certainty (O'Rourke, Penrod, Cutler, & Stuve, 1989). Similarly, the degree of fear experienced by a witness can affect memory quality and the likelihood of making an accurate identification without affecting certainty (Clifford & Hollin, 1981). Although the implications of these variables for the reliability of identification evidence should not be ignored, they are of less interest to the issue of procedural reforms. On the other hand, system-variable research has critical implications for reform efforts. Any legal procedure that alters the certainty–accuracy relation is in direct conflict with the fact-finding purposes of the legal system. Therefore, research and reform efforts surrounding system variables are directed at curbing the use of procedures that have the potential to corrupt the diagnostic utility of witness certainty.

CERTAINTY MALLEABILITY

One of the most frequently studied examples of a certainty–accuracy dissociation involves what has been termed the *certainty malleability problem*. Certainty malleability refers to the idea that an eyewitness's level of certainty can be pushed around on the basis of external factors that are unrelated to identification accuracy. Although an eyewitness's level of certainty might at first glance seem like an estimator variable (because it can only be estimated in any given case), eyewitness researchers tend to think of certainty as a system variable because it can be directly manipulated by legal system players through the timing and content of statements that are provided to eyewitnesses (Wells & Seelau, 1995). The key to understanding why certainty is susceptible to influence from external factors is that a witness's certainty simply reflects a belief held by the witness that his or her identification was an accurate one. Accordingly, any information that increases that belief can be expected to inflate the witness's certainty. Take, for example, the well-known postidentification feedback effect (Wells & Bradfield, 1998, 1999). In the original postidentification feedback experiments, witnesses viewed a crime event and then made mistaken identifications from a target-absent lineup. After making an identification, some witnesses received confirming feedback from the lineup administrator ("Good, you identified the suspect"), whereas other witnesses were not given any feedback about their identification. Witnesses who received confirming feedback later reported being more certain in their identification than did witnesses who did not receive confirming feedback. In one study, fewer than 15% of eyewitnesses who had mistakenly identified someone stated that they were positive or nearly positive in their identification. However, when given a suggestive statement that appeared to confirm their identification, a full 50% of mistaken eyewitnesses recalled having been positive or nearly positive in their identification (Wells & Bradfield, 1998). Because the confirming remark did not occur until after witnesses made identifications, the remark could not have influenced how certain the witnesses were at the time of the identification. Hence, not only did the confirming feedback inflate witnesses' current level of certainty but it also distorted their recollections of how certain they recalled having been at the time they made the identification. Witnesses could no longer remember that they were uncertain at the time they made the identification; armed with confirming feedback, mistaken eyewitnesses believed that they had been certain all along.

The distorting effects of confirming feedback on witness certainty have been replicated in numerous studies, including with real eyewitnesses to serious crimes (Wright & Skagerberg, 2007). In a meta-analysis of the post-identification feedback effect, witness certainty was shown to be more vulnerable to distortion resulting from feedback than any other variable that has been studied in the postidentification feedback literature (Douglass & Steblay, 2006). And, in a recent study demonstrating the pervasive nature of feedback effects, participant-evaluators who viewed videotaped testimony of mistaken eyewitnesses rated witnesses who had received confirming feedback more favorably than they rated witnesses who did not receive confirming feedback. Evaluators were also more likely to believe that the feedback-contaminated witnesses' identifications were accurate (Douglass, Neuschatz, Imrich, & Wilkinson, 2010). Thus, feedback given at the time of the lineup identification has pervasive effects extending far beyond the personal beliefs held by the witness to the evaluations ultimately made by observers.

Although the inflating effects of feedback on witnesses' certainty are a problem in and of themselves, certainty inflation per se is not what poses the largest threat to the diagnostic utility of witnesses' certainty statements. What is more damaging to the certainty–accuracy relation is that confirming feedback leads to stronger memory distortion among witnesses who made inaccurate rather than accurate identifications (Bradfield et al., 2002). This asymmetry creates a situation in which inaccurate witnesses can end up reporting certainty levels similar to those reported by accurate witnesses. As a result, it becomes difficult to distinguish between accurate and inaccurate witnesses on the basis of their expressions of certainty; for some witnesses, high certainty might simply be a reflection of the fact that they received confirming feedback. The problem is compounded by the fact that in real cases it is very difficult to know whether witnesses received feedback after their identification. Witnesses must not only be aware of the feedback and remember having received it, they must also be willing to report it. Research suggests that witnesses are unable to report accurately on whether and how they have been affected by feedback (Wells & Bradfield, 1998). Thus, the consensus among researchers is that once a witness has been tainted by postevent suggestion, there is no way to undo the taint.

DOUBLE-BLIND ADMINISTRATION

In light of the argument that confirming feedback causes irreparable distortions to witnesses' recollections of certainty, that it leads to more pronounced inflation among inaccurate witnesses than among accurate witnesses, and that witnesses cannot effectively correct for the effects of feedback, researchers have recommended the use of double-blind lineup administration procedures as a safeguard to protect against feedback-induced certainty inflation (see Chapter 6, this volume). A *double-blind lineup procedure* is one in which the administrator of the lineup does not know which member of the lineup is the suspect and which members are fillers (Wells, 1988). In contrast, the nonblind procedure that is used in the vast majority of law enforcement agencies is one in which the lineup administrator (usually the case detective) knows the identity of the suspect. When the administering officer is aware of which individual in the lineup is under investigation, postidentification influence is likely to occur. Not only would it be difficult for an officer who is invested in the case to resist affirming a witness's positive identification of the suspect but also witnesses themselves are disposed to the natural human tendency to look to others to assess their performance (Festinger, 1954). This is especially true if the eyewitness believes that the lineup administrator knows which lineup member is the suspect and which members are fillers, which would always be the case for a nonblind lineup procedure. For this reason, the double-blind recommendation also states that the witness should be explicitly informed that the person administering the lineup does not know the identity of the suspect. In this way, the certainty expressed by the witness will be based on the eyewitness's memory, not on the lineup administrator's expectations or on confirming feedback delivered after the identification.

With the exception of jurisdictions that have made procedural reforms, such as New Jersey, North Carolina, Connecticut, Ohio, and major cities like Boston, Dallas, and Denver, law enforcement agencies continue administering nonblind lineups despite the large body of research showing the destructive effects of using nonblind procedures (see Conclusion, this volume, for a review of identification test reforms). At best, agencies that have not implemented reforms might simply instruct their nonblind administrators to avoid influencing witnesses and to refrain from telling witnesses whether they identified the suspect. Although this recommendation stems from the legitimate goal of preventing administrator influence, psychological science has shown that people can inadvertently influence the behavior of others. In many psychological domains, it has been shown that testers influence the behavior of people they are testing in ways that are consistent with the tester's expectations and beliefs (e.g., see the meta-analysis by Harris & Rosenthal, 1985). Likewise, the body language, tone of voice, and verbal or nonverbal behavior of lineup administrators can influence witnesses in subtle yet powerful ways. A study by Garrioch and Brimacombe (2001) illustrated this phenomenon. Mistaken eyewitnesses were asked about their certainty by a lineup administrator who had either been led to believe that the witness had identified the suspect or a filler. In reality, the witnesses' identifications were always inaccurate because the lineup did not contain the culprit. It was found that the certainty statements obtained by administrators who believed that the witness had identified a suspect were much higher than the certainty statements obtained by administrators who believed that the witness had identified a filler. The power of lineup administrators' beliefs to inadvertently influence witnesses' certainty reports underscores the need for double-blind lineup administration.

RECORDING THE CERTAINTY STATEMENT

Although double-blind lineup administration eliminates issues of inadvertent suggestion and confirming feedback that occur at the time of the lineup procedure, a number of other variables have been shown to have similar inflating effects on witness certainty even in the absence of administrator suggestion. For example, one study found that repeatedly questioning eye-witnesses caused witnesses to become more certain in the accuracy of their memories (Shaw, 1996). A similar result was observed in a study in which witnesses were instructed to prepare for cross-examination. Witnesses who were warned that they were going to be cross-examined subsequently gave much more confident testimony about their identification during the cross-examination than did witnesses who were not given such a warning (Wells et al., 1981). Even instructing witnesses to think privately about their certainty has been shown to induce false certainty among eyewitnesses (Wells & Bradfield, 1999). Witnesses are also likely to make inferences based on events that follow the identification procedure. For example, if charges are brought against the identified person, the witness might infer that his or her identification was accurate. In one study, witnesses who learned that a cowitness identified the same person were subsequently more certain in their identification even though their identifications were mistaken (Luus & Wells, 1994).

Thus, even in the absence of confirming feedback administered on the part of the lineup administrator, witnesses can become increasingly certain in their identifications. For this reason, researchers have recommended that a certainty statement be secured immediately after the witness makes an identification, before external influences can influence the witness's level of certainty. In this way, even if the witness's certainty becomes inflated over time, a certainty statement recorded at the time of the identification provides prosecutors, judges, and jurors with an untainted indicator of the witness's identification-time certainty. On the contrary, a certainty statement given for the first time on the witness stand at trial might reflect any number of factors that are unrelated to the quality of the witness's memory.

LINEUP FAIRNESS AND UNBIASED INSTRUCTIONS

A number of other system variables under the control of the legal system have been shown to manufacture false eyewitness certainty. *Biased lineups*—lineups in which the suspect stands out or in which the suspect is the only one who matches the witness's description of the perpetrator—lead witnesses to make suspect identifications with greater certainty regardless of whether the suspect is guilty (Wells, Rydell, & Seelau, 1993; see also Chapter 4, this volume, for a review of the importance of fillers and filler selection strategies). A recent series of experiments by Charman, Wells, and Joy (2011) showed that putting "duds" in a lineup (i.e., fillers who fail to meet the description of the perpetrator and are never chosen) inflates witnesses' certainty in identifying an innocent person who fits the description of the perpetrator. It is therefore critical that police create fair, unbiased lineups in which all of the lineup fillers match the witness's description of the culprit (see Chapter 4, this volume, for more comparisons of filler selection strategies).

Witnesses should also be informed that the lineup might not contain the actual culprit. Recent research shows that this instruction, called the *pre-lineup admonition*, protects against certainty inflation and decreases the likelihood that witnesses make mistaken identifications (Charman, Schwartz, & Carol, 2011; see also Chapter 3, this volume). Only under conditions that adhere to these procedural recommendations should certainty be used as a postdictor of accuracy in the evaluation of identification evidence.

WHEN TO TRUST CERTAINTY

Some readers might find their heads swimming from the foregoing and conclude that there is no utility at all to eyewitness identification certainty. But that is not the message of this chapter. Instead, the message is that many variables can influence eyewitness identification certainty (e.g., postidentification feedback, poor lineup fillers), and these kinds of variables are prevalent in actual cases. But when these contaminants are controlled and the conditions are more pristine (e.g., good witnessing conditions, good fillers, absence of feedback), the certainty of the witness can be highly informative for police investigators, judges, and juries.

IMPLICATIONS AND CONCLUSION

Despite the limits of eyewitness certainty, it remains true that there is value in knowing how certain a witness is about his or her identification. Eyewitness certainty will always play a role in the court's and in jurors' evaluations of identification evidence. For this reason, procedural reform recommendations come at a critical time. Mistaken eyewitness identification is the leading cause of the conviction of innocent people, accounting for more cases of wrongful conviction than all other causes combined (http://www.innocenceproject.org). But scholars have made the argument that mistaken identification per se is not what poses the risk of wrongful conviction (e.g., Wells, Memon, & Penrod, 2006). A mistaken identification from an uncertain witness is unlikely to lead to conviction. On the other hand, a mistaken identification from a highly certain witness is persuasive to judges and jurors.

In every one of the exoneration cases uncovered through DNA testing, the witnesses were mistaken but positive. Through psychological research, psychologists now have a better understanding of how this can happen. The source of the problem lies in the fact that eyewitness certainty is susceptible to influence from external factors that are unrelated to accuracy. Some of those factors are outside of the control of the legal system (e.g., individual differences in which some people are naturally more certain about everything, coincidental resemblance that drives up certainty but not accuracy), but some of them are system variables that can be controlled. Procedural reforms such as using good lineup fillers (see Chapter 4, this volume) and assessing certainty at the time of the identification under double-blind conditions (see Chapter 6) can help preserve the diagnostic utility of eyewitness certainty. The failure to implement such procedural safeguards is a complacency that comes with unconscionable costs: the endorsement of more miscarriages of justice in the form of wrongful convictions based on the testimony of highly certain, but mistaken, eyewitnesses.

REFERENCES

Bothwell, R. K., Deffenbacher, K. A., & Brigham, J. C. (1987). Correlation of eyewitness accuracy and certainty: Optimality hypothesis revisited. *Journal of Applied Psychology, 72*, 691–695. doi:10.1037/0021-9010.72.4.691

Bradfield, A. L., Wells, G. L., & Olson, E. A. (2002). The damaging effect of confirming feedback on the relation between eyewitness certainty and identification accuracy. *Journal of Applied Psychology, 87*, 112–120. doi:10.1037/0021-9010.87.1.112

Brigham, J. C., Ready, D. J., & Spier, S. A. (1990). Standards for evaluating the fairness of photograph lineups. *Basic and Applied Social Psychology, 11*, 149–163. doi:10.1207/s15324834basp1102_3

Charman, S. D., Schwartz, S., & Carol, R. (2011, June). *The effect of biased lineup instructions on identification confidence.* Paper presented at the meeting of the Society for Applied Research in Memory and Cognition, New York, NY.

Charman, S. D., Wells, G. L., & Joy, S. (2011). The dud effect: Adding highly dissimilar fillers increases certainty in lineup identifications. *Law and Human Behavior, 35*, 479–500. doi:10.1007/s10979-010-9261-1

Clark, S. E., & Wells, G. L. (2008). On the diagnosticity of multiple-witness identifications. *Law and Human Behavior, 32*, 406–422. doi:10.1007/s10979-007-9115-7

Clifford, B. R., & Hollin, C. R. (1981). Effects of the type of incident and the number of perpetrators on eyewitness memory. *Journal of Applied Psychology, 66*, 364–370. doi:10.1037/0021-9010.66.3.364

Clifford, B. R., & Scott, J. (1978). Individual and situational factors in eyewitness testimony. *Journal of Applied Psychology, 63*, 352–359. doi:10.1037/0021-9010.63.3.352

Cutler, B. L., & Penrod, S. D. (1989). Forensically relevant moderators of the relation between eyewitness identification accuracy and certainty. *Journal of Applied Psychology, 74*, 650–652. doi:10.1037/0021-9010.74.4.650

Cutler, B. L., Penrod, S. D., & Dexter, H. R. (1990). Juror sensitivity to eyewitness identification evidence. *Law and Human Behavior, 14,* 185–191. doi:10.1007/BF01062972

Cutler, B. L., Penrod, S. D., & Stuve, T. E. (1988). Juror decision-making in eyewitness identification cases. *Law and Human Behavior, 12,* 41–55. doi:10.1007/BF01064273

Deffenbacher, K. A., Brown, E. L., & Sturgill, W. (1978). Some predictors of eyewitness memory accuracy. In M. M. Gruneberg, P. E. Morris, & R. N. Sykes (Eds.), *Practical aspects of memory* (pp. 219–226). London, England: Academic Press.

Douglass, A. B., Neuschatz, J. S., Imrich, J., & Wilkinson, M. (2010). Does post-identification feedback affect evaluations of eyewitness testimony and identification procedures? *Law and Human Behavior, 34,* 282–294. doi:10.1007/s10979-009-9189-5

Douglass, A. B., & Steblay, N. (2006). Memory distortion in eyewitnesses: A meta-analysis of the post-identification feedback effect. *Applied Cognitive Psychology, 20,* 859–869. doi:10.1002/acp.1237

Festinger, L. (1954). A theory of social comparison. *Human Relations, 7,* 117–140. doi:10.1177/001872675400700202

Fox, S. G., & Walters, H. A. (1986). The impact of general versus specific expert testimony and eyewitness certainty upon mock juror judgment. *Law and Human Behavior, 10,* 215–228. doi:10.1007/BF01046211

Garrioch, L., & Brimacombe, C. A. E. (2001). Lineup administrators' expectations: Their impact on eyewitness certainty. *Law and Human Behavior, 25,* 299–315. doi:10.1023/A:1010750028643

Harris, M. J., & Rosenthal, R. (1985). Mediation of interpersonal expectancy effects: 31 meta-analyses. *Psychological Bulletin, 97,* 363–386. doi:10.1037/0033-2909.97.3.363

Kassin, S. M. (1985). Eyewitness identification: Retrospective self-awareness and the accuracy-certainty correlation. *Journal of Personality and Social Psychology, 49,* 878–893. doi:10.1037/0022-3514.49.4.878

Leippe, M. R., Wells, G. L., & Ostrom, T. M. (1978). Crime seriousness as a determinant of accuracy in eyewitness identification. *Journal of Applied Psychology, 63,* 345–351. doi:10.1037/0021-9010.63.3.345

Lindsay, R. C. L., Wells, G. L., & Rumpel, C. (1981). Can people detect eyewitness identification accuracy within and across situations? *Journal of Applied Psychology, 66,* 79–89. doi:10.1037/0021-9010.66.1.79

Loftus, G. R., & Harley, E. M. (2005). Why is it easier to identify someone close than far away? *Psychonomic Bulletin & Review, 12,* 43–65. doi:10.3758/BF03196348

Luus, C. A. E., & Wells, G. L. (1994). The malleability of eyewitness certainty: Co-witness and perseverance effects. *Journal of Applied Psychology, 79,* 714–723. doi:10.1037/0021-9010.79.5.714

Neil v. Biggers, 409 U.S. 188 (1972).

O'Rourke, T. E., Penrod, S. D., Cutler, B. L., & Stuve, T. E. (1989). The external validity of eyewitness identification research: Generalizing across subject populations. *Law and Human Behavior, 13*, 385–395. doi:10.1007/BF01056410

Read, J. D., Vokey, J. R., & Hammersley, R. (1990). Changing photos of faces: Effects of exposure duration and photo similarity on recognition and the accuracy-certainty relationship. *Journal of Experimental Psychology: Learning, Memory, and Cognition, 16*, 870–882. doi:10.1037/0278-7393.16.5.870

Shaw, J. S., III. (1996). Increases in eyewitness certainty resulting from postevent questioning. *Journal of Experimental Psychology: Applied, 2*, 126–146. doi:10.1037/1076-898X.2.2.126

Sporer, S., Penrod, S., Read, D., & Cutler, B. L. (1995). Choosing, certainty, and accuracy: A meta-analysis of the certainty–accuracy relation in eyewitness identification studies. *Psychological Bulletin, 118*, 315–327. doi:10.1037/0033-2909.118.3.315

State of Connecticut v. Ledbetter, 441, A.2d 595 (Conn. 1981)

Wells, G. L. (1978). Applied eyewitness testimony research: System variables and estimator variables. *Journal of Personality and Social Psychology, 36*, 1546–1557. doi:10.1037/0022-3514.36.12.1546

Wells, G. L. (1984). How adequate is human intuition for judging eyewitness testimony? In G. L. Wells & E. F. Loftus (Eds.), *Eyewitness testimony: Psychological perspectives* (pp. 256–272). New York, NY: Cambridge University Press.

Wells, G. L. (1988). *Eyewitness identification: A system handbook.* Toronto, Ontario, Canada: Carswell Legal.

Wells, G. L., & Bradfield, A. L. (1998). "Good, you identified the suspect:" Feedback to eyewitnesses distorts their reports of the witnessing experience. *Journal of Applied Psychology, 83*, 360–376. doi:10.1037/0021-9010.83.3.360

Wells, G. L., & Bradfield, A. L. (1999). Distortions in eyewitnesses' recollections: Can the post-identification feedback effect be moderated? *Psychological Science, 10*, 138–144. doi:10.1111/1467-9280.00121

Wells, G. L., Ferguson, T. J., & Lindsay, R. C. L. (1981). The tractability of eyewitness certainty and its implication for triers of fact. *Journal of Applied Psychology, 66*, 688–696. doi:10.1037/0021-9010.66.6.688

Wells, G. L., Greathouse, S. M., & Smalarz, L. (2011). Why do motions to suppress suggestive eyewitness identifications fail? In B. L. Cutler (Ed.), *Conviction of the innocent: Lessons from psychological research* (pp. 167–184). Washington, DC: American Psychological Association. doi:10.1037/13085-008

Wells, G. L., Memon, A., & Penrod, S. (2006). Eyewitness evidence: Improving its probative value. *Psychological Science in the Public Interest, 7*, 45–75.

Wells, G. L., & Olson, E. A. (2002). Eyewitness identification: Information gain from incriminating and exonerating behaviors. *Journal of Experimental Psychology: Applied, 8*, 155–167.

Wells, G. L., Olson, E. A., & Charman, S. D. (2002). The certainty of eyewitnesses in their identifications from lineups. *Current Directions in Psychological Science*, *11*, 151–154.

Wells, G. L., & Quinlivan, D. S. (2009). Suggestive eyewitness identification procedures and the Supreme Court's reliability test in light of eyewitness science: 30 years later. *Law and Human Behavior*, *33*, 1–24. doi:10.1007/s10979-008-9130-3

Wells, G. L., Rydell, S. M., & Seelau, E. P. (1993). On the selection of distractors for eyewitness lineups. *Journal of Applied Psychology*, *78*, 835–844. doi:10.1037/0021-9010.78.5.835

Wells, G. L., & Seelau, E. P. (1995). Eyewitness identification: Psychological research and legal policy on lineups. *Psychology, Public Policy, and Law*, *1*, 765–791. doi:10.1037/1076-8971.1.4.765

Wells, G. L., Steblay, N. K. & Dysart, J. E. (2011). *A test of the simultaneous vs. sequential lineup methods: An initial report of the AJS national eyewitness identification field studies*. Unpublished manuscript, American Judicature Society. Retrieved from http://www.ajs.org/wc/pdfs/EWID_PrintFriendly.pdf

Wright, D. B., & Skagerberg, E. M. (2007). Post-identification feedback affects real eyewitnesses. *Psychological Science*, *18*, 172–178. doi:10.1111/j.1467-9280.2007.01868.x

Yarmey, A. D., & Jones, H. P. T. (1983). Is eyewitness identification a matter of common sense? In Lloyd-Bostock & B. R. Clifford (Eds.), *Evaluating witness evidence* (pp. 13–40). New York, NY: Wiley.

8

FIELD STUDIES OF EYEWITNESS MEMORY

DANIEL B. WRIGHT, AMINA MEMON, GARY DALTON, REBECCA MILNE, AND RUTH HORRY

Laboratory studies of eyewitness memory have been vital for understanding the causal mechanisms at play in situations in which eyewitnesses might find themselves. Much of this book describes such laboratory research. Although this research is valuable, laboratory research has difficulty answering this simple question: How good are eyewitnesses? This question is difficult to answer with any method but can be approached using data from actual cases. These are often called *field studies*. The purpose of this chapter is to discuss the differences between laboratory and field research and to examine different types of field research.

It is difficult to come up with a definition of a *field study* that can hold across many areas of psychology. One might consider a field study to be a study in which the resulting data are directly relevant to a police investigation. Even with this very specific definition, however, ambiguous examples are easily

This research was funded by the Economic and Social Research Council Grant RES 189-25-0110 to Amina Memon, Rebecca Milne, and Daniel B. Wright. All of us would like to thank the police officers with whom we have worked over the past few decades.

DOI: 10.1037/14094-009
Reform of Eyewitness Identification Procedures, B. L. Cutler (Editor)

conjured because "relevance" is subject to interpretation and disagreement. Alternative ways of classifying different types of research are by whether the research is primarily exploring causal or associative hypotheses and how representative the samples are of the populations to which the researcher wants to make inference. These ways have the advantage that they apply to other areas of science. In the first half of this chapter, we focus on these means for classifying research with respect to eyewitness testimony. In the second half of the chapter, we provide examples of field studies, discuss their limitations, and make recommendations for future field studies.

An important variable that is available in most laboratory research—and one that is critical for many research questions within memory—is what actually happened during the event that is being remembered. This is sometimes referred to as the *ground truth*. This variable is absent from most field studies, a limitation that is discussed in the second half of the chapter.

GENERALIZING FROM THE LABORATORY AND FROM THE FIELD

Memory research, in general, can be classified in many ways. Consider the following two questions:

1. Does the research address causal or associative hypotheses? (somewhat dichotomous)
2. Are the samples of people, stimuli, and situations meant to be representative of their respective populations of interest? (somewhat continuous)

Both of these require further explanation. Neither is necessary or sufficient for classifying a study as laboratory or field research, but as discussed in the section that follows, traditionally laboratory research has addressed causal hypotheses using unrepresentative samples. This compares with the smaller number of field studies, which often address associative hypotheses but use representative samples of people and stimuli. However, both laboratory and field research have ventured into the territory usually occupied by the other. The main conclusion from this taxonomy is that the differences between laboratory and field research are best thought of as a tendency to fall into different places on the basis of these two questions.

In the remainder of this section, we describe Questions 1 and 2 with specific reference to the inference that can be made from eyewitness testimony field research. An underlying theme of this chapter is that good field research is difficult, is bound to have limitations, and typically addresses different hypotheses than does laboratory research. Like laboratory research, there are good and bad examples: Good research should be praised, and bad research can mislead the field. Banaji and Crowder (1989) wrote that just because a study is done in the field, it does not mean that it should not undergo methodological scrutiny. Here we describe some of that scrutiny, with particular reference to field research about eyewitness memory.

Does the Research Address Causal or Associative Hypotheses?[1]

The purpose of science is to increase people's understanding of nature, and there are different aspects of nature that scientists try to understand. Early memory researchers like Ebbinghaus (1885/1913) adapted the experimental methods from the physical sciences. This approach was helpful in constructing causal models of the underlying processes of memory. Spearman (1904) was uneasy with this approach:

> Most of those hostile to Experimental Psychology are in the habit of reproaching its methods with insignificance, and even with triviality. . . . They protest that such means can never shed any real light upon the human soul, unlock the eternal antinomy of Free Will, or reveal the inward nature of Time and Space. (p. 203)

Spearman advocated a correlational psychology, a nonexperimental approach in which scientists tried to measure naturally occurring associations.

Cronbach (1957) described how the experimental and correlational approaches had developed into separate autonomous psychologies, one for testing causal mechanisms and one for measuring naturally occurring associations. The distinction between the experimental and correlational psychologies is not always clear-cut, and there is some interaction between the groups (Cronbach, 1975). However, it is important to distinguish between them because the methods necessary to evaluate a causal hypothesis are different from those needed to evaluate an associative hypothesis (for formal comparison, see Pearl, 2009). Sometimes a researcher may make the wrong type of conclusion. The three critical issues to consider are whether a manipulation is altering what it is supposed to be altering and only what it is supposed to be altering, whether the random allocation is used, and how the sample is gathered.

Manipulating the "Cause"

Consider the relationship between emotion and accuracy. The causal question as to whether increasing the emotional intensity of an event influences

_____

[1]For a longer and more technical account of the issues in this subsection as applied to eyewitness research, see Wright (2006).

how accurately a person remembers that event can be explored through carefully controlled laboratory experiments (and quasi-experiments). The findings show that memory is impaired in some circumstances and for some aspects but not in others (Kensinger, 2007). One type of laboratory study for investigating the effect of emotion on memory involves showing two groups of subjects the same set of slides except that for one group the slides are made emotional in some way (for an example, see the description of Cahill, Prins, Weber, & McGaugh, 1994, in the paragraph that follows). The researchers then measure memory performance. The critical aspects of making a causal attribution are that the stimuli shown to the two groups do not differ in any way that might affect memory other than emotionality and that the groups would perform similarly to each other if they were all shown the same stimuli.

Trying to change only emotion, even in a laboratory study, is difficult. For example, Cahill et al. (1994) showed all of their subjects the same series of slides, with a written story describing each slide. For subjects in the *neutral* condition, the story described a boy seeing a bunch of wrecked cars in a junkyard and then going to a hospital to see the surgical team take part in a practice exercise for the hospital to prepare in case there is a real emergency. In the *emotive* condition, the slides were the same, but the story described the boy being in a terrible accident with critical injuries. The slides, which had been used to describe the hospital exercise for subjects in the neutral condition, described the surgical team trying to save the boy's life (including reattaching severed feet) in the emotive condition. Cahill et al. showed that the emotional reaction was rated as more intense in the second condition and also that memory was better for those critical slides. However, it may also be that other aspects of the event, like how important subjects thought the event was, were also changed, and these may have affected memory.

Of course, in the laboratory at least the researchers can try to equate something between the neutral and the emotion conditions. In the field this is impossible because the researcher has little, if any, control over the events.[2] Thus, when field researchers compare identifications from crimes with a weapon versus those without a weapon, they should not assume that the only difference is the emotionality experienced in the event. Many other aspects of the crimes will be different. Without making numerous (and usually unjustified) assumptions, it is difficult to draw causal inferences about the effect of emotion on memory. If there is a memory difference it might be due to one of the other differences between the two sets of crimes. This sometimes creates

---

[2]Examples exist in which there is control over the encoding of an event. For example, a researcher could place height-marking strips on doors of randomly selected convenience stores and examine if these help with height estimation of the fleeing criminals from these stores compared with height estimation of fleeing criminals from the nonselected stores.

difficulties mapping empirical data from field studies onto the mostly causal theories about memory from cognitive psychologists.

Allocating People to Conditions

A critical assumption for causal inference from experiments is that the control condition and experimental condition are not systematically different from each other except for the experimental manipulation. This can be addressed through random allocation and is the basis for the Rubin's model of causation (see Holland, 1986, for a thorough review; Neyman, 1923/1990, for a historical precursor; see also Shadish, 2010; West & Thoemmes, 2010). As Cook and Campbell (1979) stated, "random assignment is the great *ceteris paribus* [italics original]—that is, other things being equal—of causal inference" (p. 5). In field research it is usually difficult to randomly assign witnesses to encoding conditions (though see Footnote 1). There are often ethical difficulties when manipulating anything in actual criminal investigations. For example, it would be unethical to randomly allocate an eyewitness to a condition with a biased lineup instruction. However, sometimes it is possible to assign witnesses to different retrieval or test conditions. This is what happens in most field experiments. The Wells, Steblay, and Dysart (2011) report described subsequently is an excellent example.

Randomly allocating people to conditions allows the researcher to test causal hypotheses like whether the cognitive interview produces more information than the traditional police interview or whether sequential lineup presentation produces fewer false identifications than simultaneous presentation. But not all causal questions can be addressed with field experiments. Researchers cannot in a field experiment test the causal hypothesis about whether a weapon negatively affects memory for a perpetrator's face. Some approaches that discuss reaching causal conclusions from nonexperimental data are propensity matching (Rosenbaum, 2002; Rubin, 2006) and producing causal diagrams, called directed acyclic graphs (Pearl, 2009). The books cited here provide thorough coverage of these techniques, and each stresses the assumptions that are necessary (unfortunately often users of all statistical techniques fail to consider all assumptions).

Causal hypotheses are of the form X leads to Y. Showing a situation (any situation) in which this does not occur falsifies a strict form of this hypothesis.[3] This, according to Popper (1959) and reinforced by the U.S.

---

[3]In practice, the hypothesis is not always falsified. The research community may discount the data on methodological grounds or as a statistical fluke. Alternatively, the community may reduce the situations to which the hypothesis is purported to apply. There is much philosophical debate about the role of the situations that act to complete a hypothesis (Fodor, 1991). There are also disputes about the definition of *causation;* the phrase used here, "leads to," is purposefully vague.

Supreme Court (*Daubert v. Merrill Dow Pharmaceuticals, Inc.*, 1993), is critical for science. Thus, causal hypotheses at least at some level of abstraction can be thought of as independent of the situation. Associative hypotheses, on the other hand, describe the relationship between X and Y in some set of situations. It would not make sense to refer to an associative hypothesis without reference to a set of situations. Deciding what situations the study can generalize to is the focus of the next section.

Sampling People and Stimuli

When *sampling* is mentioned in most introductory methods classes, the focus is on sampling people from a population. Most undergraduate psychologists have heard the criticism of much psychology research that the typical subject, a highly educated 19-year-old psychology student, may differ in important ways from other people. Suppose if somebody wanted to explore the association between age and memory and sampled students from a psychology course. Clearly the distribution of age in the typical student sample makes this unwise. Given that most psychologists know the difficulties of generalizing from student samples, we do not discuss this further. Instead, we focus on stimuli.

In addition to sampling people, in a typical psychology study the researchers also sample the stimuli the subjects are shown and the context in which they are tested (see Wells & Windschitl, 1999, for a discussion with respect to eyewitness research). Within psychology, Clark (1973) described how ignoring that the stimuli were sampled from some larger population could lead to incorrect conclusions. This is true also of the context in which the study takes place and the characteristics of the interviewer. This is well-known in the social sciences, and if studies are designed well, then statistical techniques are available to take into account, for example, differences among interviewers (e.g., O'Muircheartaigh & Campanelli, 1998). Clark's article was important both because he made psychologists think about sampling stimuli and because he provided statistical tests that took into account stimulus sampling. The methods Clark described were in use until fairly recently when advances in computing packages for mixed effect models were developed; these allow the user to account for both randomly sampled subjects and randomly sampled stimuli in a more flexible manner (Baayen, Davidson, & Bates, 2008; Wright, Horry, & Skagerberg, 2009).

In eyewitness research, practical considerations can often make stimulus sampling difficult. Consider, for example, the *own ethnicity bias* (also called the *cross-race effect* and the *own race bias*), whereby people can recognize faces of people from their own ethnicity more accurately than faces of people from other ethnicities. In the typical laboratory study the researchers sample a large number of faces of different ethnicities. Suppose they sample 50 faces of a particular ethnicity. At one level they are saying these 50 faces represent all faces of that population, just as when sampling subjects, researchers assume the subjects are sampled at random from some larger population. With modern statistical techniques researchers could allow the probability of a correct identification to vary both by subject (some subjects will have better face memory than others) and by face (some faces will be more memorable than others).

In some research it is difficult to have a large number of faces. For example, Wright, Boyd, and Tredoux (2001) wanted to examine the own ethnicity bias in a natural setting using a between-subjects design. They had a Black or a White confederate approach people who were either Black or White in town centers. For practical reasons they used only four confederates. Although they observed that each confederate was identified from a photographic lineup by more people of his own ethnicity (all confederates were male), they had to be careful generalizing their findings to Black and White people. For the study to be useful, they needed to describe how their research fitted within the larger literature. This is the same as, for example, what medical researchers must do when they report data from a small number of patients.

Consider another example. The postidentification feedback effect is one of the most discussed findings within eyewitness research over the past 15 years (see Chapter 7, this volume). Wells and Bradfield (1998) showed for a given stimulus (a grainy video of people walking into a shop) that telling subjects after they made a lineup identification that they either chose the suspect or made an error affects the subjects' confidence in their memory (and many other judgments). From their data they could concluded that the effect exists for subjects presented with this video and the set of photographs that they used. Because of random allocation, they could discuss the causal mechanisms involved and could argue that these same mechanisms would produce effects in many other situations. Although the Wells and Bradfield article is a landmark paper, it cannot provide an estimate for the size of the postidentification feedback effect other than for situations like the scenario used by the authors. They purposefully used a grainy video (see Wells & Bradfield, 1998, Figure 1) so that identifying the culprit would be a difficult task. It may be that difficulty is an important moderator of the postidentification feedback effect. Therefore, to make claims about the effect size for all lineups it would be necessary to have a set of stimuli more representative of all lineups.

It is important to note that combining several studies all using stimuli that are not designed to be a representative sample of the population of interest does not allow an estimate of the population effect size no matter how many studies and subjects are included. This is one of the errors some people make when interpreting results from meta-analyses. When meta-analyses are used to summarize different studies using different stimuli and methods (as opposed to multisite studies in medicine), then they should be used to explore how these differences among the studies moderate the effect size. To aggregate data from multiple studies to provide an estimate for the effect size in the population, it is necessary to argue that the collection of studies is somehow representative of the population of interest.

Field research can use more representative samples, but often it does not. As with any research, it depends how the people and stimuli are sampled from their populations. If random sampling, or something that approximates it, is used, it means that the witnesses and stimuli are likely to be representative of the population from which they are sampled.

EXAMPLES OF EYEWITNESS FIELD STUDIES

There are two broad types of field studies that we consider. The first are *archival studies* in which no experimental manipulation is done, often also called *correlational* or *observational* studies. The second are *field experiments* in which groups are allocated into conditions.

One of the biggest difficulties with field studies is not knowing whether the suspect is in fact the culprit. The difficulty is compounded because different types of evidence interact. If an eyewitness identifies a suspect, the police are more likely to continue investigating that person; the person is more likely to confess; and the person is more likely to be convicted than if he or she had not been identified. If some measure of the likelihood of being guilty is used, it is critical that this measurement be made prior to an identification so that the act of identifying or not identifying the person does not affect this measure. Further, it is necessary that the witness is not aware of this information because it could affect the witness's likelihood of making an identification. We discuss this issue later in this section.

Archival/Observational Studies

A small number of archival field studies have examined rates of suspect and filler (also called *foil, lure,* and *distractor*) identifications from various types of identification procedures. Many of these were conducted in England and were made possible by much cooperation between English police forces and academics. The samples are usually all lineups in some location for a specified time period. This means that they can be viewed as representative of that place and time. This does not mean that they are representative of an entire country or representative of future situations because characteristics of the crimes, criminals, and witnesses vary by time and place (e.g., crime statistics are different in urban than in rural areas). This is discussed next.

One of the early studies examined the identification attempts by 1,561 witnesses who inspected 616 live lineups in the London area during 1992 either at one of two specialist suites or at individual police stations (Wright & McDaid, 1996). Suspects were identified 39% of the time, fillers were identified 20% of the time, and 41% of the time no identification was made. These were all live lineups and were conducted at a time when the London police were transitioning from lineups being conducted at individual police stations to having them conducted at specialist suites.

Because it was a time of transition for how lineups were conducted in England, the original purpose of Wright and McDaid's (1996) study was to help the police decide if having the lineups in a suite caused any difference in outcomes compared with having them conducted at the stations. However, once the analyses were begun, it was clear that there were large differences in the typical cases that were handled at the stations versus those handled at the suites. The suites were then used for more violent crimes, for cases in which finding adequate fillers was more difficult (they had a much higher proportion of ethnic minority suspects), and the lineups were conducted after a longer delay. Wright and McDaid were able to covary out these variables and show that eyewitnesses at the suites were still choosing more fillers than at the stations. Given that these are known errors, if taken at face value this would have been worrying for the police who were wanting to expand the use of suites. However, a major purpose of the Wright and McDaid article was to caution researchers to be very careful making causal attributions from their data. It may be that other unmeasured variables, particularly those related to the difficulty of conducting a lineup at a station, were related to both choosing to have the lineup conducted at the suite and the high filler identification rate. This is sometimes called a *hidden variable*, and the relationship is called a *spurious correlation* (Simon, 1954). Of course, without having measured this hidden variable, it is not possible to know if this is what occurred. These types of difficulties are inherent in trying to draw causal conclusions from nonexperiments (Wright, 2006).

Valentine, Pickering, and Darling (2003) collected data from one of four identification suites in the London area using a database of 640 witnesses who attempted to identify suspects in 314 lineups (56 witnesses knew the suspects, an important consideration when analyzing lineup identification but not always indicated by researchers). In line with Wright and McDaid's (1996) findings, approximately 40% of witnesses identified a suspect, and 40% made no identification. Suspects known to the witness were, not unsurprisingly, more often identified than unknown suspects. The data were obtained through a questionnaire completed by the investigating officer and comprised a number of explanatory variables divided into witness characteristics (e.g., age, gender, race, role), suspect characteristics (e.g., gender, height, race, build), variables about the eyewitness situation (e.g., viewing conditions), the incident (e.g., offence, presence of weapon), the eyewitness's description (e.g., completeness, match to suspect's appearance), and variables associated with the identification attempt (e.g., delay, witness decision speed).

Consider the witness's gender. Female witnesses chose a filler 28% of the time; male witnesses chose a filler only 18% of the time. This is a large difference: Female witnesses were making 50% more known errors. If somebody tried to make a causal conclusion, he or she might argue that being female causes the person to have a worse memory. This is an invalid conclusion for several reasons, the most notable one being that in most of the laboratory studies that compared face memory by gender, females were better at the task (Herlitz & Rehnman, 2008). It is clear that the set of female witnesses are not in the same situation as the set of male witnesses (e.g., female rape victims are more common than male rape victims), and therefore causal conclusions should be avoided. Surprisingly, even with examples in which causal attributions are clearly unjustified, when researchers observe an unexpected association in an archival study, they often discuss possible causal mechanisms without considering whether they are needed.

Consider a recent English study. Horry, Memon, Wright, & Milne (2011) examined data from 1,039 video parades conducted in five police forces in England. Overall, suspects were identified in 39% of lineups; fillers were identified in 26% of the lineups; and no identification was made in the remainder. The authors reported the association between many characteristic of the suspect, witness, and crime with identification outcome.

We want to focus on one important variable in Horry et al. (2011). In England, the lineups are all run sequentially, but the eyewitnesses must view the entire video parade at least twice before making a choice. The eyewitnesses can also request to see the lineup again, either wholly or in part. Horry et al. (2011) found that eyewitnesses who asked to see the lineup again were approximately 2.5 times more likely to select a filler than those who did not (38% vs. 16%). In fact, these eyewitnesses were as likely to select a filler as they were to select the suspect. Does this mean that eyewitnesses should not be allowed to see the lineup again? No. It may be (and in that article, we argued) that eyewitnesses who are likely to make an error are more likely to ask to see the lineup again (see Steblay, Dietrich, Ryan, Raczynski, & James, 2011, for a laboratory demonstration). It is worth considering this "more viewings" group in more detail. It may be that there are two groups of eyewitnesses who ask to view the lineup again. One group is of eyewitnesses who have good memories and just want to make sure that they are identifying the correct person. The second group may be eyewitnesses who are not sure and may ask to view the lineup again so that they can choose the person who they think looks most like the culprit (i.e., a relative judgment rather than an absolute judgment). What can be concluded is the following association: Eyewitnesses who ask to see the lineup again and do see it again are more than twice as likely to make a filler identification than those who do not ask. This is something that police and juries should consider when evaluating the reliability of an identification. Therefore, the police should record if the eyewitness asks for additional viewings. In addition, police should try to establish *why* the eyewitness is asking for additional viewings.

So far we have just considered a selection of English archival studies. This is because more archival studies have been conducted in England compared with elsewhere in large part because of the willingness of English police forces to cooperate with cognitive scientists. Until recently it has been more difficult for researchers in other countries to attain samples that did not have clear biases. We consider just two examples to discuss sampling difficulties.

Behrman and Davey (2001) analyzed the identification attempts from 271 cases of 349 crimes in Northern California between 1987 and 1998. Several types of eyewitness identification procedures were used (some crimes had several identifications, which was not taken into account in their analyses, though it was in the English studies cited previously). The types were 258 field showups, 289 photographic lineups, 58 live lineups, and 18 single photo showups. The percentage of showups, about 40%, indicates that showups were occurring in Northern California at the time, but this figure cannot be used to say that approximately 40% of identification procedures are showups because the sample used was not a random sample of Northern Californian lineups. This study had a clear bias. About half of the cases were used because one of the authors was a consultant in the case. Given this, it is difficult to know what can be concluded from this study. In our own experiences, when a lawyer contacts one of us about a case, it is because the lawyer wants to talk about an issue with a memory expert. This means that something in the case makes at least the lawyer believe there is an issue with the eyewitness testimony. Use of a showup may be such an issue. These problems aside, one aspect that Behrman and Davey did try to address was the ground truth. They looked through police files to try to decide if the identification was accurate. Although this seems good, the problem is different types of "evidence" contaminate each other (Hasel & Kassin, 2009). Thus, if confronted with an identification, the suspect may be more likely to confess than if there were no identification and is more likely to be convicted.

The final archive to discuss in this section is the DNA exonerations (one of the largest is at http://www.innocenceproject.org). These are cases in which a person has been convicted and then DNA shows that the convicted person was not the culprit. These cases have been incredibly influential in persuading jurisdictions to reconsider cases. In about 75% of the cases, errant eyewitness testimony was part of the original exculpatory evidence (see the Introduction, this volume, for more details). Although this suggests that eyewitness testimony is the leading cause of false convictions, it is important to consider if the DNA cases are a random sample of all false convictions (see Gross, Jacoby, Matheson, Montgomery, & Patil, 2005, for more details of this argument). Unfortunately, it is likely that most false convictions will never be uncovered. The DNA exonerees in some sense are lucky because the true culprit in the crimes they were falsely convicted of left a biological marker, often semen. This allowed the exoneration to happen. Given that DNA is not available for many crimes, this shows that the DNA exonerations are just the tip of the iceberg, but the underwater part of the iceberg may have different characteristics than the portion exposed to the air. Further, it is likely that plea bargaining to lesser sentences, which will vary by jurisdiction, will affect false conviction rates. It is also important to define the population of infractions that are being considered. For example, do traffic violations count? We believe that errors by eyewitnesses are one of the largest causes of false imprisonment, but estimating what proportion of false imprisonments are caused by errant eyewitness testimony from an unrepresentative tip of an iceberg (the DNA exonerations) requires many, perhaps unjustified, assumptions about how representative these cases are of all cases (see Introduction, this volume, for more discussion).

Field Experimental Studies

In medical research a field experiment is often called a *clinical trial*. Suppose you are testing some new drug for treating heart attacks. Medical institutions describe different phases of clinical trials that need to be conducted for that drug to be accepted. Medical doctors, hospitals, and the U.S. National Institutes of Health (and similar government and charity funding agencies) conduct and fund these vital studies. There are detailed protocols for how clinical trials should be conducted and reported. These protocols are believed to be vital to ensure people's safety.

Fewer eyewitness innovations have been proposed than medical innovations. There also is less money to evaluate eyewitness innovations; the pharmaceutical companies (and their shareholders) are keen to test new drugs, but the charities involved with judicial change have much less money and have less in the way of financial rewards if they are successful. Despite these differences, the procedures in place to perform medical trials can be used to help evaluate the quality of eyewitness field studies.

We consider two eyewitness innovations that have been proposed. Wells and Bradfield (1998) described how telling an eyewitness that he or she identified the suspect increases the eyewitness's confidence (see Chapter 7, this volume), and therefore they asserted that confidence should be assessed prior to informing the eyewitness about the outcome. Lindsay and Wells (1985) proposed the sequential lineup as an alternative to the simultaneous lineup (see Chapter 5, this volume).

Consider first the postidentification feedback effect on confidence (Wells & Bradfield, 1998). Wells and many others have shown in laboratory studies that if you show people a video and ask them to identify an actor from the video, telling them that they identified the suspect increases people's confidence, whereas telling them they identified a filler decreases it. There are two questions that we can address with a field experiment. The first is whether this effect would occur with real eyewitnesses. Perhaps there is something special among student subjects that created this effect, or perhaps it occurs only for videotaped stimuli and not for witnessing real crimes. Thus, it is important to show that this effect could occur with real eyewitnesses (and this is a concern almost always raised under cross-examination if an expert witness presents laboratory eyewitness research). The second question concerns the size of the effect. Because we believe that the size of the postidentification feedback effect may vary by different characteristics of the crime, the eyewitness, the culprit, the suspect, and more, it is necessary to measure it in a sample that is fairly representative of all lineups. Most laboratory studies try to control these characteristics and so present only one (or a small number of) video(s). Even if that video is like some crime situation, it will not be representative of the array of different situations. Therefore, these laboratory studies cannot provide an estimate for the size of the postidentification feedback effect among real eyewitnesses.[4]

There has been a single field experiment of this effect, and it had a relatively small sample ($N = 134$). Wright and Skagerberg (2007), in collaboration with the Sussex Police Force, conducted it. Eyewitnesses took part in the standard English lineup, some identifying the suspect and some not. The eyewitnesses were escorted to a waiting room. They were asked several questions, but here we focus on a question about how easy the eyewitness found making the identification (on a 1–10 scale). A random half were asked this

---

[4]Under cross-examination a lawyer could ask what the effect size is for the exact circumstances of the crime. A field experiment will not provide this. No study would unless one could mimic the exact circumstances of the crime (which is likely impossible).

question before being told whether they had identified the suspect.[5] Those eyewitnesses who had identified a filler had a mean of 4.88, and those who had identified the suspect had a mean of 7.76. All the filler identifications were errors. Although some of the suspect identifications may have been errors, it is likely that most were correct. This suggests that eyewitnesses find accurate identifications easier than inaccurate ones.

Wright and Skagerberg's (2007) main interest was what happens when you tell an eyewitness that the identification was of a suspect or of a filler. A random half were asked the ease-of-identification question after being told if they chose the suspect or a filler. The mean of filler choosers had decreased to 2.75, and the mean of the suspect choosers had increased to 8.60. Because of random allocation and statistical significance, Wright and Skagerberg were able to say that the feedback had affected how easy eyewitnesses said they found the identification. Unfortunately, because of the small sample, Wright and Skagerberg were not able to provide a precise estimate of the size of the effect. Thus, further field research on postidentification feedback is needed.

The next two field experiments concern the simultaneous versus sequential lineup procedure (reviewed in Chapter 5, this volume). We start with the more recent one. Wells et al. (2011), in collaboration with four U.S. police departments, conducted an experiment to test if sequential and simultaneous lineup procedures produced different results. The four critical aspects of their study were as follows. They did not have a biased sample; they had control so that the sequential or simultaneous format was the only aspect of the procedure that was manipulated; they followed basic scientific protocol with random assignment and double-blind administration; and they accurately measured the outcomes. The lineups were administered on a computer that allowed the identification to take place without the administrator knowing the position of the suspect (thus, they were double-blind, an important aspect of the clinical trials in medicine; see Chapter 6, this volume), and the computer could control the randomization. The basic results (summarized in Wells et al., 2011, Figure 2) are shown in Table 8.1. Thus, in line with laboratory research, the fillers were identified more in the simultaneous lineups than in the sequential. Interestingly, the proportion of identifications is lower in both of these conditions than what has been found in many of the English surveys. There are several reasons why this difference could occur, including

---

[5]There are ethical or institutional review board and legal concerns with any manipulation involving actual eyewitnesses. At the time of the study, the legal rules (Police and Criminal Evidence Act, 1984) did not stipulate when the eyewitness was told about the outcome of the identification or what questions about the identification he or she was asked. In fact, the different suites handled these issues differently. Therefore, all lineups in this study were conducted in accordance with the Police and Criminal Evidence Act (1984). Further, the data were all anonymous.

TABLE 8.1

Percentage (Number) of Suspect Identifications, Filler Identifications, and No Identifications from Wells et al. (2011)

Lineup method	Suspect identification	Filler identification	No identification
Simultaneous	25 (66)	18 (47)	56 (146)
Sequential	27 (65)	12 (29)	61 (144)

Note. Frequencies are calculated from Wells et al., 2011, Figure 2. The row percentages do not sum to 100% because of rounding.

U.S. eyewitnesses feeling that they need to be more certain to make an identification and/or U.S. lineups less often having the culprit in them.

One caveat about this research is whether the power was high enough to argue that the simultaneous procedure produced significantly more filler identifications. The data were collapsed across the four sites because there were relatively few data points at three of the sites. Site could be an interesting variable because of the different types of crimes that occur in different locations (as found in Horry et al., 2011) and because police forces may vary with respect to the criteria they use to determine whether to conduct a lineup. The odds of making a filler identification in the simultaneous lineup was .22, whereas the odds of making a filler identification in a sequential lineup was .14. The odds ratio is 1:60. If one assumes that all of the lineups were sampled from the same location and that they were independent (e.g., that none were for the same suspect), a 95% confidence interval can be calculated, and it is from 0.97 to 2.63. The null hypothesis, that the conditions yield the same proportions, is 1.00, so the confidence interval includes the null value. Other methods are also available for comparing two proportions (or odds), but this approach (and other common approaches like a χ^2 test) yields a nonsignificant finding (albeit in the same direction as observed in the laboratory research). Having a larger sample might create a statistically significant result.

An earlier study was conducted in Illinois (Mecklenburg, 2006) and has been criticized by several prominent psychologists (e.g., Schacter et al., 2008) and in high-profile journals (e.g., Spinney, 2008). The Illinois study involved comparing sequential with simultaneous lineups. Like the Wells et al. (2011) study, it can be evaluated on four critical aspects (i.e., Was the sample biased? Was the sequential or simultaneous format the only characteristic manipulated? Were basic scientific protocols followed? Were outcomes accurately measured?). Unlike Wells et al., it falls short on these. We focus on two aspects. The first is that it was not a double-blind study, but, worse, it was not double-blind for only one of the conditions. If an administrator knows who the suspect is, the administrator may—consciously or unconsciously—dissuade an eyewitness from choosing a filler and may even provide cues toward the suspect. This need not be intentional. Thus, the expectation is that eyewitnesses in the nonblind condition should choose fillers less often and suspects more often than in the double-blind condition. In this study double-blind versus non-double-blind was confounded with sequential versus simultaneous. This means little can be said on the basis of these data alone about the effects of either of these. It is a particularly ill-thought-out confound because the scientific literature suggests decreased filler selection in nonblind conditions for bad reasons (the administrator at some level dissuading the eyewitness from choosing a filler) and decreased filler selection in the sequential conditions for good reasons (avoiding making a relative judgments for culprit-absent lineups).

We tried to recreate the data from the percentages in Mecklenburg's (2006) Table 3a and from the report of one of the Illinois study experts, but it appears eyewitnesses could be in more than one category (e.g., in the sequential, 45% chose the suspect; 9.2% chose a filler, and 47.2% made no identification, for a total of over 101%; see also Mecklenburg, 2006, Table 3b). Further, one of the locations had 137 simultaneous lineups and only 35 sequential lineups. For ease of comparison, the Illinois study data from Chicago, which was the largest sample, are presented in Table 8.2.

Although these data, on their own are not informative about differences between simultaneous and sequential lineups, they can be compared with the Wells et al. (2011) data. Wells et al.'s simultaneous double-blind condition had 25% suspect identifications and 18% filler identifications. These can be compared with the 57% and 1% from Chicago. If we assume the only difference between these is non-double-blind versus double-blind administration, it suggests that the administrator is dissuading almost all eyewitnesses who would choose a filler not to and persuading many to choose the suspect. This is, of course, a very dangerous bias to have. The 1% from the Chicago data

TABLE 8.2

Percentage (Number) of Suspect Identifications, Filler Identifications, and No Identifications from the Illinois Study in Chicago

Lineup method	Suspect identifications	Filler Identifications	No identification
Simultaneous/ nonblind	57 (86)	1 (1)	42 (64)
Sequential/ double-blind	43 (72)	10 (17)	49 (81)

Note. Frequencies are calculated from Mecklenburg, 2006, Table 3b, multiplying the percentage by the sample sizes (151 simultaneous, 167 sequential). Because the percentages for the sequential lineup add to more than 100%, the sample size for this row is 170).

is so far out of line with other studies that if there were no other problems with the Illinois study, it would be the strongest evidence for double-blind administration. Memory is erroneous, so to have this low a figure suggests that the bias in some administrators is large.

However, other problems with the Illinois study make reaching conclusions difficult. The first has to do with random assignment to conditions. Random assignment was not used in Wright and McDaid (1996), which was why they argued against reaching causal conclusions. In the Illinois study (Mecklenburg, 2006), the author claimed that random allocation was used: "the selection had to be random" (p. 25). However, Steblay (2011a, 2011b) was able to get ahold of some of the data and argue convincingly that random assignment was not used. If random assignment was not used, and yet the author claims it was used, this is problematic.

Second, Wells (2008) described how some of the outcomes were not coded correctly. For example, he showed that there actually were more than 1% filler identifications in Chicago for the simultaneous lineups, but they were coded as no identifications for reasons that neither Wells (2008) nor we follow. Several other authors have described the basic problems with the Illinois study, and we see no need to repeat these (e.g., Schacter et al., 2008). What is worrying is the impact of the Illinois study. As Steblay (2011a) pointed out, prior to the Illinois study many jurisdictions were adopting lineup procedures on the basis of recommendations from psychologists, but "by 2008 the argument seemed to be stubbornly stalled, without resolution. A sticking point was the question of why the Illinois data look as they do" (para. 5).

FINAL COMMENTS AND RECOMMENDATIONS

The central message of this chapter is that although valuable, laboratory and field studies are best suited to address different research questions. Although running a carefully controlled laboratory study can elucidate the causal mechanisms involved, for example, in how emotion affects memory, it does not address the associative question of whether a police officer should expect an eyewitness to an emotional crime to have a good or a bad memory. Similarly, there are so many uncontrolled (and unmeasured) factors present in most field studies that it can be difficult to pinpoint what is going on. Laboratory and field research both have advantages, and each adds complementary information to researchers' understanding of eyewitness memory.

The focus of this chapter is on field studies. There are two main considerations that researchers need to have when designing any study, including field studies. The first is whether the sample is representative of the population of interest. This is necessary if the researchers want their conclusions to apply to the whole population. It would be difficult for any eyewitness researcher to sample at random all lineups in their country. Usually the researchers are constrained to a small number of forces. If there are peculiarities of those forces (e.g., extremely high or low crime rates), these should be noted. This bias is largely unavoidable and one hopes unrelated to the main variables in which the researchers are interested. Many of the studies achieve this. Problems occur if there is a sampling bias directly related to memory issues. For example, in the study by Behrman and Davey (2001), many cases were included in the sample because one of the authors was contacted, and this may have been because somebody felt there was a problem with the identification.

The second consideration is the control that the researchers have over the situation. One problem with most field studies is that no one knows what actually happened at the crime scene. The cases in which truth is known are usually atypical of all the cases in which the researcher wants to generalize findings (e.g., Sjöberg & Lindblad, 2002, had videotapes made by the perpetrator in child sexual abuse cases). Another consideration is whether an experimental manipulation is done such that random allocation is used and the design is not confounded. As discussed previously, the Illinois study is an example that falls short on both of these counts, whereas the Wells et al. (2011) study is an excellent example.

We make two sets of recommendations. The first is for individual researchers wishing to conduct field studies. The second is for procedural reforms suggested from field research.

We have compiled the following recommendations for those wishing to conduct field research on eyewitness testimony:

1. Are you sure? Is your research question best addressed by a field study?
2. Find police officers who are also concerned with whether current procedures are the best for acquiring reliable lineup results and who are in a position to give you access.
3. Discuss the sampling issues with the police. If the police are only giving you access to a subset (e.g., only closed cases), be clear how any potential biases may affect the results. If they are selecting cases for your use, it is important to explain that this sampling will severely limit any conclusions. Conduct a power analysis to know how many lineups are needed. This is important because the uncontrolled factors in field settings will likely increase error variance and lower power.
4. Be clear what is to be measured and how. For example, it is important to differentiate filler identifications from nonidentifications.

5. If possible, follow scientific protocol by having blind administration. Otherwise, this will be a potential confound.

6. Be careful with any identifying information in the data set. Discuss this with your institutional review board or ethics board representative.

7. Take into account the nonindependence of the data. For example, often a suspect is seen by multiple witnesses, and therefore the lineups are not independent. Statistical techniques are available for this (it may be useful to have a statistician on the research team).

The second set relates to recommendations for changing lineup procedures. This type of recommendation is discussed in many of this book's chapters that focus on particular eyewitness phenomena. However, we are hesitant to make many recommendations solely on the basis of field studies for the reasons discussed throughout this chapter. We make the following three procedural recommendations on the basis of field studies (see Horry, Memon, Milne, Wright, & Dalton, 2012, for a larger set for English lineups based on both field and laboratory studies):

1. Our first recommendation is for more field research and, in particular, more field experiments. Eyewitnesses are taking part in thousands of lineups every day. Therefore, this provides the opportunity for much field research. This can be helped by more financial resources and better recognition for both academics and police involved with what, if done well, can be high-impact research.

2. Our second recommendation, which is based on our experiences with archival studies, is for standardization of recording the outcome of lineups. There are large differences in how the outcomes are recorded, including what constitutes a positive identification. Standardization would allow large-scale archival research to take place and allow changes in outcomes to be tracked over time and across jurisdictions. In addition, it would be valuable to record all information about the identification (and any interactions with the eyewitness). This would help to minimize defense attorneys speculating about biased procedures when none occur and also to identify them when they do (but, one hopes, lessen them in the long run). In some jurisdictions the identification is videotaped. Given that video recording capabilities are even on most people's phones, there seems little reason not to routinely videotape the identification.

3. Our third recommendation comes from a combination of field and laboratory studies. Laboratory studies show that double-blind procedures should be used, but many officers have said that these could be difficult to implement. Field studies have shown that this can be done without much difficulty with blind administrators (Steblay, 2011a) or with computer technology (Wells et al., 2011).

REFERENCES

Baayen, R. H., Davidson, D. J., & Bates, D. M. (2008). Mixed-effects modeling with crossed random effects for subjects and items. *Journal of Memory and Language, 59*, 390–412. doi:10.1016/j.jml.2007.12.005

Banaji, M. R., & Crowder, R. G. (1989). The bankruptcy of everyday memory. *American Psychologist, 44*, 1185–1193. doi:10.1037/0003-066X.44.9.1185

Behrman, B. W., & Davey, S. L. (2001). Eyewitness identification in actual criminal cases: An archival analysis. *Law and Human Behavior, 25*, 475–491. doi:10.1023/A:1012840831846

Cahill, L., Prins, B., Weber, M., & McGaugh, J. L. (1994, October 20). b-Adrenergic activation and memory for emotional events. *Nature, 371*, 702–704. doi:10.1038/371702a0

Clark, H. H. (1973). The language-as-fixed-effect fallacy: A critique of language statistics in psychological research. *Journal of Verbal Learning & Verbal Behavior, 12*, 335–359. doi:10.1016/S0022-5371(73)80014-3

Cook, T. D., & Campbell, D. T. (1979). *Quasi-experimentation: Design and analysis issues for field settings*. Chicago, IL: Rand McNally.

Cronbach, L. J. (1957). The two disciplines of scientific psychology. *American Psychologist, 12*, 671–684. doi:10.1037/h0043943

Cronbach, L. J. (1975). Beyond the two disciplines of scientific psychology. *American Psychologist, 30*, 116–127. doi:10.1037/h0076829

Daubert v. Merrell Dow Pharmaceuticals, Inc., 509 U.S. 579, 113 S. Ct. 2786 (1993).

Ebbinghaus, H. (1913). *Memory: A contribution to experimental psychology* (H. A. Ruger & C. E. Bussenious, Trans.). New York, NY: Teachers College, Columbia University. (Original work published 1885)

Fodor, J. A. (1991). You can fool some of the people all of the time, everything else being equal; Hedged laws and psychological explanations. *Mind, 100*, 19–34. doi:10.1093/mind/C.397.19

Gross, S. R., Jacoby, K., Matheson, D. J., Montgomery, N., & Patil, S. (2005). Exonerations in the United States 1989 through 2003. *The Journal of Criminal Law & Criminology, 95*, 523–560.

Hasel, L. E., & Kassin, S. M. (2009). On the presumption of evidentiary independence: Can confessions corrupt eyewitness identifications? *Psychological Science, 20*, 122–126. doi:10.1111/j.1467-9280.2008.02262.x

Herlitz, A., & Rehnman, J. (2008). Sex differences in episodic memory. *Current Directions in Psychological Science, 17*, 52–56. doi:10.1111/j.1467-8721.2008.00547.x

Holland, P. W. (1986). Statistics and causal inference. *Journal of the American Statistical Association, 81*, 945–960. doi:10.1080/01621459.1986.10478354

Horry, R., Memon, A., Milne, R., Wright, D. B. & Dalton, G. (2012). *Video identification of suspects: A discussion of current practice and policy in the United Kingdom.* Manuscript submitted for publication.

Horry, R., Memon, A., Wright, D. B. & Milne, R. (2011). Predictors of eyewitness identification decisions from video lineups in England: A field study. *Law and Human Behavior, 36*, 257–265. doi:10.1037/h0093959

Kensinger, E. A. (2007). Negative emotion enhances memory accuracy: Behavioral and neuroimaging evidence. *Current Directions in Psychological Science, 16*, 213–218. doi:10.1111/j.1467-8721.2007.00506.x

Lindsay, R. C. L., & Wells, G. L. (1985). Improving eyewitness identifications from lineups: Simultaneous versus sequential lineup presentation. *Journal of Applied Psychology, 70*, 556–564. doi:10.1037/0021-9010.70.3.556

Mecklenburg, S. H. (2006). *Report to the legislature of the state of Illinois: The Illinois pilot program on sequential double-blind identification procedures.* Retrieved from http://www.chicagopolice.org/IL%20Pilot%20on%20Eyewitness%20ID.pdf

Neyman, J. (1990). On the application of probability theory to agricultural experiments. Essay on principles (Section 9; D. M. Dabrowska & T. P. Speed, Trans.). *Statistical Science, 5*, 465–480. (Original work published 1923)

O'Muircheartaigh, C., & Campanelli, P. (1998). The relative impact of interviewer effects and sample design effects on survey precision. *Journal of the Royal Statistical Society: Series A. Statistics in Society, 161*, 63–77. doi:10.1111/1467-985X.00090

Pearl, J. (2009). *Causality: Models, reasoning, and inference* (2nd ed.). New York, NY: Cambridge University Press.

Police and Criminal Evidence Act. (1984). Retrieved from http://www.legislation.gov.uk/ukpga/1984/60

Popper, K. R. (1959). *The logic of scientific discovery.* London, England: Hutchinson.

Rosenbaum, P. R. (2002). *Observational studies* (2nd ed.). New York, NY: Springer-Verlag.

Rubin, D. B. (2006). *Matched sampling for causal effects.* New York, NY: Cambridge University Press. doi:10.1017/CBO9780511810725

Schacter, D. L., Dawes, R., Jacoby, L. L., Kahneman, D., Lempert, R., Roediger, H. L., & Rosenthal, R. (2008). Policy forum: Studying eyewitness investigations in the field. *Law and Human Behavior, 32*, 3–5. doi:10.1007/s10979-007-9093-9

Shadish, W. R. (2010). Campbell and Rubin: A primer and comparison of their approaches to causal inference in field settings. *Psychological Methods, 15*, 3–17.

Simon, H. A. (1954). Spurious correlation: A causal interpretation. *Journal of the American Statistical Association, 49*, 467–479.

Sjöberg, R. L., & Lindblad, F. (2002). Delayed disclosure and disrupted communication during forensic investigation of child sexual abuse: A study of 47 corroborated cases. *Acta Paediatrica, 91*, 1391–1396. doi:10.1111/j.1651-2227.2002.tb02839.x

Spearman, C. (1904). "General intelligence," objectively determined and measured. *The American Journal of Psychology, 15*, 201–293. doi:10.2307/1412107

Spinney, L. (2008, May 21). Line-ups on trial. *Nature, 453*, 442–444. doi:10.1038/453442a

Steblay, N. K. (2011a). A second look at the Illinois Pilot program: The Evanston data. *The Champion*, 10–15. Retrieved from http://www.nacdl.org/Champion.aspx?id=20652

Steblay, N. K. (2011b). What we know now: The Evanston Illinois lineups. *Law and Human Behavior, 35*, 1–12. doi:10.1007/s10979-009-9207-7

Steblay, N. K., Dietrich, H. L., Ryan, S. L., Raczynski, J. L., & James, K. A. (2011). Sequential lineup laps and eyewitness accuracy. *Law and Human Behavior, 35*, 262–274. doi:10.1007/s10979-010-9236-2

Valentine, T., Pickering, A., & Darling, S. (2003). Characteristics of eyewitness identification that predict the outcome of real lineups. *Applied Cognitive Psychology, 17*, 969–993. doi:10.1002/acp.939

Wells, G. L. (2008). Field experiments on eyewitness identification: Towards a better understanding of pitfalls and prospects. *Law and Human Behavior, 32*, 6–10. doi:10.1007/s10979-007-9098-4

Wells, G. L., & Bradfield, A. L. (1998). "Good, you identified the suspect": Feedback to eyewitnesses distorts their reports of the witness experience. *Journal of Applied Psychology, 83*, 360–376. doi:10.1037/0021-9010.83.3.360

Wells, G. L., Steblay, N. K., & Dysart, J. E. (2011). *A test of the simultaneous vs. sequential lineup methods. An initial report of the AJS national eyewitness identification field studies*. Unpublished manuscript, American Judicature Society. Retrieved from http://www.psychology.iastate.edu/~glwells/Wells_articles_pdf/EWID_PrintFriendly.pdf

Wells, G. L., & Windschitl, P. D. (1999). Stimulus sampling and social psychological experimentation. *Personality and Social Psychology Bulletin, 25*, 1115–1125. doi:10.1177/01461672992512005

West, S. G., & Thoemmes, F. (2010). Campbell's and Rubin's perspectives on causal inference. *Psychological Methods, 15*, 18–37.

Wright, D. B. (2006). Causal and associative hypotheses in psychology: Examples from eyewitness testimony research. *Psychology, Public Policy, and Law, 12,* 190–213. doi:10.1037/1076-8971.12.2.190

Wright, D. B., Boyd, C. E., & Tredoux, C. G. (2001). A field study of own-race bias in South Africa and England. *Psychology, Public Policy, and Law, 7,* 119–133. doi:10.1037/1076-8971.7.1.119

Wright, D. B., Horry, R., & Skagerberg, E. M. (2009). Functions for traditional and multilevel approaches to signal detection theory. *Behavior Research Methods, 41,* 257–267. doi:10.3758/BRM.41.2.257

Wright, D. B., & McDaid, A. T. (1996). Comparing system and estimator variables using data from real lineups. *Applied Cognitive Psychology, 10,* 75–84. doi:10.1002/(SICI)1099-0720(199602)10:1<75::AID-ACP364>3.0.CO;2-E

Wright, D. B., & Skagerberg, E. M. (2007). Post-identification feedback affects real eyewitnesses. *Psychological Science, 18,* 172–178. doi:10.1111/j.1467-9280.2007.01868.x

CONCLUSION: IDENTIFICATION TEST REFORMS

ANDREW M. SMITH AND BRIAN L. CUTLER

The preceding chapters in this volume described the research conclusions regarding system variables, both past and present. As noted, researchers' understanding of the effects of various system variables has evolved over time as new research has arisen and new meta-analyses have been published. In this chapter, we review how eyewitness identification tests have changed over time in response to the growing recognition of the role of mistaken identification in wrongful conviction and in light of the research. Just as research conclusions have evolved, the nature of the reform has evolved as well. Thus, another main objective of this chapter is to compare the reforms in place with the research conclusions reached in the previous chapters. Doing this permits us to distinguish which identification procedures are consistent with research findings, inconsistent with research findings, and not well understood from a research perspective. These comparisons can ultimately point the way for further modifications of reforms and identify important new research directions.

DOI: 10.1037/14094-010
Reform of Eyewitness Identification Procedures, B. L. Cutler (Editor)

THE TRAJECTORY OF IDENTIFICATION TEST REFORMS

The application of eyewitness research to police practices in the United States began in the 1990s, following the first 20 years of research on system variables stimulated by Wells (1978). In 1996, the National Institute of Justice released a report on exoneration cases, which indicated that 80% of these exonerees had been erroneously convicted in part because of mistaken eyewitness identification (Connors, Lundregan, Miller, & McEwan, 1996). Janet Reno, the U.S. Attorney General at the time, met with eyewitness scientist Gary Wells in early 1997 and formed a panel to address this concern (Wells et al., 2000). In early 1998, the Technical Working Group for Eyewitness Evidence was formed. The group consisted of defense attorneys, prosecutors, law enforcement personnel, and eyewitness research psychologists. In 1999, after several meetings, the group released the final product, *Eyewitness Evidence: A Guide for Law Enforcement* (U.S. Department of Justice [DOJ], Office of Justice Programs, National Institute of Justice, 1999). The DOJ guide was intended to promote best practice procedures for law enforcement personnel—procedures that protect the innocent while facilitating the conviction of guilty persons.

The scope of the DOJ guide was broad. It included recommendations concerning the establishment of rapport with eyewitnesses; the activities of officers who are first responders to the scene; and best practices for interviewing eyewitnesses, viewing mug shots, and administering field identification tests (showups), photo arrays, and live lineups.

With respect to photo arrays and live lineups, the DOJ guide recommended the inclusion of only one suspect in a lineup. This practice has been universally recommended in guidelines going forward. The guide recommended the use of unbiased lineup instructions in which the eyewitness is informed that the perpetrator may or may not be present in the lineup (see Chapter 3, this volume). The guide instructed law enforcement personnel to select fillers who generally match the eyewitness's description of the perpetrator and that additional similarity should not be sought (see Chapter 4). Consistent with the research presented in Chapter 7 of this volume, the guide instructed law enforcement personnel not to provide postidentification feedback to the eyewitnesses prior to assessing their confidence levels. For example, an officer who is administering a lineup should not inform the eyewitness that he or she has identified the right person prior to asking the eyewitness to indicate his or her level of confidence in his or her identification. The guide described both simultaneous and sequential procedures for both live and photographic lineups but did not express a preference for one over the other (see Chapter 5). The guide also did not include a recommendation for the use of double-blind lineups (see Chapter 6). The guide did not recommend the use of double-blind identification procedures because law enforcement personnel on the working group were opposed to this procedure for two reasons: First, these working group members felt that members of law enforcement would take this procedure as a sign that they are untrustworthy; second, law enforcement members pointed to practical constraints, including a lack of human resources in smaller departments, that would be necessary to administer lineups in a double-blind fashion (Wells et al., 2000).

The publication of the DOJ guide and the Innocence Project's continued attention to prominent cases of wrongful conviction led some states, police departments, and professional organizations to study the issue of eyewitness identification, the relevant research, and their own practices and recommend reforms with the overarching goal of improving justice. To better understand the current state of practice, we collected published sets of reforms at the national, state, and local levels of government from the United States, Canada, and Great Britain. Reform procedures came in the form of national guidelines of recommended best practices and mandated acts. In total, we identified 18 sets of recommendations for reform. Five sets were national recommendations or recommendations made by professional organizations (e.g., International Association of Chiefs of Police, n.d.; American Bar Association, Criminal Justice Section, 2004). Eight were recommended or mandated procedures at the state level. Four of the mandated procedures at the state level—Texas, Florida, Maryland, and West Virginia—are not included in the table on pages 206–207 because the procedures used by law enforcement agencies in these states have been relegated to individual law enforcement agencies. Although all four of these states provide guidelines for what must be addressed in reform policies, none directly specify what procedures must be used. The remaining five sets of reforms were mandated procedures adopted at the local level. The reforms adopted by the Dallas Police Department, however, are not included in the table. The department did not completely overhaul their identification procedures, but they did adopt the double-blind sequential procedure for conducting lineup identifications. Our sample is not exhaustive because the reform is a process that remains in development.

The reforms varied in their scope. For example, some mainly addressed eyewitness identification procedures, whereas others also addressed additional aspects of investigations in which eyewitnesses would be involved (e.g., interviewing eyewitnesses). Some reforms addressed a wide variety of procedures, including use of showups, prior presentation of a suspect, separation of eyewitnesses and discouraging them from discussion of the case, inclusion of only one suspect in a lineup, management of multiple eyewitnesses, lineup instructions, selection of fillers, uniformity of photos, behavior of lineup members, manner of presentation of lineup members, double-blind administration, assessment of confidence, and the documentation of lineup

Eyewitness Identification Reforms Implemented

Reform	ABA	Canada[a]	DOJ	Greenbelt, MD Police[b]	IL[c]	IACP	NJ[d]	Northampton, MA[e]	NC[f]	PACE	Santa Clara, CA[g]	Suffolk, MA[h]	WI[i]	Total (%)
Unbiased instructions	✓	✓	✓	✓	✓	✓	✓	✓	✓	✓	✓	✓*	✓	13 (100%)
Document lineups	✓	✓	✓	✓	✓	✓	✓	✓	✓	✓	✓	✓		12 (92.3)
Confidence	✓	✓	✓	✓			✓	✓	✓	✓	✓	✓	✓	11 (84.6)
Double-blind procedures	✓	✓				✓	✓	✓	✓	✓	✓	✓	✓	10 (76.9)
Match to description	✓	✓	✓	✓	✓		✓	✓	✓			✓*	✓	10 (76.9)
Minimum no. of fillers		9	5p, 4l	5		6p, 5l	5	5p, 4l	5	8	5	7p, 5l		10 (76.9)
Avoid feedback	✓	✓	✓	✓		✓	✓	✓	✓			✓		9 (69.2)
Sequential lineups		✓				✓	✓	✓	✓		✓	✓	✓	8 (61.5)
Mandated				✓	✓		✓	✓	✓	✓	✓			7 (53.9)
Previous arrests not visible			✓			✓	✓	✓	✓	✓		✓*		7 (53.9)
Suspect different positions			✓	✓			✓	✓	✓	✓		✓*		7 (53.9)
New suspect, new fillers			✓	✓			✓	✓	✓			✓*		6 (46.2)

Practice						n (%)
Separate witnesses, avoid media	✓	✓	✓	✓	✓*	5 (38.5)
Open-ended questions		✓	✓		✓*	4 (30.8)
Showups rarely	✓	✓	✓			3 (23.1)
Photo uniformity		✓			✓*	3 (23.1)
Avoid prelineup exposure, multiple identifications	✓		✓	✓		2 (15.4)
All lineup members perform acts			✓			2 (15.4)
Conduct a blank lineup		✓				1 (7.7)

Note. ABA = American Bar Association; DOJ = U.S. Department of Justice; IACP = International Association of Chiefs of Police; PACE = Police and Criminal Evidence Act (1984); p = photo lineup; l = live lineup. Recommendations in Suffolk County, Massachusetts, that are marked with an asterisk are not explicitly stated in the adopted best practices; however, the first recommendation for identification procedures is to adopt all practices recommended by the department of justice. All of these procedures are recommended by the DOJ.

[a]See Federal-Provincial-Territorial Heads of Prosecutions Committee Working Group, 2004. [b]See Greenbelt Maryland Police Department, 2009. [c]See Criminal Procedure, IL, C. S. 725, 107A (2003). [d]See State of New Jersey Department of Law and Public Safety, 2001. [e]See Northampton Police Department, 1999. [f]See State of North Carolina, 2008. [g]See Police Chiefs' Association of Santa Clara County, 2002. [h]See Suffolk County, 2004. [i]See State of Wisconsin Training and Standards for Law Enforcement, 2005.

procedures. For our purposes, we focused our review on the procedures that have been given the most attention in the eyewitness research, and we also noted whether the reforms were mandated or recommended.

The recent identification reform procedures mandated by the Dallas Police Department, Florida, Maryland, Texas, and West Virginia are not included in the table. As noted previously, the Dallas Police Department adopted the sequential double-blind lineup identification procedure but did not completely overhaul their identification procedures. Acts in the four states provide general guidelines for police departments operating within their respective states; however, each of these states relegates decisions on specific procedures to local police departments. The newly adopted Texas Code of Criminal Procedure (2011), for example, states that law enforcement agencies must adopt policies based on scientific research on eyewitness memory and relevant guidelines developed by the federal government, other states, or other law enforcement agencies. Furthermore, the act states that each law enforcement agency must address the following topics: selecting fillers for identification procedures, standard instructions that will be provided to eyewitnesses before an identification procedure, the documentation of lineup procedures including witness statements, procedures for conducting lineups with a person who has limited ability with the English language, and procedures that prevent administrators from influencing the eyewitness (e.g., double-blind procedure).

Likewise, the recently adopted act by the state of Florida (Florida Department of Law Enforcement, 2011) takes a similar form. The state of Florida recommends that standardized scripted instructions be used for conducting lineup procedures to ensure that they are complete and consistent during each identification procedure, that the administrator avoid influencing the eyewitness' identification decision, that fillers resemble the suspect, and that the words and actions of the eyewitness be documented. In addition, in 2007 the state of Maryland passed two bills (HB 103 and SB 157) that mandate that all police departments adopt written policies for eyewitness identification policies that comply with the DOJ guide's standards. The bills also include the establishment of a task force for the purpose of developing new eyewitness identification procedures.

Finally, although the state of West Virginia mandates the use of unbiased instructions and documenting all eyewitness identification procedures, the state does not specifically mandate other procedures. Instead, much like the other three states in this category, West Virginia mandates that the identification task force consider such procedures as double-blind administration, the number of and selection of fillers to be included in lineup identification procedures, sequential versus simultaneous presentation, the inclusion of only one suspect in a given identification procedure, the recording of eyewitness confidence by investigators, the provision of confirmatory feedback by officers, documenting the lineup identification procedure, and video or audio recording of the identification procedure. Eyewitness identification reform policies have been adopted at a steady pace since the recommendations made by the technical group in 1999. The figure on page 210 displays a timeline including all regions. Eyewitness reform policies have been adopted by states at a fairly consistent rate between 1999 and 2011.

On the basis of the above analyses we conclude that identification test reform is spreading. Of those regions that have adopted reform procedures, the majority have adhered to the recommendations set out by the technical group (U.S. DOJ, Office of Justice Programs, National Institute of Justice, 1999). In addition, several regions have gone beyond those procedures recommended by the technical group and have adopted additional procedures to safeguard against mistaken identification. It is also noteworthy that some states, as discussed earlier, have mandated the development of policies for identification tests but left discretion to individual districts to determine which procedures shall be adopted.

THE COMMON FEATURES OF LINEUP REFORM

The table on pages 206–207 summarizes the procedures of most interest in this volume and lists the status of each procedure in each set of reforms. A check mark means that the reform includes the procedure. The reforms are listed in the table in order of commonality, and we have organized this review by the same criterion.

The most common reforms were the use of unbiased lineup instructions (100%), documentation of lineup procedures (92%), and the assessment of eyewitness confidence without postidentification feedback (84.6%). Documenting identification procedures can take many forms, including videotaping, audio recording, or providing written reports including the photographs from the identification procedure. The next most common reforms were the requirement of a minimum number of fillers (77%), the use of fillers who fit the description of the perpetrator (77%), and the use of double-blind administration procedures (77%). Among the guidelines that included a recommendation for the use of a minimum number of fillers, the required minimum varied from five to nine with five being the most common recommendation. For live lineups, the required minimum number of fillers was four.

Less commonly recommended procedures included withholding feedback to the eyewitness concerning whether he or she had identified the suspect (69%) and using sequential lineups (61.5%). When conducting

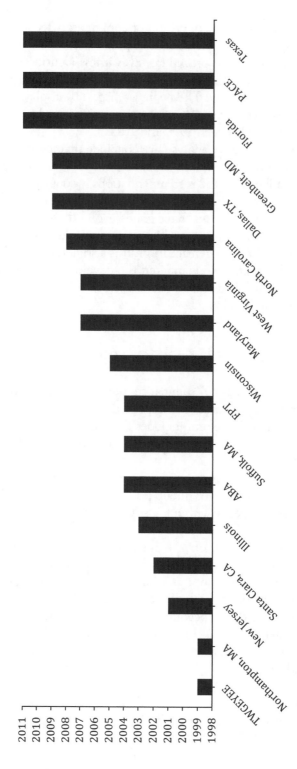

Eyewitness reform timeline. TWGEYEE = Technical Working Group for Eyewitness Evidence; ABA = American Bar Association; FPT = Federal-Provincial-Territorial Heads of Prosecutions Committee; PACE = Police and Criminal Evidence Act (1984).

sequential lineups, however, Great Britain (Police and Criminal Evidence Act, 1984) allows eyewitnesses to request to see the picture of a lineup member multiple times. In fact, in Great Britain eyewitnesses must make at least two passes through the lineup before making an identification decision. About half (53.9%) of the guidelines that we reviewed were required as opposed to recommended procedures. Reform guidelines at state and local levels were more likely to be required (75%) than recommended, whereas reform guidelines at the national level or from professional organizations were more likely to be recommended (80%) than required—notably, the only *required* reform guidelines at the national level were those adopted by Great Britain.

Seven (53.9%) reforms recommend including only one suspect in any given identification procedure. One caveat must be added to this: the Police and Criminal Evidence Act (1984) of Great Britain allows for the inclusion of a maximum of two suspects in a lineup in the rare circumstances in which two individuals suspected of involvement in the same crime closely resemble each other. And, in such circumstances the lineup must contain a minimum of 12 fillers—normally the Police and Criminal Evidence Act requires the inclusion of eight fillers in a lineup procedure.

Seven (53.9%) reforms recommend placing the suspect in different lineup positions for each eyewitness when multiple eyewitnesses view a crime. Seven (53.9%) recommend that lineup members' previous arrest records not be visible to the eyewitness. Six (46.2%) recommend that when multiple suspects are involved in the same crime, different fillers be used for each suspects' lineup identification procedure. Five (38.5%) reforms recommend separating eyewitnesses and instructing them not to discuss the case with other eyewitnesses or to avoid media accounts of the case. Four (30.8%) recommend that law enforcement personnel use open-ended questions when gathering information from eyewitnesses. Three (23.1%) sets of guidelines recommend the use of showups only in the rare circumstances in which a suspect is located near the scene of the crime in both time and space. Three (23.1%) recommend that when conducting a photographic lineup, law enforcement officers ensure that photographs are uniform (i.e., all photos are the same size and resolution, not mixing mug shots among other photos). Two (15.4%) recommend that if a witness requests that a lineup member speak or make a gesture, that all lineup members perform the same act. Two (15.4%) recommend that law enforcement personnel avoid exposing the suspect to the eyewitness prior to the lineup identification procedure and not use multiple identification procedures. Finally, one (7.7%) reform recommends using a blank lineup—a lineup that includes all fillers and no suspects—before conducting the actual lineup identification procedure.

COMPARING THE RESEARCH WITH THE REFORMS

Most of the reforms listed in the table on pages 206–207 have been addressed in the chapters in this volume. The present section is organized by reform, beginning with the most popular ones. For each reform, we draw comparisons between how the reform is used in practice and what we have learned from the research summarized in the earlier chapters.

The most common reform listed in the table is the use of unbiased lineup instructions. All reforms included unbiased instructions. Steblay (see Chapter 3, this volume) found, on the basis of her meta-analysis, that use of the may-or-may-not-be-present instruction reduces the risk of false identifications and filler identifications and increases the diagnosticity of identification. Thus, Steblay concluded that the inclusion of the may-or-may-not-be-present instruction is sound practice and policy. Instructions that are used in reformed procedures, however, often include other instructions, such as the appearance-change instruction and the don't know instruction. Given that the appearance-change and don't know instructions are such common elements of reform, research on their effects should be a high priority.

The only study we know of that has examined the appearance-change instruction was conducted by Charman and Wells (2006). They found that the appearance-change instruction increased innocent suspect and filler identifications but did not increase target identifications. In hindsight, this is not surprising given that participants in the appearance-change instruction condition were instructed that the culprit might not look the same during the lineup as he or she did during the crime. This instruction likely primed participants to expect less of a match between their memory for the perpetrator and the lineup member who best fit this description, leading to a less conservative decision strategy. Moreover, mentioning that the culprit—as opposed to the suspect—might not look the same in the lineup as during the crime might have undone the benefits of the perpetrator may-or-may-not-be-present instruction. Although Charman and Wells (2006) demonstrated the potential pitfalls with the appearance-change instruction, different operationalizations of the same concept might prove to be effective. For example, a carefully worded appearance-change instruction might be used in showups (see Chapter 2, this volume) to curtail clothing bias (i.e., Dysart, Lindsay, & Dupuis, 2006) and stress the importance of focusing on more permanent physical features such as facial features or body type. Future research should continue to explore the appearance-change instruction.

In regard to the don't know instruction, Clark, Howell, and Davey (2008) meta-analyzed 94 eyewitness experiments, 13 of which provided participants with explicit don't know options. They found that don't know responses were not diagnostic of guilt or innocence. Guided by basic metacognitive research, which suggests that don't know responses are used by individuals with lower confidence levels, Weber and Perfect (2011) hypothesized that both identifications and nonidentifications would be more diagnostic when eyewitnesses were explicitly provided with a don't know option. This is based on the assumption that some of those individuals who are less confident will opt to use the don't know response when it is explicitly provided but will make identification decisions when it is not. Indeed, Weber and Perfect found that only 2% of participants provided a don't know response when not explicitly provided with the option compared with 19% of participants who were explicitly provided with the option. Consistent with Clark et al.'s findings, don't know responses were not diagnostic of guilt or innocence; however, as expected, both identifications and nonidentifications were more diagnostic when participants were provided with an explicit don't know option. Although replication is necessary, the don't know instruction appears to be a promising avenue to consider in future research.

The next most common recommendation is the documentation of lineup procedures (92%). The rationale behind this recommendation is to document the procedure so that those responsible for evaluating the eyewitness identification can have a better understanding of the procedures that produced the evaluation. Clearly, this is sound policy, but it raises some interesting questions. What do we know about people's abilities to evaluate lineups? Are laypeople (e.g., jurors) and legal professionals able to effectively evaluate the accuracy of eyewitness identifications based on documented procedures?

The extant literature suggests that neither laypeople nor legal professionals (i.e., defense lawyers, judges) are able to fully and effectively evaluate the accuracy of eyewitness identifications based on documented procedures. Although jurors may be aware of some of the factors that affect eyewitness accuracy (Desmarais & Read, 2011), jurors' decisions to convict are insensitive to the factors that influence eyewitness accuracy (Cutler, Penrod, & Dexter, 1990; Cutler, Penrod, & Stuve, 1988). In Cutler et al. (1990) and Cutler et al. (1988), participants were presented with a video of a simulated trial in which 10 eyewitness factors were manipulated. Participants were asked to determine a verdict and the likelihood that the identification was correct. Only eyewitness confidence had reliable effects on jurors' perceived probability that the identification was accurate and decisions to convict. This is especially indicative of jurors' reliance on eyewitness confidence given that in the high-confidence condition the eyewitness was 100% confident and in the low-confidence condition, the eyewitness was still 80% confident. The results of these studies suggest that jurors are not sensitive to factors that influence eyewitness decision making and are overly reliant on eyewitness confidence.

Attorneys do show some sensitivity to factors that influence eyewitness decision making but are not fully sensitive to all factors. Stinson, Devenport,

Cutler, and Kravitz (1996) assessed attorney sensitivity to lineup suggestive-ness. Attorneys were sensitive to filler bias, somewhat sensitive to instruction bias, and insensitive to the differential effects of simultaneous and sequential presentation. In regard to instruction bias, attorneys felt that biased instructions were more suggestive but did not find them to be less fair; fairness, however, was a scaled variable on which attorneys rated fairness generally and fairness to the defendant, the eyewitness, the victim, and the public. Attorneys also felt that the sequential lineup procedure was more suggestive and less fair. Although recent research suggests that the relationship between sequential and simultaneous lineups is better typified by a sequential shift explanation (see Chapter 5, this volume) than by the prevailing sequential advantage explanation that existed at the time, it is incorrect from either viewpoint to rate the sequential procedure as more suggestive than the simultaneous procedure.

Like attorneys, judges also showed some sensitivity to the factors that influence eyewitness decision making but were not fully sensitive to all factors (Stinson, Devenport, Cutler, & Kravitz, 1997). Judges were sensitive to filler and instruction biases but, like attorneys, were insensitive to the differential effect of simultaneous and sequential presentation. Specifically, when lineups included either biased fillers or instructions, judges were more likely to suppress identification procedures and rated the lineups as more suggestive and less fair. In addition, when the lineup included biased instructions, judges felt that the likelihood of false identification was greater. With respect to presentation methods, however, judges felt that sequential lineups were more suggestive and less fair. In sum, judges were sensitive to some but not all factors that affect eyewitness decision making. Notably, they did not feel that filler-biased lineups would increase the likelihood of mistaken identification.

Regardless of people's abilities to evaluate lineups, the recording of identification procedures is sound practice. Both attorneys and judges did show some sensitivity to the factors affecting eyewitness performance. Even if knowledge is limited, access to the identification procedures leaves open the potential for attorneys to address the procedure through motions to suppress or cross-examination. If procedures are not properly recorded, there is little chance that they will come to light during trial, in which case there is no chance for them to be addressed.

The assessment of confidence is the next most commonly recommended reform (85%). Smalarz and Wells (see Chapter 7, this volume) devoted part of their chapter to explaining how our understanding of the confidence–accuracy relation has changed as the research has matured. They reviewed the impact of postevent information on confidence. The research reviewed by Smalarz and Wells supports the need to include confidence assessment in the reforms. Their review raises the question, however, of whether confidence is used properly as a diagnostic variable during investigations and trials. As mentioned previously, Cutler et al. (1990) and Cutler et al. (1988) found that jurors are overly reliant on eyewitness confidence and dismissive of other factors that they ought to consider when assessing identification performance.

The next most commonly adopted reform is the use of double-blind lineups (77%). Austin, Zimmerman, Rhead, and Kovera's review (see Chapter 6, this volume) of the general research on experimenter expectancy effects in the psychological literature and the small but growing body of research on double-blind lineups in eyewitness research supports the use of double-blind lineups as part of the reforms. They noted, however, that future research is needed to identify the factors that qualify the impact of double-blind lineups. We agree that it will be useful to better understand the psychological underpinnings of administrator influence on lineup identifications. One practically important question about double-blind lineups is whether computer-based lineups can create the same benefits as a blind lineup administrator. Some police departments are now using computers for administering lineups. Computer-based lineups are largely self-guided. The eyewitness clicks through the identification procedure, indicating whether he or she recognizes any of the lineup members. Nevertheless, an investigator must still be on hand to oversee the procedure, troubleshoot any computer problems, and answer any questions that the eyewitness may have. When overseeing a computer-based procedure, is there an opportunity for the nonblind lineup administrator to influence the eyewitness? Can safeguards be put into place to eliminate the possibility of influence by the nonblind administrator in a computer-based identification procedure? These are important practical questions for which researchers do not yet have empirically based answers.

The next two commonly used reforms pertain to the use of fillers. One reform is to use the match-to-description (as opposed to the match-to-suspect) strategy, and the other pertains to the minimum number of fillers. Clark, Rush, and Moreland (see Chapter 4, this volume) concluded that description-matched lineups yield better identification performance than description-mismatched lineups, but description-matched lineups reduce the rate of both correct and false identifications as compared with suspect-matched lineups. Clark et al. concluded that the recommendation to select fillers on the basis of their match to description rather than their match to the suspect has little or no empirical support.

Some of the other reforms also pertain to lineup composition. For example, some include the following: ensure that information about previous arrests is not visible on photo arrays, alternate the suspect's position when showing the lineup to multiple witnesses, use new fillers with new suspects, ensure photo uniformity, and ensure all lineup members perform the same acts (this is analogous to saying make sure a photo does not stand out). As noted by Clark et al. (see Chapter 4, this volume), there is a dearth of empirical research on aspects of lineup composition, such as pictorial distinctiveness, neighborhood effects, and configuration effects. The lack of empirical support for the commonly adopted recommendation and dearth of research on potentially important composition issues leads us to identify this issue as a high priority for future research. Clark et al. provided some excellent suggestions for such research.

Sequential presentation is a common component of lineup reform. Gronlund, Andersen, and Perry (see Chapter 5, this volume) reviewed the contemporary research on sequential presentation. Their detailed analysis of the study results led them to conclude that sequential presentation produces a more conservative decision strategy, which yields fewer false identifications and fewer correct identifications than simultaneous presentation (a sequential shift). They further concluded that policymakers, when considering future reforms, should give careful consideration to the sequential shift pattern associated with sequential presentation, the estimated rate at which guilty people are placed in lineups, and the relative importance of missed and correct identifications. Gronlund et al. made several additional important points relative to the reform movement. They noted that there is a growing disconnect between the manner in which sequential presentation is used in practice and researchers' understanding of its effect on the basis of research. More specifically, many of the variations used in practice are not well understood on the basis of research. Although we hope that the variations used in practice improve, or at least do not mitigate, the presumed beneficial effects of sequential presentation, we will not know for sure until the research has been conducted. We consider research on variations of sequential presentation to be a high priority as well. Gronlund et al. recommended that future research on sequential presentation (and system variables in general) be informed by psychological theory. They also identified alternative presentation methods that are worthy of consideration in both research and practice.

A few of the reforms recommend that showups be used relatively rarely. Goodsell, Wetmore, Neuschatz, and Gronlund (see Chapter 2, this volume) reviewed the research on showups. Goodsell et al. concluded that policy recommendations concerning the use of showups is premature. They concluded that showups have both benefits and drawbacks. The benefits include their efficiency in the field. The drawbacks include the potential for heightened suggestiveness and the lack of protections provided by fillers (as used in photo array and lineup procedures). Goodsell et al. suggested that policy recommendations await future research on the conditions that qualify the effectiveness of showups. We agree and consider the need for research on showups to be a high priority.

FINAL THOUGHTS

This volume has illustrated the practical application that psychological research on eyewitness identification has had and continues to have on eyewitness identification procedures used in criminal investigations. It has become clear that both eyewitness research and the reform process are not static and have great potential for mutual influence. Earlier reforms were informed by research that was recent and timely, yet the body of research continues to grow and evolve. Thus, it behooves policymakers to keep current with the research and be able to modify procedures as new techniques are developed or as evidence concerning the efficacy of techniques changes. Researchers must play a vital role in helping policymakers to stay current with the research. States that have enshrined their identification procedures in law will find it more challenging to make these changes. It behooves researchers to learn about how the techniques are used in practice as they find that the translation of laboratory research into the field sometimes evolves into modifications of practices that have not been empirically tested or not thoroughly tested. In addition, staying current with how techniques are used in the field allows researchers to learn of new research ideas from the law enforcement community—ideas that could not easily have been anticipated in the laboratory. In sum, eyewitness identification represents an area in which psychological research has made important practical contributions to criminal justice practices. A collaborative working relationship between researchers, law enforcement, and policymakers will ensure that these contributions continue.

REFERENCES

American Bar Association, Criminal Justice Section. (2004). *Report to the House of Delegates: Resolution adopting the American Bar Association statement of best practices for promoting the accuracy of eyewitness identification procedures.* Retrieved from http://meetings.abanet.org/webupload/commupload/CR209700/relatedresources/ABAEyewitnessIDrecommendations.pdf

Charman, S. D., & Wells, G. L. (2007). Eyewitness lineups: Is the appearance-change instruction a good idea? *Law and Human Behavior, 31,* 3–22. doi:10.1007/s10979-006-9006-3

Clark, S. E., Howell, R. T., & Davey, S. L. (2008). Regularities in eyewitness identification. *Law and Human Behavior, 32,* 187–218. doi:10.1007/s10979-006-9082-4

Code of Criminal Procedure, TX, 38, 38.20 (2011).

Connors, E., Lundregan, T., Miller, N., & McEwan, T. (1996). *Convicted by juries, exonerated by science: Case studies in the use of DNA evidence to establish innocence after trial.* Alexandria, VA: National Institute of Justice.

Criminal Procedure, IL, C. S. 725, 107A (2003).

Cutler, B. L., Penrod, S. D., & Dexter, H. R. (1990). Juror sensitivity to eyewitness identification evidence. *Law and Human Behavior, 14*, 185–191. doi:10.1007/BF01062972

Cutler, B. L., Penrod, S. D., & Stuve, T. E. (1988). Juror decision making in eyewitness identification cases. *Law and Human Behavior, 12*, 41–55. doi:10.1007/BF01064273

Desmarais, S. L., & Read, J. D. (2011). After 30 years, what do we know about what jurors know? A meta-analytic review of lay knowledge regarding eyewitness factors. *Law and Human Behavior, 35*, 200–210. doi:10.1007/s10979-010-9232-6

Dysart, J. E., Lindsay, R. C. L., & Dupuis, P. R. (2006). Show-ups: The critical issue of clothing bias. *Applied Cognitive Psychology, 20*, 1009–1023. doi:10.1002/acp.1241

Federal-Provincial-Territorial Heads of Prosecutions Committee Working Group. (2004). *Report on the prevention of miscarriages of justice.* Retrieved from http://www.justice.gc.ca/eng/dept-min/pub/pmj-pej/p5.html

Florida Department of Law Enforcement. (2011). *Guidelines for Florida state and local law enforcement agencies in dealing with photographic or live line-ups in eyewitness identification.* Retrieved from http://www.fdle.state.fl.us/Content/getdoc/327876c5-0464-4ecb-832a-79962c5e09a9/GuidelinesEyewitnessID.aspx

Greenbelt Maryland Police Department (2009). *Greenbelt Police Department special operating procedure: Eyewitness identification.* Retrieved from http://www.greenbeltmd.gov/police/Eyewitness_identification.pdf

International Association of Chiefs of Police. (n.d.). Eyewitness identification. *Training Key 600, 34.* Retrieved from http://www.theiacp.org/LinkClick.aspx?fileticket=568%2B005JtQU%3D&tabid=324

Northampton Police Department. (1999). Eyewitness identification procedure. *Administration and Operations Manual, 0-408*, 1–9. Retrieved from http://www.innocenceproject.org/docs/Northampton_MA_ID_Protocols.pdf

Police and Criminal Evidence Act. (1984). Retrieved from http://www.legislation.gov.uk/ukpga/1984/60

Police Chiefs' Association of Santa Clara County. (2002). *Lineup protocol for law enforcement.* Retrieved from http://www.innocenceproject.org/docs/Santa_Clara_eyewitness.pdf

State of New Jersey Department of Law and Public Safety. (2001). *Attorney General guidelines for preparing and conducting photo and live lineup identification procedures.* Retrieved from http://www.state.nj.us/lps/dcj/agguide/photoid.pdf

State of North Carolina. (2008). *Actual Innocence Commission recommendations for eyewitness identification.* Retrieved from http://www.innocenceproject.org/docs/NC_eyewitness.pdf

State of Wisconsin Training and Standards for Law Enforcement. (2005). *Eyewitness identification best practices.* Retrieved from http://www.innocenceproject.org/docs/WI_eyewitness.pdf

Stinson, V., Devenport, J. L., Cutler, B. L., & Kravitz, D. A. (1996). How effective is the presence of counsel safeguard? Attorney perceptions of suggestiveness, fairness, and correctability of biased lineup procedures. *Journal of Applied Psychology, 81*, 64–75. doi:10.1037/0021-9010.81.1.64

Stinson, V., Devenport, J. L., Cutler, B. L., & Kravitz, D. A. (1997). How effective is the motion-to-suppress safeguard? Judges' perceptions of the suggestiveness and fairness of biased lineup procedures. *Journal of Applied Psychology, 82*, 211–220. doi:10.1037/0021-9010.82.2.211

Suffolk County. (2004). *Report of the Task Force on Eyewitness Evidence*. Retrieved from http://www.innocenceproject.org/fix/Eyewitness-Identification.php

U.S. Department of Justice, Office of Justice Programs, National Institute of Justice. (1999). *Eyewitness evidence: A guide for law enforcement*. Retrieved from http://www.nij.gov/pubs-sum/178240.htm

Weber, N., & Perfect, T. J. (2012). Improving eyewitness identification accuracy by screening out those who say they don't know. *Law and Human Behavior, 36*, 28–36. doi:10.1007/s10979-011-9269-1

Wells, G. L. (1978). Applied eyewitness-testimony research: System variables and estimator variables. *Journal of Personality and Social Psychology, 36*, 1546–1557. doi:10.1037/0022-3514.36.12.1546

Wells, G. L., Malpass, R. S., Lindsay, R. C. L., Fisher, R. P., Turtle, J. W., & Fulero, S. M. (2000). From the lab to the police station: A successful application of eyewitness research. *American Psychologist, 55*, 581–598. doi:10.1037/0003-066X.55.6.581

INDEX

Canadian Wrongful Convictions study, 9t
Carlson, C., 97
Carlson, C. A., 59, 97, 117–119
Carmona, Arthur, 55
Causal models, associative vs., 181, 183–184
Ceci, S. J., 127
Center on Wrongful Convictions (Northwestern University School of Law), 132
Certainty, eyewitness. *See* Eyewitness confidence
Certainty–accuracy correlation, 164–168
Certainty inflation
    from confirming feedback, 169–170
    and recording of certainty statement, 171–172
Certainty malleability, 168–170
Certainty statements, recording, 171–172
Change-of-appearance instructions, 155
Charman, S. D., 74n6, 79, 172–173, 212
Children
    elimination lineup as aid to, 130
    may-or-may-not instruction for, 72
Chivabunditt, P., 46
Choosers, 166–167
Choosing rate
    and foil similarity, 77
    and lineup instructions, 67
    for lineups vs. showups, 52, 53
    with may-or-may-not instructions, 71–72
Clark, H. H., 184
Clark, S. E., 51–54, 92, 94, 95t, 97, 99–101, 103, 117, 118, 120–123, 125–127, 212–213
Clever Hans, 139–140, 157
Clinical trials, 190
Clothing bias, 55–56
Communication
    of eyewitness research in popular media, 36–37
    of lineup administrators and eyewitnesses, 154
Compound signal detection model, 124–125
Computer administered lineups, 158, 215

Conditional probability
    as measure of identification performance, 53
    and sequential advantage, 118
Confidence. *See* Eyewitness confidence
Configuration effects (lineup construction), 104–106
Confirming feedback
    absence of, by lineup administrators, 172
    double-blind lineup administration and, 171–172
    eyewitness certainty and, 169–170
Connecticut, eyewitness identification reform in, 37
Conroy, J., 9t
Construction of lineups. *See* Lineup construction
Control, researcher (in field studies), 196
Conviction, wrongful. *See* Wrongful conviction
Conviction reversals, eyewitness identification in, 89
Cook, T. D., 183
Correct identification, 14
    in identification performance, 53
    and probative value of suspect identification, 91–92
    terminology, 91
Correct identification rates
    and description-matched filler selection, 95, 96f, 97–98
    in eyewitness identification research, 94–98
    and filler similarity, 92–94, 93f, 95t
Correct rejections, 15, 51, 52. *See also* Lineup rejection
Criterion placement, in sequential lineup presentation methods, 129
Criterion shift, and may-or-may-not instruction effect, 73–74
Cronbach, L. J., 181
Cross-examinations
    certainty inflation for, 172
    and wrongful conviction, 11
Cross-race effect, 184–185
Cross-race identifications, as general-impairment variable, 27
Crowder, R. G., 181

Showup identification procedures,
45–59
defined, 14, 46
in the field, 47–48
guidelines for, 57
legal decisions on, 48–51
lineups vs., 51–57
policy recommendations, 58–59
reform of, 216
researchers view of, 39
variables in, 54–57
Signal detection
and may-or-may-not instruction
effect, 73–74
in sequential presentation, 125–126
Signal detection theory, 114
Similarity effects. *See also* Filler
similarity
false identification rates, 98, 99
sequential lineups and, 97
simultaneous lineups and, 97
Similar-replacement strategy, 165
Simmons v. U.S., 89
Simultaneous lineups
effect of administrator knowledge
on, 144–147, 150
field studies of sequential vs., 192–195,
193t, 194t
filler identification in sequential vs.,
40–41, 76
identification errors with, 76–77
innocent suspect identifications in, 77
lineup presentation in, 106
position of suspect in, 104–106
sequential vs., 114, 115, 192–195,
193t, 194t
similarity effects in, 97–98
suspect identifications in sequential
vs., 116
Single-blind lineups
effect of administrator knowledge in,
145–148, 151–153
innocent suspect identifications
in, 155
lineup instructions for, 77
suspect–perpetrator similarity in, 156
Single-suspect lineups, innocent suspect
identifications in, 29
Skagerberg, E. M., 191–192

Snee, T., 30
Social influence, in eyewitness
identification studies, 30
Spearman, C., 181
Spurious correlations, 187
Standard sequential lineup procedure,
114
State of Connecticut v. Ledbetter, 162–163
State of New Jersey v. Henderson, 113,
114, 143, 158
Steblay, N. K. M., 26, 51–52, 68, 69,
78–80, 115, 116, 119–121, 128,
183, 195, 212
Stern, L. B., 74n6
Stimuli, for field vs. laboratory studies of
memory, 184–186
Stinson, V., 213–214
Stopping rule (sequential lineups),
39–40, 128
Stovall, Theodore, 48–49
Stovall v. Denno, 48–49
Stress, as estimator variable, 26
Structural variables, in eyewitness
identification studies, 30
Study space analysis, for showups, 58
Stuve, T. E., 67
Suffolk, Massachusetts, 206t–207t, 210t
Suggestion, in double-blind lineups,
171–172
Suggestive identification procedures
expert testimony on, 33
pretrial, 48–49
and suppression of identification,
34–35
system variables in, 31
Suggestive lineup instruction
future research on, 78
and identification errors, 68
and lineup rejection, 66
not present option vs., 73
and witness confidence, 78–79
Suggestiveness
of lineups, 58, 88, 106n6
in reliability test, 49–50
of showups, 48, 58
Suppression, of eyewitness
identification, 11, 34–35
Suspect-bias variables, general-
impairment vs., 27–28

ABOUT THE EDITOR

Brian L. Cutler, PhD, received his doctorate in social psychology in 1987 from the University of Wisconsin–Madison. He is a professor in the faculty of social science and humanities at the University of Ontario Institute of Technology (UOIT), Oshawa, Ontario, Canada. Prior to joining UOIT's faculty, Dr. Cutler served on the psychology faculties at Florida International University and the University of North Carolina at Charlotte.

Dr. Cutler has been conducting research on the psychology of eyewitness identification and its role in conviction of the innocent for more than 25 years. His research has been funded by the National Science Foundation. In addition to this volume, he has authored and edited five books and more than 60 book chapters and research articles about the psychology of eyewitness identification. His research has been cited in court cases, the media, other research, and psychology textbooks. Dr. Cutler has also served as editor of the journal *Law and Human Behavior* and president of Division 41 (American Psychology–Law Society) of the American Psychological Association.

In collaboration with his students and other eyewitness scientists, Dr. Cutler continues to maintain an active research program, focusing on eyewitness identification. He teaches undergraduate and graduate courses on various aspects of psychology, criminology, research methods, and writing for the social sciences.